Teaching Freedom

THE FAIRLEIGH DICKINSON UNIVERSITY PRESS SERIES IN ITALIAN STUDIES

General Editor: Dr. Anthony Julian Tamburri, Dean of the John D. Calandra Italian American Institute

The Fairleigh Dickinson University Press Series in Italian Studies is devoted to the publication of scholarly works on Italian literature, film, history, biography, art, and culture, as well as on intercultural connections, such as Italian-American Studies.

On the Web at http://www.fdu.edu/fdupress

Recent Titles

Massimo Castoldi, *Teaching Freedom: Stories of Anti-Fascist Teachers in Italy* (2024)

Paola Irene Galli Mastrodonato, *Emilio Salgari: The Tiger Is Still Alive!* (2024)

Emanuele Pettener, *When We Were Bandini: Humor and Satire in John Fante's American Dream* (2024)

Julianne VanWagenen, *Mythologist in Microgroove:A Study of Italian Myths and Cultural Shifts with Fabrizio De André on Lead Vocals* (2023)

Cristina Perissinotto, *Marco Paolini: A Deep Map* (2023)

Raymond Angelo Belliotti, *Italian Rebels: Mazzini, Gramsci, and Giuliano* (2022)

Anna Camaiti Hostert and Enzo Antonio Cicchino, *Trump and Mussolini: Images, Fake News, and Mass Media, Weapons in the Hands of Two Populists* (2022)

Raymond Angelo Belliotti, *Heroism and Wisdom, Italian Style* (2022)

Joseph Francese, *The Unpopular Realism of Vincenzo Padula: Il Bruzio and Mariuzza Sbriffiti* (2021)

Marie Orton, Graziella Parati, and Ron Kubati (eds.), *Contemporary Italian Diversity in Critical and Fictional Narratives* (2021)

Giorgio Linguaglossa, *Alfredo de Palchi: The Missing Link in Late Twentieth-Century Italian Poetry* (2020)

Daniela Bini, *Portrait of the Artist and His Mother in Twentieth-Century Italian Culture* (2020)

Cinzia Russi, *Sicilian Elements in Andrea Camilleri's Narrative Language: A Linguistic Analysis* (2020)

Raymond Angelo Belliotti, *Values, Virtues, and Vices, Italian Style: Caesar, Dante, Machiavelli, and Garibaldi* (2020)

Elio Attilio Baldi, *The Author in Criticism: Italo Calvino's Authorial Image in Italy, the United States, and the United Kingdom* (2020)

Teaching Freedom

Stories of Anti-Fascist Teachers in Italy

Massimo Castoldi
Translated by Gail McDowell

FAIRLEIGH DICKINSON UNIVERSITY PRESS
Vancouver • Madison • Teaneck • Wroxton

Published by Fairleigh Dickinson University Press
Copublished by The Rowman & Littlefield Publishing Group, Inc.
4501 Forbes Boulevard, Suite 200, Lanham, Maryland 20706
www.rowman.com

86-90 Paul Street, London EC2A 4NE, United Kingdom

Copyright © 2024 by The Rowman & Littlefield Publishing Group, Inc.

All rights reserved. No part of this book may be reproduced in any form or by any electronic or mechanical means, including information storage and retrieval systems, without written permission from the publisher, except by a reviewer who may quote passages in a review.

This book was originally published in Italy by Donzelli Editore under the title *Insegnare* libertà. Storie di maestri antifascisti, copyright © 2018, Donzelli editore.

Fairleigh Dickinson University Press gratefully acknowledges the support received for scholarly publishing from the Friends of FDU Press.

British Library Cataloguing in Publication Information Available

Library of Congress Cataloging-in-Publication Data

Names: Castoldi, Massimo, author. | McDowell, Gail, translator.
Title: Teaching freedom : stories of anti-fascist teachers in Italy / Massimo Castoldi ; translated by Gail McDowell.
Description: Vancouver : Fairleigh Dickinson University Press ; Lanham, Maryland : Rowman & Littlefield Publishing Group, Inc., [2024] | Series: The Fairleigh Dickinson University Press Series in Italian Studies | Includes bibliographical references and index. | Summary: "Between 1920 and 1944, fascist Italy envisaged elementary schools as a place for constructing child-soldiers obedient to the regime. Teaching Freedom recounts twelve stories of elementary schoolteachers who opposed this model, educating their students in solidarity and awareness, and sometimes paying the ultimate price for the freedom they taught"—Provided by publisher.
Identifiers: LCCN 2024011478 (print) | LCCN 2024011479 (ebook) | ISBN 9781683934202 (cloth) | ISBN 9781683934219 (epub)
Subjects: LCSH: Elementary school teachers—Italy—Biography. | Elementary schools—Italy—History—20th century. | Anti-fascist movements—Italy—History—20th century. | Fascism and education—Italy—History—20th century.
Classification: LCC LB1776.4.I8 C37 2024 (print) | LCC LB1776.4.I8 (ebook) | DDC 372.110945—dc23/eng/20240529
LC record available at https://lccn.loc.gov/2024011478
LC ebook record available at https://lccn.loc.gov/2024011479

Bridge Book Award Winner, 2020

Insegnare libertà. Storie di maestri antifascisti [Teaching Freedom: Stories of Anti-Fascist Teachers in Italy] by Massimo Castoldi was awarded the Bridge Book Award for Nonfiction in 2020, now available in English translation.

Contents

Introduction	ix
Chapter 1: The Assassination of Carlo Cammeo	1
Chapter 2: The Sacrifice of Franz Innerhofer	11
Chapter 3: Anselmo Cessi: A Catholic Patriot Killed by the Fascists	17
Chapter 4: The Lofty Socialist Integrity of Alda Costa	25
Chapter 5: Mariangela Maccioni: The Anti-Fascist Teacher from Nuoro	41
Chapter 6: Abigaille Zanetta: A Fighter	53
Chapter 7: Fabio Maffi: The Teacher of Teachers	65
Chapter 8: Carlo Fontana: From Councilor to Mayor of Magenta	75
Chapter 9: Aurelio Castoldi: From the Typographers Union to the Publishing House Labor	89
Chapter 10: Giuseppe Latronico: Director of Studies and Gobetti's Friend	105
Chapter 11: Anna Botto and the Three Rosaries: From Vigevano to Ravensbrück	115
Chapter 12: Salvatore Principato: Setting an Example as a Form of Civic Education	127
Bibliography	145
Index	153
About the Author	163

Introduction

1. A SILENT BATTLE.

A few days after April 25, 1945, the Socialist schoolteacher Andrea Tacchinardi spoke in Milan at the first conference in liberated Italy of the Italian Teachers Union. The union, a member of the General Confederation of Labor, was founded by Socialist teachers in April 1919 and had been forced into silence by Fascism. Tacchinardi, originally from Pavia, was one of its founders; he was a convinced Socialist and had written various articles for Pavia's journal *La Plebe* and for *Avanti*! (Callegari 1991, 128).[1]

It only took a few years to suffocate the union: from the first threats in 1921 to the liberticidal Fascist laws in 1925.

An anonymous report dated June 1930 about the state of teachers, entitled *School Conditions in Italy*, is fairly eloquent: "Some had their house destroyed, some were wounded, some were forced to drink castor oil, some were dirtied and disfigured in public; women teachers were attacked in class, their hair was cut in the school hallways, and they were insulted, although they weren't killed, like [Carlo] Cammeo; at night, the front doors of single women were knocked down by trucks and they had to escape through the vegetable gardens (*Le condizioni della scuola in Italia (Da un rapporto di un gruppo di maestri italiani alla organizzazione internazionale degli insegnanti)*, in "Lo Stato operaio," May–June 1930, 338) (Vecchi 2017, 73). One of these women was the teacher from Ferrara Alda Costa, who inspired the character Clelia Trotti in *Within the Walls* by Giorgio Bassani. In July 1922, in Bologna, she was surrounded by a crowd of Fascists who "insulted her, spat on her, ripped her clothing, forced her to drink castor oil, and smeared her face with soot because she had refused to sing the praises of Fascism."

Many of these teachers didn't stop opposing Fascism in very different ways: sometimes head-on, provoking and defying the regime; sometimes in more dissimulated ways, trying to give their students an alternative education, eluding the admittedly strict control of Fascist censors. Tacchinardi was one

X   *Introduction*

of these latter teachers, and for his actions, he received the gold medal for scholastic merit from the president of the Republic, Einaudi.

In that reborn Teachers Section of the Union, Tacchinardi remembered the last twenty-three years he had spent in a condition of "exile in our homeland," made, he said, of "many shadows, very much half-light," but also "many lights," which must not be forgotten.

He added that, even though there were many who had "rushed to sell their soul to the regime for a seat or a promotion," there were also others who had "battled in silence, sometimes isolated, resisting meter by meter in ideal trenches and, until the end, some gave signs of life."

Even though he did not intend to indulge in commemorations, he remembered those teachers who had "faced greater sacrifices in the regime's dungeons, and [. . .] also given their life," such as Salvatore Principato, who was executed by a firing squad on German orders in Piazzale Loreto on August 10, 1944. As Tacchinardi explained, Principato was an "example of a teacher who has given us a way to set off toward the destinations of a better future." And Carlo Cammeo, who was "slaughtered on the threshold of his classroom by Fascists" in Pisa on April 13, 1921. He concluded:

> We began with this bloody episode in 1921 and our drama has come to an end in these days. These comrades of ours stand tall in our souls. Their bodies are no longer with us but their spirit is in our spirit, it works there imperceptibly because many of the transformations that have been preparing themselves in this period, are thanks to them.
>
> Principato was a member of the Italian Teachers Union's patrol, composed of a few young and fervent men: he was the nicest of us and, over the course of these twenty years, he showed a loyalty to the idea that bonded us together and that ended with his sacrifice.
>
> I didn't have the courage to go see him in Piazzale Loreto, now Piazzale dei Quindici Martiri;[2] I went to see him at the morgue, this gentle giant, who fought in the war of 1915–18 and earned a silver medal for valor.
>
> I went to the morgue and I saw my dear friend, this brother of mine: his swollen face and broken arm bore witness to the torture he had suffered in prison.
>
> For many days I wasn't myself: I felt revenge and hate spread inside myself. But then, the macabre image of this colleague of ours was superimposed by his true image, his open face, his sweet and boyish gaze, and I became myself once again.
>
> And I think that if he is still sending us a message, it is a message of goodwill and fraternity (Chiorri Principato 2014, 158–59).

We know a lot about the cultural models of Fascist schools, in part because they were flaunted in rallies, journals, books, and representations—often exaggerated—of themselves, but we know almost nothing about how anti-Fascist culture and awareness passed by way of elementary school teachers, the first—not only in chronological order—to form a civic conscience in citizens.

If Fascism considered elementary school the place to train and construct the conscience of the new child-soldier who was loyal to the regime, it is indisputable that there were those who, as Tacchinardi remembered, had done their utmost to achieve the contrary effect, stimulating in the children a different awareness, the opposite of the dominant one.

It is hard to estimate the quality of the results. It would require a sociological examination of the mentality, awareness, and underlying cultural orientation of Italians born between 1916 and 1938–that is, the Italians who went to elementary school during the Fascist period. The study would have to evaluate the degree to which the Fascist projects progressively affected the children, the degree to which dissident teachers affected them, and to what degree the children were affected by the inertia of the unchanged tradition of pre-Fascist, liberal Italy. And then, in all this, the study would have to isolate the role played by primary school teaching methods over other methods of teaching and persuasion. We will leave the topic to sociologists and historians of education.

In this book, I will limit myself to reconstructing and evaluating their intentions.

The extent of the phenomenon is evident, in part due to the fact that, during the first two decades of the twentieth century, the figure of the schoolteacher acquired a new centrality in Italy's socio-cultural life. Their commitment was to the fight against illiteracy and the development of Socialism, as well as of working-class Catholicism, both of which, although in mutual conflict, sensed the need for the increasingly widespread education of children and adults. Elementary school teachers were the ones who had to instill patriotic feelings in the "children of Italy" but they were also the ones who, along with pharmacists and municipal doctors, often found themselves experiencing their country's difficult conditions firsthand, starting with social diseases, malnutrition, and precarious sanitary conditions.

2. ELEMENTARY SCHOOL TEACHERS
IN PRE-FASCIST SCHOOLS.

It might be of help in understanding the anti-Fascist choices of the teachers recounted here by retracing some of the fundamental stages of the union struggles between the nineteenth and twentieth centuries, up to, and beyond, the years of World War I.

On May 6, 1900, in Parma, the first nucleus of the Teachers Association was formed; from that moment on, it began to express its demands, in order to make teachers increasingly aware that they were a category of workers with specific requests and rights (Santoni Rugiu 2007, 86–88; Ghizzoni 2003, 63–79). Soon, many journals on the topic were distributed, and conferences and debates were held. At its first congress in April 1901, the Association already had 30,180 members, more than half of the personnel working at public schools. Luigi Credaro was elected president; he was a radical member of parliament and a professor of the history of philosophy at the University of Pavia. As Carla Ghizzoni affirms, this was a sign "of the tendency of the teaching class of the time to consider itself a subordinate, passive power, inclined [. . .] to still consider its own organized action under the paternalistic protection of a strong power" (Ghizzoni 2003, 64). Nevertheless, the first decade of the 1900s saw the progressive definition of the juridical state of elementary school teachers (recruitment through competitive exams, updating salary levels, licensing and specialization courses). In 1904, the law no. 407, passed by the Minister Vittorio Emanuele Orlando, raised the age of compulsory schooling to twelve years old and dealt with the widespread problem of illiteracy by establishing courses for adults, as well (Ghizzoni 2003, 66). At the same time, the Teachers Association increasingly sided with the left-wing political forces, calling for secular and working-class schools, including kindergarten and vocational schools. A strong anticlerical push soon led to the secession of the Catholic teachers who, on July 8, 1906, in Milan, created their own teachers association: the "Niccolò Tommaseo" (Ghizzoni 2003, 68). On June 4, 1911, "the Daneo-Credaro law was passed, decreeing the passage of elementary schools from the towns to the State, except for primary institutes in towns that were the administrative centers of provinces and districts" (Ghizzoni 2003, 71).

In 1912, upon the proposal of Giovanni Giolitti, Parliament extended the right to vote—without census limitations—to all male citizens, but an elementary school diploma was needed in order to vote at twenty-one years of age, otherwise the voting age rose to thirty. Only in 1918 was universal male suffrage introduced that lowered the voting age to twenty-one for all men, eighteen for soldiers. Thus, from 1912 to 1918, elementary school education also became a means for bringing young people to the ballot boxes and it was an important opportunity to focus the attention of Socialists and Popular Catholics on elementary schools.

During the following years, while the conflict of various women's associations demanding equal pay and remuneration became more radicalized, efforts were made within the Association to increase the male presence, which was around 20 percent, to correct the critical issues of the Daneo-Credaro law, and to revise scholastic training for teachers.

Introduction xiii

The contradictions that emerged during and after the First World War led to a further secession in April 1919 and to the birth of the Italian Teachers Union. It adhered to the General Confederation of Labor and wanted teachers to be considered like every other worker, not a sort of secular priest whose task was national education. Above all, it wanted to share in the battles of those workers whose children were in the teachers' classes. The intent was to fight for the rights of teachers and support the class struggle alongside the other workers (Ghizzoni 2003, 77).[3] It was enthusiastically endorsed by almost every Socialist teacher (Tomasi 1982; Catarsi 1982). On June 11, 1919, there was an initial strike, which wasn't yet called by the Teachers Union, of elementary school teachers against the government; the Catholic Association Tommaseo also participated.

3. FASCISM, THE WARRIOR'S EDUCATION, AND THE ANTI-FASCIST SCHOOL.

But 1919 was also the year that saw the birth of Fascism, which in just a short time would oppose and quash all these battles. Much has been written on the topic and I do not want to dwell on Fascist legislation for schools (Bocchetti 2013; Maiorca 2000;[4] Gibelli 2005; Colin 2012). I will limit myself to quoting a few excerpts from an analysis made in the 1930s by the philosopher Gallo Galli regarding L'educazione guerriera [*The Warrior's Education*] in his book *I Principii della Scuola Fascista con particolare riguardo alla Scuola Elementare*, which so well interprets those fundamental nuclei of Fascist education against which our teachers felt the moral duty to rebel:

One of the fundamental characteristics—and perhaps the newest and most significant—that the Italian school has gradually acquired and is about to implement with total clarity and precision in its directive ideas and technical organization, is the mark of the warrior. In the domain of education, in which the entire life of a population reflects itself and from which it draws both sustenance and vigorous affirmation, what prevails is the categorical actualization of the national conscience, which is the mission of Fascism in Italian history. [. . .]

Military conscience, the warrior spirit, is nothing other than the national conscience; but together, they constitute a dual aspect of the elevation of the individual beyond his own particular benefit, in order to effect life's ideal justification: a dual aspect of that concept of life as a mission, in which the individual perishes in his superficial and evanescent form and substantiates himself in universal and eternal reality [. . .].

Above the nation there is—indeed, there can be—no organization that equitably directs and governs the activity of individual social-national groups

xiv   *Introduction*

and establishes a harmonious equilibrium through the composition of the contrasts. [. . .]

The possibility of, the need for armed conflict is inherent to the national conscience, it is present in its every moment; and this awareness and the preparation of the suitable spirit for this conflict are, we would almost say, a second face of the national conscience. And thus, no education is truly, vigorously national unless it is also warrior education. But that does not suffice. The specific task of warrior education, the preparation for armed conflict, has its own character—in connection with the nature and the demands of this conflict—and thus it is not only the reflection or, one could say, the shadow of national education, but it somehow detaches itself from and reacts on it, increasing and integrating its value. Moreover, it increases and integrates the value of education in general, as well.

The preparation for armed conflict is a true preparation: 1) for the most complete renunciation of one's own self, since it involves the renunciation of life, the first and highest good, presupposed by all; 2) for the renunciation—albeit momentary and as a means leading to a higher affirmation—also of one's own spiritual personality, through prompt and full obedience, since conflict is action and there is nothing more harmful and insane than discussion when it is the moment to act (Galli 1935, 67–72).

The warrior's education also passed by way of the cult of those symbols in which, Galli wrote, "an idea defines itself, consolidates itself, and is put into action:" the flag as an emblem of moral unity, uniforms and ranks, which "have the purpose of facilitating identification and rendering it more difficult to avoid discipline." The subjects most intimately connected with warrior education were history and physical education.

History helped teach the "inescapability of conflict among populations" and the productiveness of this conflict "with regard to the advance of human civilization." In history, war was to appear "in all its tragic necessity" and hence, although "the ideologies of universal and perpetual peace" represented "a nice dream," they did not stand up "to the test of history." As for physical education, he concluded:

> It supplies the agility and alacrity of movement, the resistance to exertion, and the muscular power that represent one of the most essential means of armed conflict. Moreover, because of the risk inherent in many gymnastic exercises, even if one avoids acrobatics—which lie outside the educational field—it is good battle training for the soul. The wealth and importance of warrior education is infinitely superior to that of physical education, which is perforce a component.
>
> Lastly, it will be helpful to mention sports, since they do not signify virtuosity, or rather, technical ability and physical capability as an end to themselves, but take their place within the general framework of education as a stimulus to the development of men. In this case, they are the natural outcome of physical

Introduction xv

education, or better, physical education in the fullness of its realization, since they accentuate the moment of risk and the ensuing need for self-control.

But one mustn't exaggerate the value of sports in warrior education, which is based on an ideal world that is completely extraneous to them. It refers to a state of things in which much more is at risk than a few sprains or bruises, in which the hero does not expect applause but consecrates himself serenely and confidently to a sacrifice that might also remain unsung (Galli 1935, 77–78).

This was the primary significance of Fascist education and, in 1926, of the creation of the Opera Nazionale Balilla, which obliged every boy to undergo paramilitary training with uniform and musket, starting at eight years of age. Fascist legislation did not hesitate to consider schools the most important instrument for training the Fascist, nationalist, and soldier citizen, disdainful of their own life and that of others, annulling every form of critical capacity, social awareness, and feelings of human solidarity.

Part of the match was played on the interpretation and success of the book *Heart* by Edmondo De Amicis. In June 1961, the pedagogist Mario Valeri, speaking at a conference in Turin on juvenile literature, recalled how reading the book *Heart* was often "a challenge launched by anti-Fascist teachers" because it glorified the pre-Fascist era, with its social life, and showed a "human side of the army" which the regime tolerated poorly (Valeri 1962, 67).

The anti-Fascist spirit also established itself in a number of editorial initiatives for elementary schools, of which only a few, rare examples still exist. This is the case of the anthology by Casimiro Casucci and Gildo Enrico Fiorelli, *Luci d'alba. Corso di letture per le scuole elementari maschili e femminili* (Palermo: Remo Sandron, 1921). I am familiar with the volumes for the first, second, and fourth grades; the second edition of this latter book finished printing on August 31, 1921. The socialist slant is evident, not only in the total absence of religious topics (no readings about Christmas or other recurring events of the liturgical calendar except Easter, but only as the holiday of springtime and love), but also in scattered indications, such as in the first-grade book on *School Lunches*, which notes that "at the same dining table, the children of the poor eat the same soup and the same bread, but with the children of the rich: the former for free, the latter for a fee," because "Town Hall knows that instruction and education are necessary for all" (40). The fourth-grade book features a passage by the socialist Gaetano Zibordi entitled *Work Must Be Law for All*, which begins thus: "Work is distressing when it is not a common law; work becomes odious when those doing it see others who are not working, and have the impression that their *toil* is for the *idleness* of others" (76). Further on, we also find a page by Filippo Turati, who recalls Edmondo De Amicis (115–16) and even—the only holiday celebrated—two pages dedicated to *May Day*, written by De Amicis himself: "On

xvi *Introduction*

that day, throughout the world, in one hundred different languages, legions of workers, in the form of assemblies, gatherings, symbolic marches, country festivals, and solemn chants, express one single idea and one single hope" (179); four pages follow dedicated to Andrea Costa, with the reminiscences of Giovanni Pascoli, Leonida Bissolati, and Pio Schinetti (199–202), and on page 209 there is a reproduction of *The Fourth Estate* by Pellizza da Volpedo. This should suffice to give the reader an idea but the anthology merits specific research. Both authors were elementary school teachers. Casimiro Casucci, born in 1885, was a Socialist and the leader of the maximalist wing in Bologna; in 1920, he was elected to the town council and the provincial council. He was present at the session when Fascists attacked Palazzo d'Accursio on November 21, 1920, causing the death of ten Socialist supporters. He was arrested in December and set free almost one year later, in November 1921, but was suspended from teaching for a long time. The next year, on December 26, 1922, he was severely beaten by Fascists on Via Indipendenza. He survived Fascism and died in 1967. Enrico Gildo Fiorelli, born in 1887, was a union manager and a journalist. In November 1920, he was elected to the provincial council for the San Giovanni in Persiceto constituency. He was a fugitive after the massacre at Palazzo d'Accursio. He was persecuted by the regime and died in 1928 (D'Ascenzo 2013; D'Ascenzo 2006).

There are also clear signs of Socialism in the series "Museo di Scienza Minima," directed by Virginio Carnevali for the Florentine publishing house Vallardi. Besides the small books by Abigaille Zanetta *L'apiario (sorgenti neglette di agiatezza patria)* and *La seta (umili istinti ed opere magnifiche),[5]* which offer cues for discussing the social redemption of the proletariat, there is also a book written by Carnevali himself, *I Danni dell'Alcoolismo. Una guerra santa* (Milan: Vallardi, 1924), for third- and fourth-grade children. It tells the story of the son of Signor Carlo Amadori, young Mario, who reads a newspaper account of the case of two children who contracted alcohol poisoning after eating a large quantity of cherries preserved in alcohol. Mario begins to investigate what alcohol is, how it is produced, and its effects on the human organism. He goes to the League Against Alcoholism and, with his own eyes (the images are in the book), sees drawings of the stomach, liver, and heart of a man who was ruined by alcohol, as well as a series of panels that recount the social disaster of a family destroyed by an alcoholic father. These were a few of the most advanced points of the civic education taught by anti-Fascist teachers.

During the 1930s and 1940s, people opposed Fascism by not talking about it and talking about other topics, instead—subjects which, by their very nature, taught an awareness that was the opposite of the regime's. For example, the editorial choices of teachers like Fabio Maffi, Aurelio Castoldi, Carlo Fontana, and Giuseppe Latronico, collaborators at the Milanese

Introduction   xvii

publishing house Labor, which published works of cultural propagation that were calibrated to pass Fascist censorship but at the same time protect Italian history and culture from the contagion of the cultural politics imposed by the institutions. These included the *Dizionario Enciclopedico Moderno* and the *Enciclopedia del Ragazzo Italiano*, both of which started being published in 1938.[6]

Salvatore Principato read Emilio Salgari to his students; the author was tolerated by Fascism because he was anti-British but it was an excellent pretext to talk about the struggle for freedom of an oppressed people or to highlight anti-colonial feelings at the time of the war in Ethiopia. He taught lessons on the *Risorgimento*, describing—with anti-Fascist intent—Mazzini and Garibaldi; he also gave dictations on the need to respect the elderly, while the other Italy ribaldly sang "Giovinezza, giovinezza!" ["Youth, youth!"]. Giuseppe Latronico provided an interpretation of the figure of Balilla as a boy who had rebelled against the oppressor, aside from all the Mussolinian super-fluities; Carlo Fontana did the same with *The Parliament* by Carducci, which became an ode to liberty and the people's pride. Aurelio Castoldi had his students perform a comedy in which a helmet and musket were nothing more than a carnival costume for a young member of the Fascist youth group, who threw them away in order to save a boy who had fallen into a small lake and to take a bouquet of flowers to his mother. With Fascism in full swing, Fabio Maffi wrote about the solidarity between richer children, who brought white bread to school, and children who were already working as day laborers and ate "black bread"; and about a blackcap's yearning for freedom. In a dictation, Anselmo Cessi had his students write that "intolerance offends justice"; Abigaille Zanetta had her students write that "blessed will be the day when egoism and hate disappear from the world as the reason for fierce conflicts, and iron and steel will not be used to forge instruments of death but plows for the earth and machines for free and redemptive work"; she also recounted a poverty-stricken girl's social redemption through beekeeping. Alda Costa refused to take her classes to a movie about the war because, to her, there was no identity-forging relationship between patriotism and military nationalism. Mariangela Maccioni refused to teach a lesson about the Duce, and when she was forced to do so, she rushed through the lesson during the last hour of class; her students were also caught singing the song *Bandiera Rossa*. In 1944, Anna Botto took her students to the funeral of a partisan who had been shot by the Fascists.

xviii

Introduction

4. THE BOUNDARIES OF THE STUDY. THE
TWELVE TEACHERS AND ALL THE OTHERS.

I decided to talk about twelve teachers—almost all of whom were active at school during the Fascist period—whose stories represent different ways of opposing the regime: the more head-on opposition, which I found above all in the female teachers—Alda Costa, Mariangela Maccioni, Abigaille Zanetta, and Anna Botto—and which resulted in their expulsion from school and internal exile, and in other cases in their assassination or deportation; and the more calculated and even covert opposition to the institutions, which allowed Aurelio Castoldi, Carlo Fontana, Giuseppe Latronico, and even Salvatore Principato to continue teaching. I also examined political leanings that differed from those of the predominantly socialist teachers, from Carlo Cammeo to Abigaille Zanetta and Salvatore Principato: the liberalism of Giuseppe Latronico, the Catholicism of Anselmo Cessi and Anna Botto, or Franz Innerhofer, who simply discovered his own anti-Fascism while defending his traditions and homeland. A different case is Fabio Maffi, the oldest of the twelve teachers; he was born in 1863 and conducted almost his entire career as a teacher and politician before the rise of Fascism. When Cammeo was killed in 1921, Maffi was already fifty-eight years old, even though he had spent almost the entire Fascist period working in the background with younger teachers, above all in the initiatives of the publishing house Labor. He was still fully active when he died in 1955. I didn't investigate other experiences similar to his, such as the Socialists Linda Malnati (1855–1921) and Emilia Mariani (1854–1917) (Bertolo 2017, 67–88), because they died before 1922 and thus barely overlapped with the rise of Fascism.

Similarly, I did not take into account important episodes of deportation and Resistance that were experienced by teachers, both male and female, who taught only after the Liberation. This is the case of the young teacher who was deported to Ravensbrück, Lidia Beccaria Rolfi. She was born in 1925 and graduated in 1943, and returned from the Lager to become one of the most important female witnesses of concentration camps. She died in 1996. In 1944, she had yet to complete her first year of teaching in an elementary school in Torrette, a district of the Municipality of Casteldelfino in Valle Varaita (Beccaria Rolfi and Bruzzone 1978, 10), because she was arrested for her activity in the Resistance on March 13. Even though her contribution was fundamental, I cannot include her teaching experience in the group of teachers studied here, in part because of the subsequent reflection on the conditions of children under the dictatorship (Beccaria Rolfi and Maida 1997; Greco 2005; *Lidia Rolfi. Una memoria per il futuro* 2016).

Introduction xix

The same thing can be said for Vera Vassalle, who was born in Viareggio in 1920, received her teaching degree, and then was employed at the savings bank in Lucca. After September 8, 1943, she became a partisan fighter and kept in contact with the Allies, constructing an efficient information network using a radio transmitter known as Radio Rosa. Her story was remembered and described by Mario Tobino in the novel *Il Clandestino* (Milan: Mondadori, 1962). She received a gold medal for military valor and only became a teacher during the post-war period. She died in 1985 (Bertolo 2017, 215–17).

Instead, I could have recounted many teachers' stories that are similar to the twelve profiles presented here, all of which are marked by strong and specific identities: Andrea Tacchinardi, who is frequently mentioned in this book; Maria Giudice (1880–1953), whose exemplary story is well told in the book written by her daughter Goliarda Sapienza, *Lettera aperta* (Milan: Garzanti, 1967); the communist teacher from Bologna Adalgisa Breviglieri (1874–1924), who taught in Ancona, was fired during Fascism, was severely beaten in 1924, imprisoned for two months, and died prematurely, in part because of the suffering she endured (Bertolo 2017, 173–74). Or the Slovenian teacher from Pirano, Antonio Sema (1888–1945). A socialist born into a poor farming family, after earning a living as an unskilled worker and a fisherman, Sema became a self-taught elementary school teacher. He also organized classes for adults, following a model that was shared by many of his colleagues with similar ideals. He was also a director of studies, always following the line of proletarian Internationalism. At school, he fostered dialogue between teachers and students, the exchange of ideas, and the development of an informed critical sense. At the end of World War I, he was harshly attacked, first by nationalist associations and later by Fascist ones (Sema 1995).

Another elementary school teacher was Camilla Ravera, born in Acqui Terme in 1889, the second of seven children from a cultured, middle-class family; she taught in Turin and in 1921 was one of the founders of the Italian Communist Party. She fought for women's rights and published articles in *L'Ordine Nuovo*, edited by Antonio Gramsci. She was persecuted by Fascism and spent thirteen years between prison and internal exile. She was in Ponza and in Ventotene with Sandro Pertini, who nominated her Senator-for-life in 1982. She died in 1988 (Ravera 1973). More or less her same age, Elvira Berrini Pajetta was born in Novara on March 23, 1887; she was the daughter of Mosè Berrini, a liberal democrat engineer working for the railways, and of Mariuccia Berrini, and was a convinced Catholic. She became a teacher in 1904 and, starting in 1909, she taught in Turin in the schools of the city's San Paolo district. She took a stance against the war and in 1909 joined the Teachers Union. In 1927, her eldest son, Giancarlo, was accused of anti-Fascism and suspended from the "Massimo d'Azeglio" high school and then from every school in the kingdom for three years. Elvira was considered his accomplice and fired "for having refused to collaborate with the police in suppressing criminal activities." She also experienced the Resistance as a mother, through the persecution of her three sons, who were imprisoned (Giancarlo), deported to Mauthausen (Giuliano), and died in combat (nineteen-year-old Gaspare, killed on February 13, 1944) (Goria 1964; Berrini Pajetta 1981; [Berrini] Pajetta 2015). Elvira died in 1963.

Elvira's experiences interweave with those of Clelia Montagnana, the sister of Rita, who was married to Palmiro Togliatti. A socialist Jew, she was born in 1892, was very active in the defense of women's rights and, during Fascism, in helping prisoners and persecuted anti-Fascists. She was removed from school as a result of the 1938 racial laws and was sent into internal exile in Ateleta, in Abruzzo, where she remained until the Liberation. She died in 1962 (Arian Levi and Montagnana 2000).

One anti-Fascist teacher who was severely persecuted by the regime was Rita Majerotti, who, like Camilla Ravera and Elvira Berrini Pajetta, has been the focus of various important studies (Majerotti 1995; Bertolo 2017, 188–97).[7] Born in Castelfranco Veneto on August 27, 1896, she was the daughter of Eugenio, a socialist teacher and admirer of Garibaldi. She received her teaching degree in 1896 and, thus, conducted a good portion of her teaching activity at pre-Fascist schools. She was widowed at a very young age when her husband, Giuseppe Tonon, died, leaving her with two children aged three and four. She was in good relations with Angelica Balabanoff and moved first to Milan and later to the province of Mantua. She published her autobiography, *Il romanzo di una maestra* [*The Novel of a Teacher*] in installments in the journal "La Difesa delle Lavoratrici" between 1913 and 1915, but then distanced herself from the magazine and assumed positions that were increasingly against the war. In 1915, she moved to Bari, where she continued to teach a fourth-grade class of girls and where she met Filippo D'Agostino, who shared her socialist ideas and project. They married in 1918 and, in 1921, they both joined the Italian Communist Party. From that moment on, their lives and their political and social battles became difficult. As disciplinary actions against her increased in number, Rita wrote several articles about school, women's conditions, and against the war for *Puglia Rossa*, a socialist bimonthly magazine published in Bari that was shut down by the Fascists in 1923. Her director of studies wrote that "the teacher has a vast culture, easy eloquence, and would have been a good teacher if she had taught her lessons willingly and hadn't been distracted by sectarian associations" (Majerotti 1995, 50). In May 1921, she was temporarily suspended from her duties; she was arrested in August 1922 and, on October 31, was attacked by roughly one hundred Fascists who devastated her house. She was able to escape through the window but her hair turned completely white. She left Bari, joined her

Introduction xxi

husband in Trieste, and was soon fired by the school for subversive activity; after various appeals, the situation was resolved in 1927 with a perpetual ban from teaching. She left Italy with her husband but they remained only a short time in France, from which they were deported. Filippo D'Agostino was first arrested, and then sent into political exile in Ustica, Favignana, and Ponza until 1932. He was ultimately deported to Mauthausen, where he was assassinated in Hartheim Castle on July 14, 1944. Rita faced a period of isolation, which nonetheless didn't prevent her from returning to Bari and continuing her political activity there. She died in 1960.

Many other elementary school teachers were active in the Resistance and combined their teaching activity, in places that were often impoverished, with their struggle against Nazi-Fascism, in many cases offering a logistical base to partisans. For example, Ernesta Cena (1924–2015), a teacher at Rifreddo, in the province of Cuneo. Ines Poggetto (1919–2007), a teacher in the Lanzo Valleys in the province of Turin, in areas where helping and collaborating with partisans was a daily activity. She was the daughter of Moïse, a Jew who was deported to and died at Auschwitz, and the cousin of a partisan commander; she was repeatedly arrested and experienced firsthand the entire anti-Fascist struggle. Fausta Petri (1894–1966), who lived in Rome and was expelled from school for anti-Fascism in 1926; she was one of the women who protested against the Ardeatine massacre in 1944 (Bertolo 2017, 208–09, 226–29). Cesira Fiori (1890–1976), who taught first at Velletri and then in Rome, until she was removed from school in 1928 and made political conspiracy her prime activity as a member of the Communist Party. In 1933, she was arrested and, in 1934, sent into internal exile on Ponza, Ustica, and in Maratea, until she joined her husband, who was also in internal exile, at San Demetrio ne' Vestini, in Abruzzo (Fiori 1965). He became the mayor of the town for five months in June 1944, even before the Allied troops arrived.

The examples could be extended to lesser-known cases, all the way to completely forgotten examples that surface from the memories of numerous witnesses and, above all, from archives, helping us create active memories that would otherwise be lost forever. I will offer only a few examples but there are many teachers' names in the archives of Fascist police headquarters, some of whom were only reported as suspects.

At Rivisondoli, a small town in Abruzzo in the province of L'Aquila, the elementary school teacher Ettore Ramicone, the founder and organizer of an association named after Karl Marx, was attacked by Fascists in January 1923, after the club was destroyed by the Blackshirts of Pràtola Peligna on December 18, 1922 (Puglielli 2003, 144).[8] Giacomo Matteotti wrote:

A squad of Fascists invades the house of the teacher and veteran captain Ettore Ramicone and, after dragging him into the piazza, they tie him to a tree. The xxii *Introduction*

attempt to shoot him by firing squad was deflected by the intervention of a Fascist who limited himself to whipping Ramicone. That same night, a poor woman had to submit to the sexual desires of about twenty Fascists before the eyes of her own husband (Matteotti 1983, 193).

Not far away, in the municipality of Balsorano, in November 1922 the teacher Agata Zega was forced to "swallow castor oil for not having participated at a Fascist rally" and Fascists tried to "invade the house of the teacher Antonio Durante because he hadn't bared his head at the sound of the hymn" (Matteotti 1983, 169). In Cremona, in October 1923, the Republican teacher Sandro Borghi was attacked and beaten by Fascists (Matteotti 1983, 246).

The State Archive of Naples conserves files regarding two teachers from the town of Poggiomarino, Giovanna Annunziata and Anna Bonaguro, who apparently were investigated as subversives and condemned to several months in prison "for the crime of instigation and offense to the person of HE the head of State" because, in 1931, a few of their students supposedly ripped a photo of the Duce out of their textbooks and one of them even tore it in two and threw it from the balcony.[9]

The State Archive of Milan conserves the file of the Carabinieri of Monza dated December 20, 1926, regarding the teacher Maria Viganò from Albiate, who supposedly didn't hang the portrait of Mussolini on the main wall, but "in the right-hand corner at the back of the classroom," and who, on November 4, attended a rally with her students to celebrate the victory without the "banner" that had been supplied to the class. "The incident" supposedly demonstrated her "scarce patriotic feelings," but wasn't serious enough to take action. At Nerviano, always in the province of Milan, the *podestà* indignantly reported to the prefect on May 23, 1928, that the teacher Armida Maurelli had her students recite prayers for the liberation of a certain Dr. Niccolini, an anti-Fascist who had been arrested in Rho, and that she had organized a petition requesting his release. Reported by her fellow teachers, she continued to teach, leaving in the town a "disgusting impression, that could only be canceled by an immediate, just, and exemplary measure!" The teacher from Codogno, Vincenzo D'Angelo, "of good moral conduct," but "with subversive ideas, in part due to friendly relations with a fervent Communist, a certain Prof. Mattioli Tito, who used to teach at the officially-recognized high school in Codogno," was investigated by the Royal Carabinieri on August 14, 1927, because, since he had expressed "inopportune comments" in public regarding the general secretary of the National Fascist Party, he was supposedly "slapped [. . .] before his class by a group of Fascists," even though, after this episode, he was no longer "molested, since he conducted a very secluded life."[10]

Introduction xxiii

5. TEACHERS WHO WERE VICTIMS
OF THE DICTATORSHIP.

In his above-quoted speech to the Teachers Union just after Italy's liberation, Andrea Tacchinardi remembered two teachers who were among the most representative victims of the dictatorship and who were killed during the regime's most extreme moments: as it rose, Carlo Cammeo (1921) and as it set, Salvatore Principato (1944). But there were also many others, all barbarically assassinated by Fascists or Nazis, starting with three of the teachers whose stories are told in this book: Franz Innerhofer, who, eleven days after Carlo Cammeo, was killed on April 24, 1921, in Bolzano by Blackshirts commanded by Achille Starace during a parade in traditional costume that was one of the events held during the town's yearly fair; Anselmo Cessi, who was assassinated by two Fascist hit men on the evening of September 19, 1926, as he and his wife were walking down a street in Castel Goffredo, near Mantua; the teacher from Vigevano, Anna Botto, who was possibly burnt alive in the German concentration camp of Ravensbrück. Her prison mates saw her for the last time in November 1944, in the so-called sick ward, which SS troops burnt down with flame-throwers before the camp was liberated.

Three teachers were also killed during the Nazi-Fascist massacres on March 18, 1944, in the Emiliano Apennines, at Monchio, Costrignano, and Susano: Teobaldo Ferrari, Giovanni Battista Ceccherelli, and Camillo Baldelli.

Teobaldo Ferrari was born in Montefiorino, in the province of Modena, on February 3, 1918; even though he did not have a teaching degree, he taught at the school in the small town of Campagna. He lived in San Vitale (Fantozzi 2006, 299, 312, 314, 464), and according to information supplied by the Modena chapter of ANPI [National Association of Partisans of Italy], starting on October 11, 1943, he was a partisan in the "Dragone" brigade with the nom de guerre "Baldo." He was a member of the Resistance in the Upper Secchia Valley and was killed at Monchio.

Giovanni Battista Ceccherelli was born in Modena on August 24, 1921, and was a resident of Modena; in December 1943, he began teaching at the Cà Vecchia school in Costrignano, where he was killed (Fantozzi 2006, 91, 123, 280–81, 296, 299, 411, 452, 466; Cozzi 1964).

Camillo Baldelli, born in Modena on March 14, 1916, was the son of Maria Luisa Baldelli, father unknown; he was a resident of Modena and after September 8, 1943, he was an elementary school teacher at the school in Susano (Fantozzi 2006, 280–81, 294, 299, 410–11, 467; Cozzi 1964). Sister Imelde Ranucci, who was also an elementary school teacher at Palàgano, was possibly an eyewitness and recounted:

xxiv *Introduction*

> At Susano [. . .] even the teacher, an excellent young man from Modena, whose only thought was his teaching duties, was arrested and violently hit with a rifle butt. He was left on the ground horribly massacred (Ranucci 1979, 23).

At Marzabotto, in the small town of Cà Beguzzi, near Casaglia, on October 4, 1944, a young teacher who was active in the Resistance, Ginetta Chirici, born in Pistoia, was massacred on November 24, 1924. The same fate awaited Graziella Giuffrida, who was born in Catania in 1924 and went to Genoa to teach. She was found in possession of a weapon and is said to have been raped, brutalized, and tortured by several German soldiers on March 24, 1945; her body was found in a grave after the Liberation. Rita Rosani, a Jew of Czechoslovakian extraction (originally Rosental), was born in Trieste on November 20, 1920; she was a teacher at the city's Hebrew school and chose the path of armed resistance to fight racial persecution; she was killed on Mount Comun di Negrar, near Verona, on September 17, 1944.

Cecilia Deganutti was a few years older; she was born in Udine on October 26, 1914, and taught at the elementary school at Castions di Strada; she was also a Red Cross nurse, a partisan courier in the "Osoppo" group, and was also active in providing nursing aid to the partisans. She was arrested in Udine on January 6, 1945, accused of espionage, tortured, locked up in the Risiera di San Sabba compound, and killed that same year on April 4. Her body was burned in the crematory (Bertolo 2017, 212–24).

6. THE CIVILIAN RESISTANCE OF ELEMENTARY SCHOOL TEACHERS.

The scope of this book is not to provide a list of the elementary school teachers who opposed or were victims of the Fascist dictatorship between 1921 and 1945, but, if a list were to be compiled—and sooner or later this will have to be done—the numbers would certainly be higher than expected. When this data is available, we will better understand the extent of the phenomenon and will be able to evaluate what can only be surmised today: the extent to which teachers were reference points in their communities—above all, in rural areas but also in cities—and inevitably helped define their cultural orientations and, particularly in small towns, followed their destiny.

But the history of these teachers hasn't been written, in part because it is very hard to write. The documents are few, if not nonexistent, and testimony is patchy. The archives of schools in general—and elementary schools, in particular—are often poorly conserved or have been destroyed.

At any rate, from this initial study, we can conclude that the didactic experiences of anti-Fascist teachers show that anti-Fascism cannot be resolved in an

Introduction xxv

unambiguous perspective of militant politics, first in opposition from abroad and clandestine propaganda, and later in armed struggle against the regime during the War of Liberation, even though many teachers were involved, as instigators and as victims. Moreover, they also bear witness that Fascism can also be opposed in a less direct and head-on manner, through language and cultural models. To do this, they offered their young students examples that often came from the past, from the pre-Fascist culture whose values were antithetical to the dominant ones and, thus, rejected: values such as freedom, independence, solidarity, and social aspirations.

The teachers' actions were certainly much more than a challenge. Their objectives were lofty and very noble. There is still much to investigate but I hope I have helped illuminate, to a small degree, an eclipsed page of Italy's history.

* * *

This book would not have been possible without the trust and support of the Fondazione Memoria della Deportazione, which believed in the project right from the start, and without the fundamental contribution of the Ministry for Cultural Heritage and Activities (MiBAC). A special debt of recognition to all those who, through their suggestions and bibliographical recommendations, helped me explore the world of these teachers and their memory, from Carla Giacomozzi to Simone Zecca, Natalia Tunesi, Carlo Morani, Manuel Delogu, Katiuscia Di Rocco, Valentina Bianco, and the witnesses quoted in the book—of whom I would like to name at least the last one I interviewed, Danilla Gaviglio, who studied under Anna Botto. My thanks also go to Daniela Bianca Maria Di Vaio, who helped me translate the German-language research, and to Ludovica Holz for her rereading and precious advice during every phase of the work. Lastly, I cannot help but thank the editor Carmine Donzelli, who immediately accepted my editorial proposal, and Marianna Matullo, for her painstaking and competent editorial revision.

NOTES

1. Andrea Tacchinardi, the son of Pietro and of Maria Borra, was born on March 2, 1884, in Pieve Porto Morone, in the province of Pavia, where he lived throughout his childhood; he spent time with the Hon. Emilio Canevari, who was also from Pavia, and followed his political line. He became a member of the Socialist Party, was elected a member of the town council at Pieve Porto Morone and a member of the provincial council for the district of Corteolona. With the rise and consolidation of Fascism, he was attacked and escaped punitive raids that, not finding him, threatened his family. He aided and housed people who were wanted and persecuted by the

xxvi   *Introduction*

Fascists. He never became a member of the National Fascist Party. After the war, he focused on union activity. He died in Milan on September 2, 1969 (and not in 1989, as is written in the book quoted: Callegari 1991, 128).

2. During the days of the Liberation, by popular demand Piazzale Loreto in Milan was renamed Piazza Quindici Martiri [Piazza Fifteen Martyrs—translator's note]. We can read the honorific in "L'Unità. Edizione dell'Italia Settentrionale," April 29, 1945, 2: *In piazza Quindici Martiri. Una grande manifestazione delle donne milanesi,* and also, outside Milan, on the front page of the newspaper published in Modena, "L'Unità Democratica. Organo del Comitato di Liberazione Nazionale di Modena," April 30, 1945: *Il cadavere di Mussolini giace in Piazza XV Martiri.* The Municipality of Milan subsequently preferred to maintain the piazza's historical name.

3. The essay by Carla Ghizzoni, from which I have taken only this small amount of information, is an important synthesis of the evolution of teachers' conditions during the first two decades of the twentieth century.

4. Highly precious research for a scrutiny of news reports and final reports of teachers regarding Fascist liturgy in elementary schools, which, in contrast, highlight the teaching activity of the teachers presented here.

5. See *infra*, chapter VI.

6. This topic is dealt with more in depth in chapters 7 and 9.

7. The Gramsci Foundation in Rome houses the archive given to them by her granddaughter Anna Tonon, who is very active in conserving and valorizing the memory of Rita.

8. The episode is documented at the State Archive of L'Aquila, *Fondo Questura,* cat. A8, b. 129, fasc. 5.

9. State Archive of Naples, Police Headquarters of Naples. Archivio di Gabinetto, second part, *Schedario politico. Sovversivi radiati*, b. 12, fasc. 163.

10. State Archive of Milan, Gabinetto prefettura I versamento, b. 754, *Segnalazioni di sospetti (1926–1928).*

Chapter 1

The Assassination of Carlo Cammeo

You were a teacher, teach us to live!

—Giuseppe Emanuele Modigliani

Among the tombs at the Jewish cemetery in Pisa, one in particular stands out; it belongs to the elementary school teacher Carlo Salomone Cammeo. Next to his photograph is the historical symbol of Socialism, the hammer and sickle resting on an open book. Underneath, a long inscription reads: "Per sicaria mano fascista/ cadeva assassinato/ il 13 aprile 1921/ Carlo Cammeo/ glorificando col sangue/ la santità della scuola/ e la sua fede/ nell'idea socialista/ Occhi di bimbi/ che vedeste morto il maestro/ dite agli uomini esterefatti/ quanto amore irradiasse/ la mite anima sua/ poi con le mani avvinte/ ad uno ad uno/ promettete o bimbi/ che sarete buoni/ come lui fu buono."["By the hand of a Fascist hired killer / on April 13, 1921 / Carlo Cammeo / was assassinated / glorifying with his blood / the sanctity of schools / and his faith / in the Socialist idea / You children's eyes / who saw your dead teacher / tell the horrified men / how much love was radiated / by his gentle soul / then with your hands gripping / each other's / promise, oh children / that you will be good / like he was good."] This same inscription, with the addition "The municipal council of Pisa / at the dawn of freedom / interpreting the sentiment / of the townspeople," is written on a commemorative plaque that was placed in 1945, I believe, in the sixth borough on Via Contessa Matilde, on a building that used to be the school where Cammeo taught and where he was killed.

He was born in Libya, in Tripoli, on May 6, 1897. He had yet to turn twenty-four when he died. A Jew, a socialist, a valued teacher, despite his young age he graduated in 1917 with a thesis that had an unusual title for the time: *Punishments and Rewards in Elementary School* (Galoppini 2006,

2 *Chapter 1*

215). Like many other socialist teachers, on December 26, 1919, he left the National Teachers Association. He sent a letter to the president of the association's Pisa chapter, Ugo Tagliagambe, that was published on the third page of the weekly *L'Ora Nostra* on January 1, 1920, and dated December 26, 1919:

> Seeing as how the National Teachers Association suffocates those elements that try to introduce new ideas, the undersigned sends this respectable Board of Directors his resignation as a member, in order to renew the teachers' conscience.

Tagliagambe replied to Cammeo in the next issue, on January 10, denying that he had ever "expressed an idea" during the meetings at which he had participated, and that he had ever "asked to speak about the questions under discussion." This was the first time Carlo Cammeo's name appeared in the journal *L'Ora Nostra*; within one year, Cammeo would become the journal's editor. In July 1920, Amulio Stizzi was replaced by Dino Cassoni, who in turn resigned as editor in favor of Cammeo on January 28, 1921.

Always in January 1920, the byline "Libicus" appeared in the journal, a signature that was ubiquitous in the publication and generally believed to be Cammeo's pseudonym. Sometimes, "Libicus" and "Carlo Cammeo" signed different articles in the same issue and even on the same page. No historical research has been conducted to this regard, but we must always distinguish between the articles signed by "Libicus" and those signed by "Carlo Cammeo." In fact, the "Libicus" byline implies, if not a different author, collaboration with others in writing the article, or at the least a different participation than when Cammeo himself wrote.

On April 3, 1920 (page 2), "Libicus" praised the founding of the Teachers Union in Pisa:

> Thus, an initial nucleus of avant-garde teachers has been formed in Pisa, too.
>
> Nauseated by the feeble, dilatory, and uncertain methods of the Teachers Association, they didn't hesitate to distance themselves from the ranks of an organization that has no reason to exist in our era. With faith and enthusiasm they, the laborers of the mind, sided with their brothers, the physical laborers.
>
> These teachers are convinced that, only by supporting the proletariat in the struggle they have engaged for its conquests, will they in turn achieve better economic and moral conditions.
>
> I am persuaded that only by participating effectively in the class struggle of the exploited against the exploiters, can they aspire to that material well-being to which every worker is entitled, to that moral consideration which must derive from their delicate, vital function.
>
> This first nucleus of teachers in Pisa has abandoned the old pathway and, courageously, by divesting itself of prejudices, sophistries, and past traditions,

The Assassination of Carlo Cammeo

is fraternally extending its hand to workers and farmers and saying, "My interests are in common with yours alone! He who exploits your work also exploits me: he who tramples on your rights, who fattens off your sweat, is the same person who makes me the poorest and the least-considered of workers. My place, oh worker with calloused hands, is at your side."

Whether or not he was "Libicus," Carlo Cammeo was one of those teachers; in early 1920, he had already become the secretary of the provincial federation of the Socialist Party and was striving for the unity of all workers.

On the first page of the issue dated February 4, 1921, in an article entitled "The Two Views," Cammeo, using his full name, began a dispute with the secessionists from Livorno, "excellent minds," "ardent polemicists," "marvelous writers of articles," but lacking "marked talent for action." He called for the unity of the movement in order to render its revolutionary power truly active, whereas the secessionists had supposedly weakened or, in any case, delayed it, during a difficult moment for the country and for Europe, when the Socialist revolution was anything but imminent and had to be laboriously prepared by coming together and not dividing themselves. The following February 18, he called for the party's internal reorganization in an editorial entitled "Let's Close Ranks!" On March 18, in an article entitled "Workers and Farmers," he once again called for the unity of the laborers in the factories and in the fields.

In the meantime, in almost every small town in Tuscany, Fasci of Combat were formed, while acts of fascist violence multiplied with the aim of progressively weakening the democratic forces. Attacks and devastation were repeatedly inflicted on municipal administrations, leagues, cooperatives, factory workers associations, newspaper headquarters, and even societies of Catholic inspiration, such as the one in Vicopisano, which was burned down (Vanni 1967, 45).

Giuseppe Emanuele Modigliani wrote Cammeo a letter that was published in *L'Ora Nostra* on February 18, 1921, in which he declared he was deeply concerned about the complexity of the historical moment:

Dear Cammeo, of course I would gladly come to your provincial congress! The moment is so serious, because of what is *smoldering* against the Socialist workers' movement, that I would like to say what is in my heart—everything I have in my heart—to everyone, and especially to those who have asked me to represent them. [. . .] We have been dreaming for so long, that upon wakening, we realize that, instead of the assailants, we have become the assailed. We must take remedial action. The municipalities, which we conquered yesterday, are threatened; already the cooperatives are undermined [. . .]. Thus, remedial action, and all united, without personal or sectarian ambitions, without bluster

4 *Chapter 1*

and without escape, with full solidarity for everyone who has been struck; for those who dare and for those who only suffer.

On March 4, 1921, just over one month after the Party was founded in Livorno (January 21), Enrico Ciampi, who had left the Socialist Party and founded the first chapter of the Communist Party in Pisa, at Barca di Noce in the hamlet of San Frediano Settimo, was shot to death by the Fascist marquis Domenico Serlupi, who, it was said, "had also killed a local girl with his car near San Prospero" (Vanni 1967, 47). The *squadristi* attacked the entire town of Barca di Noce, arrested Ciampi's children and other anti-Fascists, and severely beat them. They destroyed the headquarters of the Communist and Socialist parties, as well as the workers' recreation center. In early March, Fascists invaded the Confederated Trade Union in Florence and assassinated the Communist Spartaco Lavagnini and the Socialist railway worker Gino Mugnai (Vanni 1967, 48).

At the end of March, during one of the many raids the Blackshirts conducted and that often sparked armed and violent defensive reactions, a Fascist from Pisa, Tito Menichetti, was killed in a clash at Ponte a Moriano.

Menichetti's death heightened the tension. The Fascists distributed a pamphlet that read "Tito Menichetti will be avenged. Without mercy!" On April 1, 1921, Cammeo intervened on the front page of the weekly *L'Ora Nostra*, openly denouncing the danger and the contradictions of the moment. The following is the entire article he wrote, signed with his full name and entitled simply "Recklessness":

A small banner surreptitiously printed and affixed, under the noses of the obliging authorities, to the walls of Pisa's main streets warns: "Tito Menichetti will be avenged. Without mercy!"

Knowing the valor and heroism of Pisa's Fascists, valor that has earned them the excessive praise of Fascism's every committee and subcommittee, we should logically shrug our shoulders and let the youngsters vent and bark at the moon. Instead, we do not want that small banner to go unobserved because we're too fed up and indignant at seeing how they ride public opinion and prepare, at least in their intentions, the foul deed that will spark new bereavement and new pain.

The greater public—which comprises the categories of the indifferent, the reactionaries, the tardy, and the conservatives-come-what-may, who are moved when they read the oversize titles and consider Socialist-eaters the saviors of family serenity—are invited to reflect on the three lines of that concise manifesto.

With regard to the brief life that was cut short, we do not intend to offend a death by shamefully speculating over his still-warm corpse.

On the contrary, our soul is deeply pained to note how the folly of destruction and death leads to a dispersal of energy that is useful to all of humanity, and continuously emerges in the tears and bereavement of hundreds of families.

But why did the Fascists go to Ponte Moriano? What high ideal did they have to defend, what noble action did they have to accomplish, what useful benefit did they intend to receive from their punitive foray?

Destructive mania, the desire to impose their will on those who think differently, the acrid satisfaction of sowing terror in a peaceful hamlet, whose inhabitants are only guilty of having a Socialist association, on which, as a sign, they placed the emblem of the *soviets*.

Didn't those irresponsible people think that someone, crazed at the sight of the destruction of their own home, built through their sweat and toil, might respond to this supreme offense with an inhuman gesture, and sever lives in a savage but superhuman outburst of their own indignation? Didn't the promoters of that grievous expedition think that, after their crazed violence, a mother might find herself in eternal mourning?

Now, a father, petrified by pain, after having accompanied the flesh of his flesh to its final resting place, doesn't know whether he should curse the assassin or those who wrested his son from home and conducted him to his death!

And the irresponsible people demand and swear revenge and, horrible to say, promise new, insane, and criminal acts.

Against whom?

Against the workers who struggle to break their chains and don't want to see their meeting places destroyed and sacked. Against men who have families, who want to emancipate their children, and who are forced to extreme acts of defense that expose them to the cruelest persecution, to the most tragic and infinite torture.

Let the flags fly at half-mast, and bare your head at the passage of the young man who was killed; but may curses and disgrace await the cowards who turn death into an ignoble patriotic speculation, on those who, after having had him killed, want to inflict on other mothers the harrowing torment of losing their children.

Honest people, those who look with horror on the perpetuation of this fratricidal violence, must feel their souls fill with repugnance when they read that short, irresponsible manifesto.

Words of peace, but also a firm and indignant *j'accuse* against Fascist excesses. The following April 8, on the eve of the political elections, in an article entitled "Eve of Arms" on the front page of his weekly paper, Cammeo outlined the country's difficult situation, threatened by Fascism and violence. He expressed the sincere hope that the Socialist project might, despite everything, come true, but also great concern about the international scenario, with the prophetic statement that

6   *Chapter 1*

the World War, *the final war for the liberty, redemption, and self-determination of the people* might prove to be only the first of a long series of wars that will further afflict a bleeding Europe, and might also have repercussions in the Far East, which emanates a threatening and latent odor of gun powder that is about to explode.

Cammeo concluded:

And domestically?

Fires, massacres, devastation: these are the means that a class intoxicated by power and ill-gotten wealth uses to suffocate the aspirations of the working masses who want to break the chains of their own bondage. And thereby reveals, at home and abroad, the inability of the middle class to continue dominating the people.

With every passing day, through the tragic events that overshadow the civilization of this century in which we live, the middle class shows it is increasingly incompetent, increasingly vile, increasingly and selfishly ferocious.

And thus, as the proletariat is believed to be bewildered and terrified by the storm that has been unleashed, Italy inaugurates its electoral phase.

The proletariat that sees its organizations destroyed or threatened from within, that sees how middle-class domination is, everywhere, a sign of bondage, war, and horror, will know where to find its battle position.

And from the ballot box that opens before us, like a snare and a vendetta, the symbol of the people's international and its flaming flag will emerge victorious.

That same day, April 8, 1921, on the fifth page of *L'Ora Nostra*, a short satirical article entitled "The Valkyries" was published. It was signed "Libicus" and was widely considered the pretext under which, five days later, a number of female Fascist students participated in organizing Cammeo's murder. Without a doubt, Cammeo was responsible for the article since he was the journal's editor; it is harder to say whether he was its sole author. The satire against the female Fascist students from Pisa, new Valkyries, was very harsh: "These little girl warriors who have learned to say *Ejà!*, perhaps between one kiss and another from a Fascist boyfriend, [. . .] with their physics and history textbooks under one arm and the novels by Guido da Verona under the other, and the tricolor badge on their breast."

On the morning of April 13, 1921, a number of female Fascist students, accompanied by sixty-year-old Mary Rosselli Nissim—a Jew and the daughter of Pellegrino Rosselli, a patriotic follower of Mazzini, in whose house Giuseppe Mazzini had died—and by Giulia Lupetti, entered Cammeo's school on Via Contessa Matilde. They knocked on the door of his classroom and asked the teacher to come out into the courtyard. Before the teacher could realize what was happening, he was being held firmly so a group of comrades could shoot him twice with a revolver (Sarfatti 2000, 24–25; Peretti 2006, 119–20 and note n. 159).

Cammeo fell at the foot of an acacia. The anarchic railway worker Cafiero Ciuti immediately ran over; among the assassins, he recognized a certain Elio Meucci, a pharmacy student. Ciuti took Cammeo's body to the emergency room at the Santa Chiara hospital, but it was too late (Vanni 1967, 50).

Meucci was indicted but soon acquitted (Matteotti 1983, 169).

A few months later, Giulia Lupetti, the daughter of the garrison's commander, was nominated secretary of the women's Fascist party for her merits. The Fascists destroyed the printing press of the journal *L'Ora Nostra*.

There were various eyewitnesses to the crime, including the students. Cammeo had just written a poem dedicated to mothers on the blackboard: "And it was the nest where I was born / that called me back to your sky [. . .]. / Only here the sweet love / of my mother speaks to my heart." It was ten thirty in the morning, "the custodian let four or five young ladies, accompanied by an elderly woman, into the garden," "the teacher was four paces from the first window of his classroom, just to the left when entering," "from the first two rows of desks in the third grade class, anyone can see what is happening in the garden, even without going right up to the window," the young ladies were joined by a young man "who held the teacher firmly by the arms." The students saw everything from the window. A boy declared: "After killing the teacher, the one who shot him went over to a young lady and shot her in the leg that she held out to him." No weapon was found on the teacher's body. Thus, the Fascists simulated an act of legitimate defense, which was contradicted by the testimony of the students and the other people present. What is certain is that Cammeo was killed by Fascists under the eyes of his own students.

His funeral was imposing, thanks to the great participation of the people and associations; a number of political exponents spoke, including the Socialist Amulio Stizzi, the Communist Italo Bargagna, and the anarchist Gusmano Mariani (G. Ciucci, *Ai bimbi, La nostra inchiesta sull'uccisione di Carlo Cammeo, I funerali della vittima*, in *L'Ora Nostra*, April 22, 1921, 1–2).

The following May 20, *L'Ora Nostra* promoted a subscription organized by the Teachers Union in Cammeo's name to help his parents, who were left without financial support. Participation began in Bologna and spread widely throughout Italy. Each issue of the journal published a list of the participants in the subscription until September 2, when the total sum of 22,416.50 lira was reached. It is impossible to count all the names, but there were at least six thousand individual participants, plus associations, institutions, and cooperatives throughout the country. Tangible evidence of the broad consensus the Teachers Union enjoyed at the time.

8   *Chapter 1*

Numerous commemorations were also held for Cammeo, not only because he was one of the first victims of violent Fascist arrogance but also because he was unanimously recognized as a model of coherence, honesty, and loyalty to his Socialist values, a true life teacher. Giuseppe Emanuele Modigliani wrote of him: "Our Cammeo, you were a teacher, teach us to live!" (G. E. Modigliani, *Insegnaci a vivere!*, in *L'Ora Nostra*, April 13, 1922, 1–2).

In Milan, on January 8, 1922, in front of a large audience in the Hall of Statues in the Castello Sforzesco, Gustavo Sacerdote, Claudio Treves, and the teacher Andrea Tacchinardi remembered Carlo Cammeo at the conclusion of the congress of the Teachers Union. The congress was also attended by Cammeo's father and by Giuseppe Ciucci, from Pisa, a close collaborator of the murdered teacher, whom he called his "brother of choice." On the occasion, Treves also remembered the murder of the Socialist teacher Lorenzo Panepinto, which had occurred in 1911 in the province of Agrigento, at Santo Stefano Quisquina. Right in front of the entrance to his home, Panepinto had been killed by two rifle shots to the chest, an example of the category's long tradition of coherence and sacrifice. In his speech, Treves hoped for the end of that "black night of hate, ignorance, and crime," and the birth of a "civilization of free and equal people, of brotherhood [. . .] in the new light of history." Only then, he concluded, "our valiant and good Cammeo, can we say we that we have avenged you worthily and well, in Socialism, with Socialism."

His words sparked indignant cries of "Cowards! Assassins!" among the participants; Cammeo's father joined in, after which, "overcome and devastated," he broke out in a "flood of tears and pain" (*La commemorazione di Carlo Cammeo a Milano*, in *L'Ora Nostra*, January 13, 1922, 2). The dictatorship would soon destroy these hopes and consign Cammeo to oblivion, rather than to history.[1]

It is difficult to reconstruct Cammeo's teaching method; his students' tribute, which was made public one year after his death, offers us few details, only the essence: "*The Children to their Teacher*. On this sad anniversary, your students, too, oh Carlo, want to pay tribute to the memory of their beloved teacher and they have asked us to make public their renewed promise: that their lives will conform to the principles of goodwill and rectitude, which you taught them with such love" (*I Bimbi al Maestro*, in *L'Ora Nostra*, April 13, 1922, 1).

To this regard, his colleague and fraternal friend Giuseppe Ciucci published a very interesting article on March 4, 1921, always in *L'Ora Nostra* (3), entitled *Freedom to Teach and the Union's Program*. It is as though Cammeo himself were writing and outlining his didactic goals, which can be summarized as the essential principles of a universal school that complies with "its natural, human mission," a school that believes in the dual objectives of "valorizing to the highest degree the innate potential of every individual and their conscious freedom, to achieve the highest individual and social dignity," and of "preparing people to live economically in a universal civilization, based on the sole right of the people, under a system of the just distribution of their productive endeavors and the enjoyment of the fruits of their labor."

To Ciucci, this formulation would safeguard people from every threat tending toward the "insinuation of beliefs that transcend scientific knowledge and probative possibility (the one dignity of human thought)," because he believed that coercion was a "pedagogical crime," used during the formative period of human reasoning by reactionary powers that imposed "programmatic content, a form of educational propaganda (which they interpreted in their own way), an evocative environment, printed and decorative material, masterfully designed and organized to neutralize the natural emancipating power of education."

He added:

To us, the child of man—the object of the teacher's educational and informational care—divests himself of any destiny of privilege or inferiority that social infamy has created over the centuries, and remains, in the inner sanctum of our laboratory, a value that is intrinsic to itself.

We are obedient interpreters of the pure etymological meaning of the word 'educate:' *educere*, to draw out, to conduct the potential activities of the intimate, of the exterior, in the active communion of the id with all.

And absorbed in our scientific commitment (which becomes passion when we are propelled by vocation and conscience), we recoil at the painful discovery of every degenerative stigma we discover in the child, and we interpret his rights when we denounce the affront he received and receives from atavistic and contingent misery, from alcoholic legacy, from hygienic negligence, from the obscure crassness of the intelligence of those who reared him, from malnutrition, from the rickets he contracts already at the breast of his mother, who is exhausted by blind exploitation in the rice paddies, in the fields, in the factories, at the workbench, at the office, and at the . . . teacher's desk. [. . .]

Or instead, before a marvelously valid subject, if we feel the affront of the brusque interruption of his culture because the bulwark of social inequality raises itself fiercely between his potential and his effective destiny, the need to immediately sell his labor to a master, to deform him through contact with other deformed subjects in the toil and profanity of the alcoholic and uncivilized workplace. If, ironic, we see school taxes arise that defend this golden privilege of the wealthy . . . then ours is still the revolt of the dispassionate scholar, of the artist of education, in the pure, superior state of civic awareness. [. . .]

Of course, if dogma—for the very learned middle class that rules the land of Campanella and Galileo—is admissible for the experts of the minds of the people, the "beloved people of our grand Homeland;" if critical freedom isn't a

10 *Chapter 1*

right of human intelligence; if food, health, superior civilization are not the right of every human being, in particular of those who directly produce the wealth, then, in the eyes of holy democracy and teachers, certainly our rebellious scientific neutrality is the worst sectarian crime because this neutrality arms its defense in the name of unarmed children, and acts (how could it be otherwise?) also outside the school, participating with the proletariat in the historical class struggle to remove every order of obstacle that opposes the egalitarian right to education, a necessary vehicle for the superior civilization of future society.

I think these words suffice, above all if compared to Gallo Galli's on the *Warrior Education* of the Fascist schools quoted in the introduction, to help us understand the profound echo of rebellion that Carlo Cammeo's assassination caused in the Teachers Union. It was the first, tragic signal of the decline of an ideal of the school that truly wanted to change the world and that was quashed by Fascism and all those who permitted and fostered its rise.

NOTE

1. In this book (chapter 6), the forgotten commemoration the teacher Abigaille Zanetta gave on the first anniversary of his death is published.

Chapter 2

The Sacrifice of Franz Innerhofer

The Fascists declared they weren't throwing bombs, only firecrackers.

—Gigi Michelotti

It had only been eleven days since Carlo Cammeo was killed in Pisa when, on April 24, 1921, Fascist squads led by Achille Starace killed another elementary school teacher, Franz Innerhofer, in Bolzano (Lechner 2014; Di Michele 2014).

As opposed to Cammeo's murder, it wasn't a carefully premeditated crime, and Innerhofer might not have been involved in the struggle to block the advance of the Fascists, as Cammeo was. But the merciless violence of the episode, its historical context, and its dramatic consequences make Franz Innerhofer one of the first Italian martyrs in the fight for liberation from Fascism and, I believe, the first victim of Fascism in South Tyrol.

That day, Innerhofer became the symbol of a type of nineteenth-century patriotism that represented love for one's homeland and the desire to combat despotism; it opposed the emerging Fascist nationalism, interpreted as an all-out war against cultural fusion, heterogeneity, and cultural and religious diversity.

His story still needs to be written in full, but his participatory involvement in Bolzano's city fair in April 1921 was surely a sign of his desire to safeguard the autonomy and tradition of his mother tongue, his culture, and his own minority and diversity that Fascism planned on annihilating, obliterating, and destroying in its cult of a uniformizing, and historically nonexistent, Italianicity.

Between April 19 and April 26, 1921, Bolzano's town fair reopened for the first time since the end of the war. It was a traditional showcase of local products, accompanied by a full program of events that would culminate on Saturday, April 24, in a parade in typical Tyrolean costume.

12 *Chapter 2*

That same day, on the other side of the Brenner Pass, a referendum was held to decide on Germany's possible annexation of Austria. This event obviously created tension in South Tyrol, where many people considered the newly established border on the Brenner Pass an arbitrary imposition.

This is reflected in the considerations Leonida Bissolati made during her speech at the Teatro alla Scala in Milan on January 11, 1919, when she expressed explicit reservations about the border on the Brenner Pass, which was intended to divide the cultural unity of the Tyrolean people between two different countries, and, instead, affirmed the right of the entire German people to their own national unity (Bissolati 1919, 20–21). The Fascist attack that prevented Bissolati from completing her speech was one of the first signs of the political line of the Fasci of Combat, which were formed only two months later in Piazza San Sepolcro and made the myth of the so-called mutilated victory one of their reference points. To the Fascists, not only was the border on the Brenner not under discussion, but Italy should legitimately extend its own border along the eastern coast of the Adriatic Sea, as well.

Even though the local authorities and Bolzano's Chamber of Commerce repeatedly declared that the fair was nothing more than a popular and commercial initiative, its timing with the referendum on the other side of the Brenner Pass and the orientation of many Tyrolean political forces, from the Volkspartei to the Liberals, who were in favor of German annexation, could only generate intolerance in the nascent Fascism, which didn't consider the parade in traditional costume a random coincidence but instead an anti-Italian, programmed action by the Pan-Germanists of Bolzano and Innsbruck.

Therefore, the Fasci of Combat of Bolzano, founded that same year on February 19 during a meeting at the Hotel Kaiserkrone, decided to concentrate a large number of forces in the city on April 24. On April 16, Attilio Crupi, a member of Bolzano's Directory, went to Milan to discuss their actions with the Central Committee of the Fasci of Combat. The management gave Crupi a note addressed to the political secretaries of the Fasci of Combat of Brescia and Verona, Augusto Turati and Italo Bresciani, inviting them to take part in the punitive expedition, which at that point was already planned. Crupi met with Turati, Bresciani, and Achille Starace, the political secretary of Trento, to organize the presence of Fascist squads in Bolzano during the fair.

Acts of vandalism had already taken place in town at night; for example, street signs in German were removed, and written declarations exalting nationalism appeared on the walls of buildings.

Rudolf Carli, the president of the fair, met with the lieutenant colonel of the Carabinieri Quinto Guerri and with representatives of the Municipality to find a way so that both manifestations, the parade in Tyrolean costume and the Fascist march, could take place without incident.

According to police dispatches, around eight in the morning on Saturday, April 24, a train arrived in town carrying two hundred and ninety Fascists from Verona, Vicenza, Brescia, Bergamo, Riva, Rovereto, and Trento; these men joined the one hundred and twenty Fascists of Bolzano. Overall leadership of the expedition was entrusted to Achille Starace.

The city was defended by one hundred and seventy Carabinieri, one thousand soldiers, one hundred and fifty customs officers, and thirty members of the local police force. Every strategic point was guarded.

The Blackshirts mustered near the station and, carrying cudgels and spiked bludgeons, marched in close formation toward the center of town, chanting slogans against the mayor, Julius Perathoner. Their plan was to occupy the town hall and hang an Italian flag from it. Against the mayor's advice, a flag was, in fact, hung in Piazza Walther, where numerous other flags were already waving to celebrate the fair.

In the meantime, the city was filling with visitors: Italian merchants and tourists from northern Italy who had come to the city to attend the characteristic parade in costume.

When the parade in Tyrolean dress had already crossed Piazza Walther, a group of Fascists arrived and fell in behind the parade, defiantly flaunting a tavern sign featuring the Imperial Hapsburg two-headed eagle, which had been stolen early that afternoon.

As soon as the marching band in front of the Fascists crossed Piazza delle Erbe and began to play the Austrian national anthem, one of the *squadristi* struck the eagle sign with a club, and the situation veered out of control.

The inhabitants of nearby houses began to throw bottles, potatoes, and pails of water from their windows at the Fascists, who seized the opportunity to start shooting and then throwing a few hand grenades, one of which killed Innerhofer. About twenty-eight people suffered gunshot wounds, the majority to the legs; fourteen were hit by hand grenade shards. Recent studies have revealed that another man died of his wounds, even though the district court of Bolzano tried to cover up the incident (Fontana Josef 2010, 239). Four Fascists were also wounded, including Cesare Prosdocimi, twenty-one years old, and Gino Pollini, twenty-two.

Franz Innerhofer, who was born on August 18, 1884, was thirty-six years old at the time, and he was a drummer in the musical band of Marlengo. According to newspaper reports of the time, he was hit while attempting to help a boy, perhaps one of his students, seek cover from the shooting. He was taken to nearby Palazzo Stillendorf but died almost immediately.

At their headquarters, the former Hotel Kaiserkrone, the Fascists celebrated their victory; then, escorted by the police, they left the city around 4:40 p.m., taking a few costumes they had stolen during the parade as trophies.

14 *Chapter 2*

The reaction of the local South Tyrolean population was indignant, firm, and forceful.

That same evening, April 24, South Tyrol's Union Commission proclaimed a general strike; first the railway workers joined in, followed by the postal service, and then many other workers.

That day, the Socialist cause of the so-called subversives and the patriotic, Pan-Germanic spirit of the South Tyroleans joined forces in an anti-Fascist demonstration that was held on the afternoon of Monday, April 25, at the Viehmarktplatz (the cattle market square, today Piazza Verdi) and numbered over ten thousand people. The leaders of the Socialist workers, Franz Tappeiner and Carlo Biamino, plus Eduard Reut-Nicolussi of the Deutscher Verband, spoke from the balcony of the tavern "Zur Sonne." The mayor, Julius Perathoner, also spoke and accused the Italian police of complicity with the Blackshirts. Stores remained closed, the newspapers were not published, and black flags were displayed throughout the city in a sign of mourning. The flag flew at half-mast on the tower of the town hall.

At the time, Gigi Michelotti was a special correspondent for the daily *La Stampa* and on April 26, he wrote a long, front-page article about the events. The article, entitled "German Demonstration in Bolzano Ends Tragically Due to Fascist Intervention," reported "bombs and gunshots" during the "picturesque parade," one death and "eight severely wounded people," the indignation of the citizens, the strike, and also how the Fascists declared that "they weren't throwing bombs, only firecrackers."

The next day, it was decided that the strikers would return to work, but only after Innerhofer's funeral was over, and that a general mobilization would be called in the event of new Fascist attacks. Roughly fifteen thousand people attended the funeral, both German- and Italian-speakers.

Innerhofer's body was transported from Bolzano to Marlengo in a solemn ceremony, during which the symbolic ties to the heroic era of Tyrol's 1809 revolt against Napoleon's army were remembered.

Austrian hymns were played, and the *Andreas-Hofer-Lied* was sung in every town in the Adige valley. Roughly ten thousand people gathered in Merano alone. On April 28, Innerhofer was buried in Marlengo's cemetery.

On June 21, 1921, during his first speech in Parliament, Benito Mussolini took moral responsibility for Bolzano's "Fascist bomb," without making any reference to Innerhofer's death:

I come to the facts of April 24, when a Fascist bomb, rightfully placed for the purpose of retaliation and for which I claim my portion of moral responsibility, marked the limit beyond which Fascism does not intend to allow the German element to go. The demonstration on April 24 in Tyrol was nothing other than a demonstration that took place at the same time as the referendum held that same day on the other side of the Brenner. Because, in South Tyrol, the Pan-Germanists resort to this subtle trick: they have the same demonstrations coincide under different guises. [. . .] After all, when the Fascists showed up in Bolzano, they found the police force equipped with helmet and bow; and when they were arrested, the inquest was entrusted to Count Breitemberg, who, as everyone knows, is a member of the Deutscher Verband. [. . .] I don't know what measures the Government will adopt but I here declare, without any solemn posturing, and I declare it to the four German parliamentarians, that they must say, and make it known on the other side of the Brenner, that we are on the Brenner and will remain there, at all costs.

He also wrote in the newspaper *Popolo d'Italia* that the bomb in Bolzano was a first solemn warning and that the Fascists' daggers and gasoline were always at the disposal of the Germans of South Tyrol (Gruber 1979, 15).

As Mussolini declared, an investigation was conducted the same day the incident occurred, by order of the president of the Council of Ministers, Giovanni Giolitti.

The young man was located who had hung the eagle tavern sign—which had been stolen on the day of the parade—in the Fasci headquarters in Verona. In police records, his name was already associated with violent behavior during other punitive expeditions. A certain Bruno Zeni, twenty-two years old and from Turin, was also identified as the alleged perpetrator who had thrown the bomb in Piazza delle Erbe. But no specific recommendations were ever made regarding the murder of the teacher from Marlengo.

On October 2, 1922, seven hundred Fascists divided into squads and led by Alberto De Stefani, with Achille Starace, Roberto Farinacci, and Francesco Giunta, returned to Bolzano, occupied town hall, and forced Julius Perathoner, who had been mayor for twenty-eight years, to resign.

A short time earlier, they had occupied the "Elisabethschule" and forced it to change its name to "Regina Elena."

In Bolzano, the Fascist squads had proven that their targets were no longer only private homes, Chambers of Commerce, cooperatives, farmers leagues, mutual aid societies, Socialist chapters and clubs, and newspapers, but institutional buildings, as well, or rather, the Liberal state itself, by way of its representatives.

These were dress rehearsals for the March on Rome, the following October 28.

On August 16, 1923, the Fascist sub-prefect Giuseppe Bolis ordered the disbandment of Liberal unions. On August 18, Fascists sacked the union headquarters. A small quantity of explosives was smuggled into the building, discovered in the attic "by chance" during a subsequent search, and used as a pretext to accuse the union officials of conspiracy.

For the region, it was the beginning of a harsh process of the cancellation of its historical independence, of forced Italianization, of the cancellation of the German and Ladin languages, all the way to the programmed immigration of Italian work forces and the distortion of the areas' historical place names (Scarano 2012).

By then, Franz Innerhofer had become a symbol of South Tyrolean anti-Fascism.

Chapter 3

Anselmo Cessi

A Catholic Patriot Killed by the Fascists

Intolerance offends justice.

—Anselmo Cessi

On September 19, 1926, at Castel Goffredo, a town thirty-seven kilometers from Mantua, the Catholic elementary school teacher Anselmo Cessi was killed by two Fascist hit men as he was walking home with his wife. That same year, Piero Gobetti, an exile in Paris, had been killed on the night between February 15 and 16. He had never recovered from the beating he had received a year and a half earlier in Turin, when four squadristi had violently hit him in the face and chest.

By then, Fascism was firmly in power. Its opponents—liberal, catholic, and socialist—were considered enemies of the State and, in order to reinforce the regime in power, they were to be eliminated through force, if necessary.

There was nothing random about Cessi's murder. Everything was premeditated and carefully organized. The teacher was born on November 8, 1877; he was forty-eight years old when he died. He was at the peak of his professional career and was also the secretary of the People's Party and the local credit institution of Castel Goffredo. He was a member of the Party's provincial committee, and president of the Vittorino da Feltre Provincial Catholic Teachers Association, which had been created after their secession from the Teachers Association.

Cessi was a leading figure in Mantua's Catholicism (Telò 2000).[1] The son of Gelasio, a baker, and Maria Mazzuconi, an elementary school teacher and Franciscan tertiary, he had two older sisters, Iginia and Giulia, and a younger brother and sister who died prematurely. His grandfather, Carlo, was a patriot

18   *Chapter 3*

who had been involved in the Belfiore anti-Austrian conspiracy and was a cellmate of Tito Speri, before he was pardoned.

The Cessi household was influenced by the Risorgimento spirit on his father's side and great religious devotion on his mother's; she was also the secretary of the local Women's Catholic Society of Mutual Help. Moreover, during the years straddling the nineteenth and twentieth centuries, when Anselmo was growing up, the parish of Castel Goffredo stood out for its significant social work, promoted by its parish priests, Don Alessandro Mori (1891–1895) and Don Domenico Bodini (1895–1906), who interpreted the essence of the message of Pope Leo XIII and his encyclical *Rerum novarum*. First, the parish promoted soup kitchens, offering the poor free food; then, the Women's Catholic Societies of Mutual Help; and lastly, credit institutions for farmers, which lent money and fought usury but also helped them purchase seed, fertilizer, and farming machinery. The parish priests demanded salaries for field hands and, in 1896, founded the League for Sunday Rest. In 1911, the parish priest even created a Consumers Cooperative. In short, it was a very active and social-minded Catholicism, which aimed to compete with the Socialist movement—and did.

Anselmo Cessi spent his childhood and youth in this world. Initially, he chose to enter the seminary, where he spent his high school years and studied alongside Francsco Orsatti, who later became the town's parish priest. Cessi and Orsatti became lifelong friends.

Another one of his companions was Eugenio Leoni, born in 1880; he, too, became a priest and was later killed by the Germans with a shot to the neck on September 12, 1943, behind Mantua's train station, perhaps because he helped an Italian sergeant flee or because he refused to provide the name of a partisan fighter who had disarmed a German motorcyclist.

Anselmo was deemed unsuitable for the priesthood and chose to become an elementary school teacher instead. He interned in the classroom of the teacher Luigi Bonfanti at the boys' elementary school in Castel Goffredo. Bonfanti, a follower of Garibaldi who had fought at Milazzo and Bezzecca, helped strengthen Anselmo's Risorgimento ideals and made him his heir. Cessi began teaching the boys' fourth and fifth grade classes in Castel Goffredo during the school year 1903–1904. Like many other schools in Italy, the classes were overcrowded; the rooms were inadequate in the building located on Via Parrocchiale, near Porta Mulina and not far from where the Cinema Smeraldo would be built during the 1930s.

We have the outlines of two dictations he had his fifth-grade students write as a farewell in July 1904. One, a penmanship test, was about Garibaldi and confirmed the teacher's ardent patriotic and Garibaldian spirit, something that was not to be taken for granted in Catholics at the beginning of the twentieth century:

When you grow up, remember the virtues of the citizen who sleeps in eternal rest under the cliffs of Caprera, and your soul will rise to desire good deeds, and your actions, if they cannot be notable, will be noble and generous.

The other was a farewell before the exams and it reveals his Catholic sensitivity, as well as a strong sense of responsibility for his own civic role:

Adieu! Children, the year is over, *adieu!* Until now, we have cultivated: what remains is to reap the harvest. I was your teacher until now: soon, I will be your judge. But do not be dismayed by this thought. I am well aware of who has worked, and I will keep it carefully in mind. Therefore, return home serenely and come to the exam with confidence. But before I leave you, let me assure you that I have already forgiven those who, through their negligence, grieved my soul so often and, for the last [time] I give them an affectionate warning: "out in the world, your shortcomings will not be so easily forgiven."

In 1906, Anselmo married Erminia Schinelli, who shared his principles and values, but she died prematurely in 1919. They had seven children. His daughter Maria, who died on August 8, 1999, cultivated and bore witness to the memory of her father her whole life long.

Social Catholicism was so strong at Castel Goffredo, and in general throughout Alto Mantovano, that during the first decade of the twentieth century, it hindered the rise of the Socialist movements, which were, on the whole, anti-clerical. But conflicts between clericalists and Socialists, which were widespread throughout Italy, did occur, even though, until 1913, the most authoritative political figure of reference at Castel Goffredo was the Liberal-Radical Alceo Pastore, who was very close to Giuseppe Zanardelli, to the point that he was jokingly called the "Pastor fido."

During those years, Anselmo Cessi started becoming interested in political activism in the ranks of the nascent Christian Democracy movement. Initially, his main reference point was Romolo Murri, until Pope Pius X condemned the man, suspended him *a divinis* (1907), and excommunicated him the same year he was elected to the Chamber of Deputies (1909).

Even though Anselmo Cessi never filled the role of municipal councilor, he was on the committee for public housing, on the committee that calculated the taxes on commercial activities, and, inevitably, on the oversight committee for compulsory schooling. He also dedicated himself to the area's main social problems, starting with the fight against pellagra.

He was active in propaganda actions to spread the principles of Social Catholicism throughout Mantua and environs. He was a member of the Teachers Association until, on February 7, 1919, Mantua's Vittorino da Feltre Catholic Association, a section of the "Tommaseo," was founded. Anselmo Cessi soon became one of the members of the board of directors, and then, on

20   *Chapter 3*

July 27, 1913, he was elected its president. He opposed the Roberto Ardigò Teachers Association, which was affiliated with the Teachers Union but more oriented along secular and Socialist positions.

On December 2, 1914, Monsignor Orsatti, his classmate, became the town's parish priest, and together they launched joint policies in defense of civil and social Catholicism, just when, for the first time, Castel Gofrfredo was led by a Socialist, Omero Franceschi, who remained mayor until 1918.

The war broke out, and even though many Catholics and Socialists of Castel Goffredo soon took a public stance against intervention, it appears that, thanks to his Risorgimento patriotism, Cessi was an interventionist. On August 30, 1920, he became the secretary of the local chapter of the Popular Party and also organized a number of chapters in nearby towns; in 1921, he became a member of the Party's provincial committee. Under his guidance, Castel Goffredo was one of the few Mantuan towns where the Popular Party won the elections in 1920, with the new mayor, Enrico Gandolfini.

He was also the director of the Cassa Rurale, the farmers' credit institution, and he continued to run the Vittorino da Feltre Catholic Teachers Association, whose focal point was his own home, at Vicolo Frutta 2 (a cross street of present-day Corso Vittorio Emanuele II). Starting in June 1916, they began printing a monthly magazine, *Il Pensiero Magistrale*. Cessi fought for the right to education, which, to him, was also a recognition of private schools, but on the union level he demanded better pay and pensions for teachers. He dedicated himself to after-school institutions, organizing summer courses, building a theatre for children, and creating school libraries.

Nor did he neglect to fight their Socialist enemies, their positivism, materialism, and different concept of school.

The contrasts between Socialists and clericalists were harsh and sometimes merciless, but they were basically honest and fair, and were founded, above all, on cultural confrontation. In this climate, the local Fascio was founded in Mantua in April 1920, and the real enemies began to show up.

On March 13, 1921, Fascists attacked the Socialist Chamber of Labor at Poggio Rusco, causing many casualties. For Mantua and environs, it was also the start of a countless series of acts of violence, led by Antonio Arrivabene and Giuseppe Moschini, twenty-five and twenty-two years old, respectively. At Castel Goffredo, the Fascio headquarters was founded in June 1921; it was run by the engineer Achille Nodari, who would later become mayor and then *podestà*.

In the face of Fascist violence, the need grew for solidarity among honest people. In May 1921, the teacher Maria Mazzola Zanetti, vice president of the Vittorino da Feltre chapter, wrote to all her colleagues, urging them to cultivate tolerance and reciprocal respect:

Anselmo Cessi

Let us not facilely condemn those who do not see things our way [. . .]. Everyone who is sincerely convinced of an idea merits respect. And, above all, let us not expect to make people accept our ideas through violence. [. . .] Through words [and] examples, let us propagate among ourselves the healthy principles of justice, and true and sincere brotherhood, of well-meaning love. [. . .] It is hard and difficult to shake the hand of those who have offended us: and yet only in this way can we obtain a true and perfect peace in our hearts, regenerative social peace.

In an open letter to Renato Camosci, the editor of the daily *Il Maestro Mantovano* published by the rival Roberto Ardigò Teachers Association, Maria Mazzola Zanetti asked that the Vittorino da Feltre chapter and the opposing organization exchange copies of their respective publications and proposed a joint agreement to defend the interests of the teachers category (M. Mazzola Zanetti, *L'ora che passa*, in *Il Pensiero Magistrale*, May 1921, 33).

These were clear signs that the cultural climate was rapidly changing.

The increase in acts of violence was implacable: on May 15, 1921, a group of young Communists (*A Castelgoffredo*, in *La Voce di Mantova*, May 18, 1921, 3) was attacked and beaten. But young members of the Don Bosco Catholic society of Castel Goffredo were also beaten, as were several parish priests in the area (Telò 1987, 195–212).

Anselmo Cessi firmly condemned all this and also declared, as did many Catholics, that, although initially in favor of anti-Bolshevik Fascism, he had soon changed his mind, in view of the facts. On February 25, 1922, Achille Nodari replied in a harsh and explicitly threatening way in *La Voce di Mantova*: "Sometimes, Fascists, the local ones, can also be (is it permitted to say so?) obliging, and if you truly want their services . . . they will do their best, at the earliest occasion" (A. Nodari, *Ad un maestro*, in *La Voce di Mantova*, February 25, 1922, 3). Cessi began to be accused: of having taught anti-Fascist songs to his son Alessandro, of having removed Fascist symbols from the walls in town, etc.

In June 1922, the teacher Edoardo Rossi of the Roberto Ardigò Teachers Association was attacked by Fascists, and the Catholic journal *Il Pensiero Magistrale* publicly and firmly defended him:

More than any others, teachers have the right to be respected, and in the act that was committed against our colleague Rossi we see an insult against those who carry out a public function of such a high order that their person is rendered inviolable. Moreover, as Christian teachers, strong and free, we cry aloud that neither Fascism nor any other type of faction will bring peace and well-being to the people (*Una protesta*, in *Il Pensiero Magistrale*, June 1922, 46).

22   *Chapter 3*

A dictation has been conserved in the *Registro generale dell'anno scolastico 1921–1922, classe quarta maschile* of the Education Department Archive of Castel Goffredo; Cessi gave his students this dictation as part of a make-up exam, and it is emblematic of the atmosphere during that period:

> Tolerate the defects of your companions if you want your own to be tolerated. When you are an adult, respect the opinions of others even if they are contrary to your own. You will encounter people who believe in a faith in which you do not believe. You will find others with political ideas that are the opposite of yours; respect them and admire them if they are honest; judge people by their daily actions more than by their words. Intolerance is an offense to justice (Telò 2000, 97–98).

An excellent synthesis of what anti-Fascism could be considered at the time. Quite different from the Fascists' intentions when they took Mantua with three thousand men, right when the March on Rome took place, on October 28, 1922. Antonio Arrivabene became the head of the National Fascist Party for Mantua, and Giuseppe Moschini was put in charge of its union.

In the area around Mantua, a few "social action" parish priests were forced to leave their parishes, and at Ponti sul Mincio, Don Angelo Lizzeri was repeatedly beaten in December 1923 and January 1924. At Castel Goffredo, both Monsignor Francesco Orsatti and Anslemo Cessi were in the Fascists' sights. The walls of Piazza Mazzini filled with writings against the parish priest, such as "If you don't keep silent, we'll silence you with the holy cudgel" or "He who preaches from the pulpit, preaches lies." On December 2, 1925, the Don Bosco Young People's Society ceased its activities; the Fascists had accused it of conducting political propaganda and immoral acts. Despite Cessi's firm stance in the name of its autonomy, time was almost up even for the Vittorino da Feltre Catholic Association, which was dedicated to a type of education that was exclusively inspired by Christian principles. It closed down in July 1925.

On September 19, 1926, Cessi had just concluded an important deal with the rural bank, selling thirty tons of lime for fertilization to a client from Mantua. Around 8 p.m., he accompanied the client to his car, in the company of his second wife, Santa Dalzini, whom he had married just a year before, on February 17, 1925, after his first wife, Erminia, died in 1919. They went into town, where his wife's family owned a small restaurant.

His wife recounted, "We were walking home arm in arm and had just passed the mill [belonging to Poino], when one of the strangers we had noticed a short while earlier came up alongside me, while the other one waited about twenty meters ahead. I was scared and made a sign at my husband. I saw him turn pale."

Anselmo Cessi 23

A neighbor passed by but they only exchanged a few words. One of the two strangers ran toward Cessi and began to beat him. The teacher reacted and grabbed his attacker by the neck, while his wife tried to hold the man's arm. The other man came up and shot Cessi in the head. He died almost instantly.

A sixteen-year-old boy, Nello Spalla, was sitting on the wall near the mill and saw everything. He ran into town, shouting that the teacher Cessi had been killed. He was immediately stopped and accompanied to Cirié, near Turin, where he was given the documents he needed to emigrate to France, then ordered to leave and never come back. Nello Spalla died in Ambert, France, in April 1998.

The *podestà* Nodari prohibited that it be written on Cessi's gravestone that he had been killed. Thus, two lines of sixteen dots each were engraved on his tomb to indicate the silence that had been imposed by the Fascist authorities. Still today, at the cemetery of Castel Goffredo, the tombstone reads: "CESSI ANSELMO / TEACHER / AGE 48 / 19-IX-1926 /. . . . . /. . . . ."

In the Deaths Registry of the Municipality of Castel Goffredo, Anselmo Cessi is listed as having died of natural causes; but in the parish register, someone wrote next to his name "Violenta manu occisus," that is, "Killed in a violent manner."

In any case, it was impossible to keep the episode a secret. On September 25, the daily *Corriere della Sera* interviewed Cessi's wife, Santa Dalzini, and she reconstructed the murder in detail. The customary trial was held, and all the defendants were found innocent: the instigators, Achille Nodari and Enrico Bresciani; and the killer, the young Fascist Umberto Vescovi. Even though Cessi's wife identified Vescovi without hesitation, he was exonerated because the Fascists Arrivabene and Moschini declared the young man was in Mantua that day.

NOTE

1. I owe almost all my information to the meticulous book by G. Telò and to its bibliography.

Chapter 4

The Lofty Socialist Integrity of Alda Costa

She had always preserved her soul in all its purity.

—Giorgio Bassani

The fourth story in *Within the Walls* by Giorgio Bassani recounts the last years in the life of Clelia Trotti, an elementary school teacher from Ferrara who lived during the first half of the twentieth century. She was persecuted by Fascism, and before Italy's Liberation from the dictatorship, she died in forced solitude, as Bassani explains, "in the prison of Codegoro, during the German occupation" (Bassani 2016, 98; Bassani 1956, 159).

The story, entitled *The Final Years of Clelia Trotti*, is constructed upon the contrast between its opening description of the posthumous and solemn funeral that the city dedicated to her in the fall of 1946, attended by a large portion of the population, and the extreme, desperate solitude of her final years, when, after her imprisonment and internal exile, Clelia lived in total, enforced isolation in her home in Ferrara.

Bassani was interested in highlighting this contrast, which seems to indicate a type of insincerity that is not infrequent in human relations; this is also reflected in a quote by Italo Svevo in an epigraph of the short story, "the people whose affections are won through a ruse are never sincerely loved."[1]

In the story, the funeral seems like "one of those then typical and frequent examinations of the collective conscience by which an old, guilty society desperately tries to renew itself":

No sooner had one noticed the thicket of red flags which followed the coffin, and the scores of placards inscribed with an assortment of slogans: ETERNAL GLORY TO CLELIA TROTTI or ALL HONOUR TO CLELIA TROTTI, SOCIALIST MARTYR or VIVA CLELIA TROTTI HEROIC EXAMPLE TO

26 *Chapter 4*

THE WORKING CLASS etc., and the bearded partisans who carried them aloft, and above all the absence in front of the carriage of priests and clergymen, than one's gaze hurried ahead to where the procession was making its way: a grave, that is, dug in the portion of the cemetery exactly in front of the main entrance to the church of San Cristoforo where, apart from an English protestant who had died from malaria in 1917, no one had been buried for more than fifty years (Bassani 2016, 94; Bassani 1956, 154–55).

Instead, Clelia is described in her final years as a "small, withered woman, nearly sixty, who didn't take care of herself, with the look of a nun," forgotten and abandoned by everyone, including those who had fought by her side against the early manifestations of the dictatorship:

> On the other hand, who in Ferrara at that time could claim to know her personally, or even remember that she existed? Even the honourable Bottechiari, despite having acted a bit in his youth, and at the beginning of his political career having directed with her the legendary *Torch of the People*—they'd even been lovers, according to the whispered gossip, at least until the First World War broke out—even he, at the outset, gave the impression of having completely lost touch with her (Bassani 2016, 102–03; Bassani 1956, 165–66).

"Clelia Trotti lived [. . .] on Via Fondo Banchetto, in a small, two-story house that was almost on the corner of Via Coperta" (Bassani 1956, 168).[2] After all, barely twenty years had passed since then but it seemed like much longer. As Bassani wrote, they had seen the "progressive degeneration of every human value," "nothing, oh nothing—and Socialism with all the rest—had actually been able to conserve itself pure, intact!" (Bassani 1956, 170).[3]

"Clelia Trotti had never bowed her neck, had always preserved her soul in all its purity," but, Bassani muses, "the better world, the just and decent society of which Clelia Trotti represented the living proof and the relic," would never return (Bassani 2016, 115; Bassani 1956, 185).

After returning from her internal exile, Clelia "had been sentenced to ten supplementary years of enforced residence with a daily obligation to be indoors by dusk and to report every week at the police station to sign in the special register of the 'cautioned'" (Bassani 2016, 121; Bassani 1956, 194).

Bruno Lattes, the other protagonist of the story and the author's alter ego, manages to visit her in her solitary prison, and Clelia tells him about the books she used to read, "Comte, Spencer, Ardigò and Haeckel with his Monism"; about her difficulty in reading Benedetto Croce (Bassani 2016, 126; Bassani 1956, 201); about how she knew she had become an "old school" Socialist; about when, in 1922, as she was leaving the "Umberto I" elementary school, on Via Bersaglieri del Po, Fascists forced her to "drink a half ounce of castor oil" and covered her face "with soot." In one of the last pages of the story, Clelia reminds Bruno:

> If it hadn't been for the children who were standing there watching, and many of them crying from fear, it wouldn't have upset me that much, I can assure you. There was hardly the call to come in a group of twenty or thirty, with cudgels, daggers, skulls on their berets, to subdue a woman on her own. A nice show of force! While I was swallowing my portion of castor oil, I knew that the Blackshirts would have achieved nothing by it except to heap general disapproval on themselves (Bassani 2016, 128–29; Bassani 1956, 205).

But this didn't happen. Given the circumstances, Fascism was accepted to an unimaginable degree, in particular during the decade following these despicable episodes.

It is a known fact, and Bassani himself declares as much, that the character Clelia Trotti was based on the teacher Alda Costa. "Since we were bound by friendship and a shared political faith, I wrote this short story [. . .] in part to commemorate her," wrote the author, who knew her and visited her between 1936 and 1943 (Quarzi 2004, 57).

She was born in Ferrara to Vincenzo and Caterina Zaballi, who was also an elementary school teacher, on January 26, 1876. She had an older brother, Alessandro, and two younger sisters, Amelia and Linda (Cazzola 1992, 9, 35). After receiving her diploma as a teacher, she taught at various schools in the province of Ferrara, at Fondoreno, Marrara, and Boara. Starting in October 1895, and after passing her qualifying exam in March 1897, she taught at Fondoreno, Quacchio, and Spinazzino, until she was appointed a teaching job by the City Council of Ferrara, where she moved in 1903 and lived at Via Fossato dei Buoi no. 3.

Starting September 1, 1899, she taught a co-educational first grade class at Vigarano Mainarda, where two of her siblings, Amelia and Alessandro (Quarzi 2004, 84), were already teachers. Then, starting in 1904, Alda found herself teaching a first grade class in Porotto composed of ninety-nine boys (Quarzi 2004, 89). In 1908, she began teaching at the town school of Borgo San Luca and then at the "Calcagnini" elementary school; starting in 1912, she taught at the "Guarini" and then, later, during the war years, at the "Umberto I" (Quarzi 2004, 90–98).

During this period, she followed the reformist line of the Socialist Party with Amilcare Storchi and the lawyer Francesco Baraldi, and helped found the journal *Il Pensiero Socialista*, which survived just over one year, until November 24, 1906, when it merged with another journal that followed the party's national line, *La Scintilla*.

28   *Chapter 4*

Alda's byline appears several times in *Il Pensiero Socialista*. On November 11, 1905, in an article entitled "In iscuola (Dal vero)," she openly took a position against the hypocrisy of the textbook then in use, an emblem of false Catholic and bourgeois morals, which obliged miserable, famished children to read conscience-numbing sentences such as "Those who toil don't beg," "An industrious man was never poor!" and "Up in the sky is the father of all the poor people . . . " These readings gave the false idea that all it took was simple industriousness to redeem the condition of extreme indigence of people who had no more than a bowl of cornmeal mush to eat, and only every other day at that. This situation led to the well-known risk of contracting *pellagra*, which was widespread in those years in the area surrounding Ferrara, and in particular around Comacchio:

> When I entered the school—or rather—the low, dark, and damp room that served as a school, Pierino was crying desperately.
>
> I went over to him and before I could ask, four or five children nearby informed me confusedly about what had happened, "He wants his trumpet, Beppe took his trumpet away. No ma'am, he gave it to him, now he wants it back."
>
> "He gave it to him for a piece of bread," one of the more intelligent students corrected them. The loving reproach I was about to direct against the adversaries died on my lips. A toy for a piece of bread!
>
> The greatest, the only joy of a child surrendered to satisfy his hunger! Ah! How powerful that hunger must have been! I leaned over the small boy, who was still crying (the other child, whether out of fear of being punished or as an act of exquisite delicacy, had given him his toy back), I caressed his small, tousled head, and I asked sweetly, "Don't you have any bread at home?" He raised his large, damp, tired eyes to my face: "No ma'am," he replied, "all we make is polenta, every other evening." "Doesn't your daddy work?"
>
> "Yes, ma'am, daddy goes to work far . . . far . . . (his eyes gaze into the void) . . . he comes home late at night . . . there are lots of us who eat!" He spoke in fits and starts . . . his voice was still broken by sobs, and his last words were followed by a long, pained sigh. He was doubtless thinking about the small portion of steaming polenta on the cutting board, which disappeared so fast into the many, avid mouths. Of course, that long sigh not only held the memory of suffering but also the desire for a good, abundant meal . . . at least once! . . . I kissed him piously (his pain was sacred and a tear remained on that small, tousled head!).
>
> "Those who toil don't beg . . . ," another small boy read a few minutes later, loudly and enunciating the syllables clearly. On his face were the stigmata, the indelible sign of poverty. And the small voice continued, a bit stridently: "An industrious man was never poor!"
>
> Lies, lies, my exasperated soul shouted in a legitimate moment of rebellion. Evil, stupid hypocrisy! [. . .]

My poor creatures, starving and tired, you don't understand the meaning of the words you are mechanically reading, and my words would be in vain; but in a few years you will still find in that deceitful book the phrases suggested by hypocritical, bourgeois morality! Ah! May you then find an honest soul who will make you think about its cruel irony . . . , may you find a good soul who will bring your minds back to the thought of the sad reality, may you yourselves understand, remembering the small portion of steaming polenta on the cutting board, and the old father returning from his exhausting job every evening more tired, every evening older!

The future is yours—this is my vow—you will become aware and strong, you will strive so that privilege and heinous injustice will soon fall, and the day will dawn when the phrases that are mechanically read in the lying book, will no longer be a cruel, atrocious irony (Cazzola 1992, 57–60).

On February 24, 1906, in a similar tone and always in *Il Pensiero Socialista*, Alda wrote an article entitled "Refezione, teatro e scheda [School Meals, Theatre and Ballots]," about the great dissimilarity between the amount of public funds earmarked for a lovely theatrical play in the city and the misery of her young students, who were famished and didn't have adequate school lunches. She put the blame on the workers themselves, since they hadn't been capable of making a courageous political choice when they elected their representatives:

The ballot! This is the powerful weapon, this is salvation, this is the future! And the ballot is yours. Yours through the will of the people, through the blood and tears of the people.

And you sell it. By selling your ballot you aren't just selling your conscience, but your own interests; you are depriving your children of school meals, bread, shoes, warm clothes. You are selling relative, material well-being which could be provided by an administration that is supported by your representatives. You are not only ruining yourselves and your families, but the families of those honest and aware people who, by disdaining base compensation and compromising their future, continue proudly on the path of honesty and duty.

A disgrace and a crime!

A disgrace, to sell for a pittance your conscience and a right that was gained with your fathers' lives; a crime, to condemn your children and those of others to hunger, to poverty, whereas, if you had honestly exercised your right, they could have enjoyed those material benefits that are even allowed by today's social regulations.

[. . .]

At last, show that you are free, conscious, and proud citizens.

Don't ask, don't implore the ruling class anymore for school meals for your children. Gain them yourselves.

30   *Chapter 4*

You have the most powerful and surest weapon in your hands. You have the ballot—what else do you need! (Cazzola 1992, 71–73).

Alda Costa's sensitivity to the social condition of her students is obvious; but so was her sensitivity to the exploitation of women. This convinced her to write an article on April 14, 1906, published in *Il Pensiero Socialista*, entitled "Né la culla né la tomba [Neither the Cradle Nor the Tomb]," in which she denounced, on the one hand, the exploitation of two penniless girls, barely ten years old, who were forced to dance suggestively in public squares for money, thereby sacrificing their own fundamental right "to sunshine, love, pure kisses, to grow up kind, good, and wise"; and on the other hand, the condition of an old man, "tattered, with an emaciated face," who begged Alda to give a few coins to the girls, for he, too, was basically the victim of a society that didn't allow him any possibility of redemption:

"Be generous, sirs, please."

The two little girls picked up the small plate and began to make the rounds. They were two poor proletarian girls, about ten years old or just a bit more. They danced in the squares and taverns and thereby earned a living for themselves and perhaps for others, who preferred the torment of their children to a job; or perhaps for others, who, in a moment of supreme desperation, had grasped that heinous method as their only means of salvation.

Naturally, they were two victims. An old man with a tired smile, whose listless gaze occasionally lit up when he looked at the two girls, plonked away on his battered barrel organ. And the little girls danced, with flowing hair and naked arms. They danced with rhythmical motions of their hips, which were precociously developed; they contorted themselves in countless poses and multiple positions, purposefully raising their short, pink dresses up to their waist and revealing their green silk panties embroidered in gold.

Sometimes, their clear, little-girl eyes revealed smiles or flashes of women whose souls were already corrupted, for sure, and perhaps, who knows . . .

At every daring gesture they made, someone in the crowd tossed out a remark, an obscene word, and, as though encouraged, the two girls continued to contort their poor tired bodies.

When the final notes of the barrel organ finished, as dejected as a sob, the two girls performed an agile cartwheel—which once again displayed their bodies wrapped in green silk to the waist—and ended their dance. The crowd applauded and the two girls smiled victoriously, with unhealthy pride; without a doubt, they were smiling at bigger and more complete conquests of which their small minds were already tacitly dreaming and which they awaited with infinite desire. [. . .]

"You give them a coin, too; poor things, they have the right to live, as well," shouts a voice behind me to someone who was doubtless standing on the other side of the crowd. I turn to see who spoke. A wretched old man, tattered, with

The Lofty Socialist Integrity of Alda Costa 31

an emaciated face, his yellow skin all wrinkles and folds. He is famished. I take a long look at him and his tired voice rings in my ears: "They have the right to live, as well." Yes, they have the right to live, but they also have the right to remain honest, they have the right to sunshine, love, pure kisses, to grow up kind, good, and wise . . . And this is the right that society denies them when it doesn't try to snatch them away from the path they are on . . . And you, too, should have the right to live, poor man! Can you tell me about the furrows that have been dug, the earth that has been plowed, the harvested crops, the wheat threshed by your calloused hands, throughout your painful life? Can you tell me about the wealth produced and the misery you have suffered? Can you tell me about the joy you have given, the pain you have endured? The tears, the difficulties, the blasphemy, the curses? Can you tell me?

You, too, like those poor little girls who dance for a snatch of life, you have a right to rest; you, who have given society your health and your youth. It is a crime to make you drag your decrepit old age to work. But society doesn't protect you, on the edge of the tomb; just like it doesn't protect two girls on the threshold of their lives.

Neither the cradle, nor the tomb. Society only knows how to toss disdain onto the wretched girls when they fall, without ever holding out a rescuing hand, just like it will cover you with abuse if you are unable to honestly conclude your miserable life, if you dare take back a tiny portion of that which you have produced.

No, society doesn't protect you; it stares at you threateningly; it anxiously waits for you to fall so it can shout anathemas against you and chase you from its bosom like an unworthy creature.

The dance ends once again and the plea begins again, insistently: "Be generous, sirs, please." Thus, faced with the painful scenes that ceaselessly torment our soul, faced with every new form of injustice, evil, exploitation, or compassionate thoughtlessness, the unvanquished need for this struggle grows inside us; a firm desire to start anew, faith in the future. And each time, our soul dedicates itself entirely to high ideals and feels the duty to devote all its efforts to changing a social order that only knows how to bestow injustice, pain, and tears (Cazzola 1992, 85–87).

Another anecdote sheds light on the personality of the teacher and her social conscience, which was able to go beyond the rhetoric of the "mother figure," a cornerstone of Italian elementary schools. On July 14, 1906, an article appeared in *Il Pensiero Socialista* with the first depiction of a series of *distressing figures*. Always at school:

Among the benches. The pale, distressing figures ceaselessly pass through. It is a boy; wretched, thin, but his eyes are lively, his features are candid, open.

I enter the school and someone says to me: "Madam Teacher, Virginio doesn't have his mother anymore, she has gone away." I turn to him, I look at him questioningly; he bows his head but he isn't emotional, he smiles. "Tell me,

32   *Chapter 4*

Virginio . . . ," and the boy talks; in bursts, without sobs in his throat, without tears in his eyes, almost smiling, sometimes stopping as though to think . . .

"They beat each other yesterday evening, mother and father . . . they always beat each other . . . they shouted a lot . . . father wanted to kill her . . . mother, too, threw a chair at him . . . she went up into their room . . . she got her new slippers and she went away . . . " And he doesn't cry. My heart aches at his indifference and I caress him. I'm certain you're sorry that your mother has left you, I ask him with a tremble. But his lips twist into a sad smile: "No," he replies curtly. "No?" He continues as though talking to himself: "There were two of them beating me, they beat me every day, now only father beats me . . . father always gets drunk; he comes home late . . . I go to bed early and sleep . . . "

"Oh! Your mother will return home and she'll be so good to you!" It seems as though his brow wrinkles in doubt, with an unpleasant fear . . .

To him, his mother was the woman who beat him . . . nothing more (Cazzola 1992, 90–91).

These were the foundations of Alda's teaching, and during the years of the Great War, they couldn't help but make her a proud antagonist of all those political and social orientations that were a prelude to Fascism and that Fascism skillfully exploited between 1919 and 1926 in order to affirm its totalitarian politics. She wrote for *La Bandiera Socialista* between 1914 and 1917 and for *La Scintilla* between 1919 and 1921,[4] fighting to obtain, first of all, a dignified level of hygiene in the schools and a qualified school cafeteria for all the children, with assistance for the neediest.

Alda also supported the young people's need for an adequate education, a far cry from the widespread habit of graduating as many students as possible to avoid overcrowding; it followed that new classes and new teachers had to be introduced. In her opinion, what was needed was a museum, a library, a recreation room, a gym, a bathroom, and movie projections, "a powerful aid in teaching history and the sciences." On the contrary, by simply aiming to "empty out" the schools and by creating classes numbering over seventy students per teacher, the young people who graduated were "incapable of assimilating the programs" and were still half-illiterate (A. Costa, "Salviamo la scuola di Ferrara," in *La Bandiera Socialista*, September 6, 1914) (Cazzola 1992, 110–12). Alda's great attention to the effective quality of young people's education dovetailed with her interest in developing schools for "deficient and abnormal" children, as they were called back then, anticipating the timing and orientation of her own political party (Cazzola 1992, 117). On these topics, she sided with the well-known positions of Maria Montessori.

Nor did she or any other Socialist teacher during those years ever abstain from battling for teachers rights, from making her own interests those of the proletariat in its entirety, going beyond the corporative interests of the school.

The war years arrived, and Alda Costa always and unhesitatingly sided, first, with the anti-interventionist front and then, once the war was underway, with all those who tried to bring the war to an end as quickly as possible, in the wake of the international conferences of Zimmerwald and Kienthal. Alda played a decisive role in the antimilitaristic unrest in January 1917, at Berra, Copparo, at the Argentano, and in the area around Codigoro, and for the first time, the prefect of Ferrara reported her to the ministry as a "subversive," who, as a captain of the Carabinieri noted, "has a bad reputation in the public opinion because she is haughty and conducts such an equivocal private life that she must be considered of dubious morality" (Roveri 1972, 313; Ravà n.d.).

Fascism was still two years away, but it was already manifesting its first explicit signs: it was trying to weaken its political adversaries by using the method of disgrace and defamation. For Alda Costa, it was the beginning of a series of persecutions that continued throughout her life. Above all, she was never forgiven for her proud stance against the war.

At the end of March 1917, Alda refused to take her class to the cinema to attend the projection of *La Presa di Gorizia* [*The Storming of Gorizia*], a film that celebrated the ongoing war (Cazzola 1992, 18).

Regarding this matter, Alda wrote to her colleagues at the "Umberto I" elementary school:

> Colleagues, we are invited to accompany our students to the cinematographic show of the Storming of Gorizia. This means watching scenes of brutality and blood that are sure to profoundly upset young imaginations, inclined to violence through atavism and domestic education. This does not mean being patriotic; it means, subconsciously or not, preparing for future wars: contributing to increase the painful statistics of juvenile delinquency. Let us show ourselves worthy of the name of educators and refuse to go. It is time for the educational direction of the schools to understand our thought and for our will to make itself felt (Cazzola 1992, 37, note 52).

L'Avvenire d'Italia praised the initiative (Cazzola 1992, 19), but Alda was violently attacked in the rest of the local press, starting with Catholic publications. On April 8, 1917, in an article entitled "Il cittadino analfabeta . . . scrive!," published in *La Domenica dell'Operaio*, a certain Monsignor Tullio Gamberoni, pretending to be illiterate and signing himself "Cro+ce," wrote:

> That elderly spinster they call Mistrss Ada Costa, whose one of those fanatic Sotialist who don't want the war, didn't want to company her publik school kiddies to see the battle of Gorizia at the movies, [. . .] in my opinion it means she made a demonstration against our war, a big load of rubbish just now [. . .] But

34 *Chapter 4*

she was understood wrong because she did it out of sentimentalism (Cazzola 1992, 18).

But above all, the weekly *Il Fascio*, whose title was a harbinger of future Italian events, attacked Alda Costa on April 1, in a decidedly violent manner, for her *Agguato socialneutralista* [*Social-neutralist Ambush*], for not having let "the children's souls vibrate before the magnificent examples of heroism and daring," accusing her—using the recognizable tones of proto-Fascist language—of being dominated by her friend, the Socialist Gaetano Zirardini, like a "slave" who "has sucked the drool, bile, and rage saturating the beard of that human body staggering through the local political life" (Cazzola 1992, 19).

On March 27, *La Provincia di Ferrara*, known as the "daily newspaper of democracy," in an article entitled "L'atteggiamento antipatriottico di un'insegnante [The Anti-patriotic Attitude of a Teacher]" didn't hesitate to accuse Alda Costa of "an act of anti-patriotic propaganda, conducted through the school, which cannot be an enemy of the Homeland," of being hostile to "those principles the school ought to teach students to love and to hold up as an example, and to the gratitude of those young people who obtained the best fruits from the sacrifice of their fathers" (Cazzola 1992, 20).

At that point, the atmosphere was saturated with Fascist rhetoric.

Alda replied in a letter she sent to *La Gazzetta Ferrarese*, which didn't publish it. But the letter was printed in *La Bandiera Socialista* on April 1, 1917:

Dear Mr. Editor of the *Gazzetta Ferrarese*:

The other day, the newspaper "La Provincia" published a short article entitled *The Anti-Patriotic Attitude of a Teacher.*

I am that *Teacher*; and since the newspaper is trying to use the unpleasant light of the usual hackneyed anti-patriotism to present an act that actually has a different meaning in the field of the school's educational orientation, I ask that you allow me a bit of space for an explanation.

By now, it has become a habit to divide all human actions into two large categories: patriotic and anti-patriotic—or, in a newspaper, didn't I read praise of a shoemaker's patriotism because he displayed a pair of shoes adorned with a cockade of the Italian flag?

Thus, in contrast to the shoemaker, my action—not having accompanied my students to the cinematographic show of the *Storming of Gorizia*—would be an anti-patriotic act. As though an event, which entails extremely high and complex questions of an educational nature, can be judged on the basis of such exclusively superficial criteria, as was the case with [. . .] the shoemaker.

But truly, is it impossible to talk about the homeland without talking about war? And can't we teach children to love their fatherland, and appreciate its beauty, and see it civil and esteemed, without ceaselessly flashing in front of

The Lofty Socialist Integrity of Alda Costa 35

their eyes images of ruin, brutality, and death? Does the love for one's homeland, thus, lie entirely in an exaltation of war? What use is it, then, to deprecate German schools that spark warmongering spirits and an urge for conquest, and don't disassociate the concept of a necessary war to make it strong and feared, if we, basically, follow in the same footsteps and form the child's soul in the same way?

This poor child's soul that, by now, is too undermined by images of violence and blood? Everything, everything speaks to the child's mind and soul of the insanity of violence: from newspaper articles to the stories they are told; from games they play with soldiers, rifles, and cannons to the cinematographer's scenes; from illustrated postcards to the engravings of *Domenica del Corriere*; it is a persistent snare that disturbs the child's conscience, inclines his soul toward violence, and, unfortunately, helps increase the painful statistics of juvenile delinquency.

This action of mine is a reaction to this entire educational inclination and an affirmation that the school must be humane and universal, and not foster hate and a desire for revenge. And, by maintaining an aura of serenity and calm that is undisturbed by faraway or nearby echoes of massacres and ruin, it must be, first of all, a creator of those feelings of human brotherhood that, it seems, will have to rule the world someday.

I am happy that the exquisite feelings of camaraderie that convinced some colleague of mine to denounce me have taken this action of mine outside the narrow walls of the school and have led it to an open discussion about ideas and principles that are of crucial importance for the future.

I could not have hoped for a better result.

I thank you, Mr. Editor, for your hospitality.

Alda continued her Socialist political militancy as one of the driving forces behind the new journal *La Scintilla*; starting in July 1919, it replaced *La Bandiera Socialista*, which was opposed on various fronts and, after repeated censorship, closed down.

Above all, after the 1920 elections, which were a triumph for the Socialists, she polemicized in *La Scintilla* against the party's pseudo-revolutionary illusions, in the absence of qualified methodological lines and the professionalism and correctness that were meant to be an example for the proletariat. Alda understood that this Socialism, wavering uncertainly between reformism and revolution, would never be able to truly contrast Fascism. It would take coherence and unity (A. Costa, "Attenti al timone," in *La Scintilla*, July 31, 1920; "Per chiarire le idee," in *La Scintilla*, August 7, 1920).

To Alda, the school could have represented a valid antidote to the growing climate of hate in society. During the first months of 1920, she became the secretary of the steering committee of the newly created Teachers Union and left the Teachers Association, where her brother Alessandro remained. She was convinced they had to react against a school that made young people

36   *Chapter 4*

"slaves to the dominant authority," that offered a "false love of the homeland and created small human machines that were unaccustomed to criticism and observation" (A. Costa, "Per il rinnovamento della scuola," in *La Scintilla*, January 17, 1920) (Quarzi 2004, 119).

On May 9, the first public assembly of Ferrara's Teachers Union was held; the Milanese teacher Abigaille Zanetta also attended. The program began with the need to abandon the false apolitical stance of the Association and, instead, identify more determinately with the demands of the proletariat. The school should provide everyone, without class distinction, with an adequate education, thereby ensuring that young people were not forced to work before graduating.

But Fascism was almost in power by then. In keeping with a typically Fascist habit of attacking adversaries, not on the political topics being discussed, but in their private, intimate sphere and, in the case of a woman, her femininity, an article published in *Balilla. Settimanale del Fascio Ferrarese di Combattimento*, dated January 22, 1922, and entitled "Istantanee Alda," presented Alda Costa as an "elderly virago of politics, who pours her weekly uterine outbursts into long columns in 'La Scintilla,' which by now has become her most seductive organ" (Quarzi 2004, 145).

In July 1922, while Alda was in Bologna, where she had gone in search of a printer for *La Scintilla*, she was surrounded by three hundred Fascists who insulted her, spat on her, ripped her clothing, forced her to drink castor oil, and smeared her face with soot because she had refused to sing the praises of Fascism (Quarzi 2004, 144; Cazzola 1992, 25).[5]

On October 4, 1923, she found herself involved in a discussion about a possible reduction—proposed by the Directory of Fascist municipalities—in teachers' salaries in general, and those of female teachers, in particular— because they were usually unmarried and lived with their parents, or depended on their husbands. Alda hurled her accusation against "an administration that is under the system of a dictatorship and that has taken away every freedom," thanks to which "salaries are cut, but they pay no mind to wasting money in fuel for airplanes" (Cazzola 1992, 28, 39, which refers to a document signed "dir. gen. dell'Uff. Pubbl. Istr. of the Municipality of Ferrara," dated January 9, 1924, conserved at the municipal historical archive of Ferrara).

The Fascist reply appeared anonymously in the *Gazzetta Ferrarese* on October 9; it was entitled "Interessante adunanza all'Unione magistrale [Interesting meeting at the Teachers Association]," and it expressed all of emerging Fascism's disdain for Alda and for dissent:

> You should know, Madam Teacher, that the Fascist Government [. . .] wants public money to be spent well and not fatten the pockets of inept and turbulent demagogues. If you think the Italian Fascist Government isn't paying you

according to your merits, go to Russia where, surrounded by supreme ignorance, you will certainly feel at ease. It is known that the majority of the teachers who have gone along with the teacher Costa's rambling speeches certainly weren't the Municipality's best. It won't be out of place to remind them that the May 27 Decree gives the municipal body the power to do away with elements that are unproductive and detrimental to the school (Quarzi 2004, 152–53).

We still have the program Alda prepared—following the governmental directive for elementary schools in 1923—for the final trimester of a girls' third-grade class. No concessions to war and incipient Fascism. Religious education was thorough, albeit entrusted to another teacher. Singing included the national anthem and the hymn to the flag, along with the popular song "Gli Scariolanti." Ample space was given to freehand drawings of naturalistic subjects (a garden, a basket of flowers). All the readings were by Edmondo De Amicis: the books *Heart*, *From the Apennines to the Andes* and *The Little Florentine Scribe*, and the poem "To My Mother."

Regarding the Italian language: dictation, translation from the dialect, useful correspondence (for example, telegrams). Arithmetic: the number system, mental calculations, and even practical exercises. Industry, agriculture, and commerce. Hygiene: tuberculosis and a description of the damage caused by alcoholism (Quarzi 2004, 148–50, which references the municipal historical archive of Ferrara, the section *Pubblica Istruzione, Scuola elementare*). The Socialist inspiration is evident, both in what was said and even more in what wasn't said, as was often the case.

On June 25, 1925, the prefect of Ferrara, Giovanni Gasti, indicated her as a "fiduciary" of the local chapter of the Socialist Party and a person who "has never ceased her subversive propaganda directed at the organization of the working masses, and taking an interest in subversive political prisoners." She was considered a threat to law and order and was put under surveillance (Roveri 1976).

In December 1925, a certain Dr. Zuffi, a school physician, reported to the town's health inspector that the teacher wasn't respecting the mandatory Roman salute, even though she had taught it to her students as required. Alda declared she was willing to teach it to her students but stated that it was not her intention to personally submit to that regulation (Quarzi 2004, 73). She received an official warning from the mayor of Ferrara.

In March 1926, the *Corriere Padano* denounced the inadmissibility of the pledge to the regime that Alda Costa had made with reservations ("Giuramenti con riserva," in *Corriere Padano*, March 16, 1926). Alda's home was searched; she was interrogated; and portraits of Matteotti, journals, membership cards, and various materials that were considered "subversive" were found in her home.

38   *Chapter 4*

During the interrogation, Alda once again proclaimed her consistency and her Socialist faith:

> I am a maximalist Socialist and a fiduciary of the Italian Socialist Party for the province of Ferrara. I have professed these ideas for many years and have never renounced them. To the best of my abilities and the possibilities offered by the present political situation, I have always been active in propaganda, trying, within the legal limits, to maintain the faith of my ideas vivid in all those followers who profess it. Therefore, I was and still am in relation with the highest exponents of the party and with the national and regional leaders of the maximalist Socialist movement. I have overseen the distribution of membership cards among party members of the province of Ferrara, I have promoted subscriptions to the journal "Avanti!," and I have fostered everything that has to do with the party's activities. I have never believed in the existence of an incompatibility between my capacity as a militant Socialist and my profession as a teacher, which I have always scrupulously conducted without ever having received a reprimand on the part of the scholastic or municipal authorities. In fact, I specified this concept when I made the well-known declaration before recently swearing my oath in Town Hall as a teacher (Inzerillo 1976; Inzerillo 1980).

The mayor of Ferrara decided to suspend the teacher and informed the prefect and the region's commissioner of education. Alda didn't lose heart; she once again picked up her pen and replied. It was March 19, 1926:

> Most illustrious Mayor,
> In acknowledging receipt of the letter dated March 17, in which I am informed of the measures you feel the need to take on my behalf, I cannot help but reject, with all the power of my soul, the accusation of perjury that has been hurled at me just when, because of my frankness and loyalty, I lose my sustenance. There is no need to remind you, Mr. Mayor, how the swearing-in ceremony was conducted on my behalf, and the way you replied to the honest doubts I expressed with equal honesty and loyalty, putting my conscience perfectly at ease. My conscience is still at ease today, in the certainty that I have scrupulously carried out my duty as an Italian teacher, woman, and citizen, without any hypocrisy, in either my thoughts or my actions.[6]

On August 7, 1926, the prefect of Ferrara, Cesare Bertini, fired the teacher for her "open and explicit profession of the Socialist faith." Alda moved to Milan in search of a new job, but by then the persecutory judicial machine was in motion. It did not let up, and a few months later, on November 21· she was condemned to five years of internal exile on the Tremiti islands.[7]

Alda was arrested in Milan on December 9 and sent to the prison in Ancona, where she was locked up in the women's section. Her journey

The Lofty Socialist Integrity of Alda Costa

continued to the prison in Foggia and ended on the small island of San Domino alle Tremiti, where she was separated from the other prisoners. There, she treated a prisoner's wife who had gone blind and tried to go to San Nicola to meet with other prisoners and her own lawyer, Mario Cavallari, who attempted to have her sentence reduced. This led to her return to Ferrara, following another period of internal exile at Corleto Perticare in the province of Potenza. Alda returned in 1928 and was contested by the *podestà* Renzo Ravenna; she was forced to request early retirement. Her request was granted in 1932, forcing her into that isolated life, probably at the home of her brother Alessandro—and not with her sister Amelia, as Bassani notes, since Amelia died on December 17, 1932 (Quarzi 2004, 76, 81, 157)—but under the strict control of the Fascist police headquarters, where she was always considered "subversive and mentally unbalanced."

The Fascists arrested her once again in 1942 because she was caught talking with a group of Socialists; she was imprisoned for one month on bread and water. Freed but in increasingly poor health, she still had the strength to join the National Liberation Committee after July 25, 1943. Following the killing of the Fascist provincial party secretary Igino Ghisellini on the night between November 14 and 15, 1943, Alda was once again arrested, along with seventy-nine other people, eleven of whom were killed in retaliation. This was the episode that inspired Giorgio Bassani to write the short story "A Night of '43" in his book *Within the Walls*, which Florestano Vancini then transposed into his 1960 movie, *It Happened in '43*.

It was the end for Alda, who, weak and sick, was first transferred to the San Paolo prison on Via Piangipane, and then to the prison in Copparo. She died in the hospital of Copparo at 2:30 p.m. on April 30, 1944. The police commissioner forbade her funeral to be held on May 1 and ordered that it take place the next day, in strictly private form.

Carlo Lega, who was a student of Alda Costa's during the years 1913–1914, remembers her thus:

> She stood out for her personality, marked by her great candor, which shone through her open gaze that was illuminated by a deep interest in her interlocutor, whoever it might be. She had a high, broad forehead, crowned by thick, chestnut-blond hair, which was always very neat. People took a liking to the teacher Costa just by looking at her and as soon as they spoke with her for a while, this feeling became even greater [. . .]. Each time she heard me cough, she checked to see that I was well protected with adequate clothing; when, at the end of the lessons, the students swarmed home, she would stand at the main door and make sure that everyone went in the right direction and she even chased after those students who didn't intend to go straight home and instead took a side street. She would catch up with them and give them the dressing down they deserved [. . .].

40   *Chapter 4*

My dear, good, affectionate Teacher! Once again, I see your large eyes ready to seize every attitude, even interior, of the students who were entrusted to you, your maternal smile that illuminated your every gesture; even after so much time has passed, I still appreciate your teaching method, that watchful tolerance you adopted toward the less docile but that did not exclude, when needed, a firm stance in line with the necessary discipline (Lega 1981, 93).

NOTES

1. This epigraph is missing from the English translation of the book, but it continues: "I remember that a dying man even refused to speak with the people who loved him because he had made them think he loved them" (Svevo 1954, 320).

2. The English translation of this book was based on a later edition, which did not have the sentence in question (*translator's note*).

3. This quote, too, was missing in the later edition of the book (*translator's note*).

4. The articles can be read in full (in Italian) in Cazzola 1992, 93–312.

5. The Fascists themselves called the episode a "merry ruckus." See "Nero fumo e olio di ricino," in *Balilla. Settimanale del Fascio Ferrarese di Combattimento*, July 23, 1922.

6. Letter conserved in the Municipal Historical Archive of Ferrara, b. 25, f. 1, *Causa Alda Costa-Municipio di Ferrara* and published in *Donne ferraresi nella resistenza: esperienze nelle scuole, testimonianze*, edited by the Union of Italian Women and the Ethnographic Center of Ferrara, Ferrara: the Municipality of Ferrara, 1975.

7. I base the entire sequence of events of her being charged as a "subversive," of her sentence of internal exile, and of her final arrests, on the information provided by Cazzola 1992, 31–35, 40, note 122, who also used documentary material conserved at the State Archives of Ferrara, Prefettura, Gabinetto, a. 1926 (but merged with 1929), cat. 30, fasc. maestra Alda Costa.

Chapter 5

Mariangela Maccioni

The Anti-Fascist Teacher from Nuoro

Inside, she had the ancient strength and kindness of the olive tree.

—Salvatore Cambosu

In Nuoro, on May 17, 1929, Carmelo Cottone, the director of studies of the local elementary school, wrote to the *podestà* Francesco Bandino regarding the noncompliance of the teacher Maccioni, who refused to teach a lesson about the Duce:

> Yesterday, in the Principal's office, I was giving the teacher Maccioni Mariangela recommendations and advice about completing the programs and fulfilling the duties of her office, and I commented on the evaluation I had made during my visit to her class (girls' first grade), which took place on the 14th of this month. I pointed out to her, among other things, that, according to reports and to the students, it appears she had never made any mention of the DUCE.
>
> When, during the visit, I asked Maccioni if the students knew something about the Duce, she replied that "she couldn't lower herself to teaching mechanical things that didn't touch the spirit" [sic]. On a different occasion, in the head office, as she was handing me the minutes of the visit to read, she returned to the reason for her historical assessment and told me that she did not consider Fascism historical because "the verdict is entrusted to posterity" . . . !
>
> To fill a gap left in the education of the students entrusted to her, and to see whether this deficiency was due to a potential sentimental theory or to a more or less willful omission, I invited her to teach a lesson—on a day that best suited her—about the Duce, after having pointed out the heroic, legendary, and poetic characteristics of this figure. Maccioni replied scornfully that she did not intend to teach this lesson. [. . .]

42   *Chapter 5*

Maccioni [then] became excessively energetic in manifesting her resistance and defending the "freedom of offended spirits," protesting a patriotism that was extremely abstract and extraneous to Fascism.

I feel the need to point out that I repeatedly invited Maccioni to reflect on the decision she had made, sparking her increasing disdain for my directive.

Since this episode—like other manifestations which I, as director, must not ignore—clearly reveals the teacher's tendency to defend herself, even in the face of the pressing duties of her office and, when possible, tacitly [?], but also her firm antagonism to every manifestation (of thought or organization) of the regime: I report the teacher Maccioni to your illustrious attention for the appropriate measures (Maccioni 1988, 115–16).[1]

That same day, the *podestà* summoned Mariangela Maccioni at 5 p.m. "for a communication" and initiated actions of "censure" and condemnation for the teacher's lack of discipline. He invited her once again to teach the much-requested lesson about the Duce and to inform the director of studies ahead of time.

On May 31, 1929, during the final hour of lessons, the teacher Maccioni thus taught her lesson about the "Duce of Fascism" to her first grade class, numbering forty-one girls, and in the presence of the director, who expressed his satisfaction (Maccioni 1988, 118).

In short, the first-grade girls of Nuoro, too, had to be taught about the Duce. It was certainly the first and last lesson, but it had to be held, albeit during the final hour of lessons.

Mariangela was born in Nuoro on April 17, 1891. In 1929, she was living alone with her mother, Giuseppina, who came from a family of small landowners. Her father, Sebastiano, an elementary school teacher, a follower of Mazzini who later became a Socialist, and the only "istudiàu" [educated] child in a sizeable family of small landowners, had died in 1918. He had been one of the driving forces of Nuoro's first workers association and had inspired his daughter's substantial anti-Fascism. The inscription on his tomb at the cemetery reads: "Educator of the people" (Maccioni 1988, 38, notes 1 and 3). Her two brothers, Bachisio and Pietro, died prematurely in 1918 and 1920. Their mother died in 1943.

That first year, after receiving her diploma and her qualification to teach, on October 1, Mariangela found herself at Mamoiàda, a town in Barbagia, teaching a class of roughly ninety "boys and girls six, seven, eight, and even ten years old [. . .], who were crowded into a small room in a private home." The year was 1908, and Mariangela was seventeen years old. She wrote:

There were barely enough desks for half of the students; I began to seat the girls, who sat properly with their hands under the apron of their traditional Sardinian costume and stared at me, their astonished faces framed by a cloth bonnet. It was quite hard to seat the boys, who talked and laughed, pushed each other, sat on the desks, and, in the end, were able to find some room on the red tile floor. They made themselves comfortable with great simplicity, crossing their ankles the same way as their fathers, who were shepherds and farmers.

But after managing to put some order into that chaos of faces and legs, and as I moved toward the teacher's desk, I stopped, overtaken by sudden dismay: what was I supposed to say now, what was I to do? Filled with confusion and fear, I tried to call to mind the scholastic "governing" methods I had been taught: among the *despotic*, *patriarchal*, *artificial*, and *civil* governing methods De Domenicis mentioned in his manual (De Dominicis 1906, 261), which was the most suitable to adopt? The young people took advantage of my confusion and recommenced their ruckus and I began saying: Quiet! Silence! But it was like talking to the waves of the sea. Desperate, I sat down; then, luckily, I remembered that, first of all, I was supposed to ask for their first and last names and write them down in the class register. This is how I passed my first morning at school (Maccioni 1988, 43).

The town's municipal secretary reassured her that her ninety students would become fifteen in the springtime because the work in fields and farmyards created scholastic dispersal. And in fact, that is what happened, and this was the situation at schools in Barbagia during the first decade of the 1900s. Two years passed, and Mariangela obtained a teaching post in Nuoro, at the same school where she herself had studied. It was the period between the venture in Libya and World War I, and everybody at school talked about war. Only one of her old teachers argued for peace at all cost, in the name of her deep-rooted evangelical principles, "which she followed with her monastic way of life, all humility and devotion"; everyone else, including Mariangela, let themselves be swept away by interventionist enthusiasm:

Years before, at the time of the war in Libya, I let myself be kindled by "Tripoli, Beautiful Land of Love" (forgetting the teachings of my father, who was also a teacher and a follower of Mazzini, and who had taught me to abhor colonial wars), and now I was enthralled by the blaze of patriotism that was spreading throughout Italy and had made its way to our remote land of Sardinia. And I spoke of irredentism and the danger of German hegemony to my teacher, who listened to me with small exclamations of pain and imploration. She was alone in her position of evangelical pacifism; at school, everyone—professors, teachers, and students—were in favor of intervention. We even explained the need for war to the children, withholding the horror; on the contrary, the horror didn't make an impression on our generation, which had only seen war in the pages of schoolbooks. With enthusiasm and faith in victory, we rolled up newspapers to heat meals, we knitted for our soldiers, we made the rounds of the houses to ask for gold for the homeland.

44   *Chapter 5*

Everybody offered something; the women of the farming landowners, whose sons were in the trenches, offered their old family jewelry (Maccioni 1988, 47).

When the war ended, all the contradictions exploded in the space of just a few months and were soon resolved with the rise of Fascism. In Sardinia, its methods of affirmation were similar to those on the continent, even though it was more prudent, under various aspects. As Mariangela recalled:

> The war that had seemed endless came to an end, it ended in victory and many people in Sardinia didn't return. We had hoped for peace, prosperity, glory; the Fascist era began. In the newspapers, we began to read stories about purges, attacks, murders. The "squads" were rampant. "This is the result of your war," my fourth-grade teacher said to me one day. "You wanted national unity, sacred borders, and here are your Fascists" (Maccioni 1988, 48).

In Sardinia, like in South Tyrol, an identitarian and autonomist wave began to rise against a type of Fascism that many people felt had not responded adequately to the needs of a population debilitated by the war. The Sardinian Action Party was organized and Mariangela initially manifested her support. Its first congress was organized in Nuoro. Mariangela recalled:

> A large, glorious procession, with white and red flags dominated by the heads of the "four blindfolded Moors," marched through the city streets: the Fascists, who are just a handful of discredited men here, were still in a defensive position. The schoolchildren didn't keep themselves apart from this great movement, which had all the air of a colorful country festivity. They made their own small flags, they adorned themselves with poppies and other red flowers, they wore the badge of the four Moors on their chest. And they already knew how to make the Sardinian salute, by striking their chest forcefully with their hand to indicate their commitment to fidelity, honor, and friendship, in life and in death. Only a few young men dared to pin the Fascist gimcrack on their jacket: they were the sons of the local Fascist party's "founders." For a long time, the Sardisti [members of the Sardinian Action Party—translator's note] were in the majority at school and almost all of them were the children of farmers, shepherds, artisans, the nephews or godsons of lawyers. Heatedly, and sometimes violently, each one of them defended their side; one day a girl ripped a Fascist badge off a classmate, trampled it, and spat on it (Maccioni 1988, 48).

But despite the opposition of the Christian, Socialist, and even the strong Sardinian movements for self-determination, fascistization arrived inexorably. Toward the end of the first decade of the Fascist government, it had become impossible to openly rebel against the regime. In her *Memorie*, Mariangela highlighted how, in Nuoro, as elsewhere, the gym teacher was the fiduciary of the Fascist party, the educational reference point for the entire school:

> Physical education surpassed every other subject matter. The gym teacher had become a demigod everyone was supposed to obey, teachers and students alike. And since he had to prepare all the students in every school for the "great display" on May XXIV, the demigod would muster them at the most unexpected moments. The classes gathered in a vast courtyard that was still full of holes and stones, which they called a gymnasium. The gymnast, brandishing a megaphone, gave the orders from a high podium. He was young, handsome, athletic, and imperious, as befitted a pure champion of the Roman world. It was impossible to resist the imperiousness of such a commander, and thus, elderly female schoolteachers could be seen following the march and marking time, partly dismayed and partly reluctant, whereas the younger ones marched along happily in a martial manner.
>
> Then came the order to wear uniforms and badges of rank; I believe that we teachers were entitled to the rank of second lieutenant. At the time, young and old teachers were happy to wear a black suit with a white dicky, and they wore it gloriously; for some, who were mothers, the cost of that parade outfit was almost impossible to sustain, and they whispered as much to a few trusted colleagues. But the scholastic journals offered it at a convenient price, on an installment plan, and so even those poor mothers could be seen bundled up in that cheap black cloth which soon turned greenish through wear and tear.

The victorious arrogance of the gym teacher was contrasted by the suffering resignation of the elderly pacifist teacher, a silent and powerless victim of this new school:

> One morning, I saw the elderly fifth-grade teacher, who is so proud, sobbing into her hands, all alone in a corner of the corridor. Frightened, I went over to her and tried to make her talk. She didn't reply but made an effort to hold back her sobs. When she had calmed down, she reticently confided to me that the principal had ordered her to take off "this bulky jacket" (it was her black widow's jacket) and wear the uniform. Her white head was bent, overwhelmed by the humiliation (Maccioni 1988, 50–51).

In 1926, a group of students from Mariangela's co-ed third-grade class was heard singing *Bandiera Rossa* and *Bandiera Sarda* as they returned from a walk in the outskirts of town. The teacher who was present chastised them and they stopped singing. But the event did not go unobserved and the news reached the scholastic inspector of Nuoro and even the commissioner of education of Cagliari. The inspector wrote to the commissioner on May 7:

46 *Chapter 5*

In itself, the small episode would not be of any importance—in that the phrases unconsciously repeated by the small group of students are the final residue of the common people's political repertory—if there weren't already precedents regarding the teacher Maccioni Mariangela, who was, for a long time, notoriously and inflexibly linked with the Sardinian party headed by the hon. Mastino, and still today conserves feelings of opposition toward the general directives of Fascism.

Mariangela was questioned and admitted the incident, but she also explained—not without irony—that even though the children had begun the song, they didn't get as far as the words "will triumph!"

Obviously, she didn't say anything about who might have taught those songs to the children.

A request was made to suspend Mariangela for ten days from work without pay, "for having been unable to avoid the reported incident, creating in the souls of her students purer and deeper feelings of love and devotion to the Homeland and to the new regime" (Maccioni 1988, 111–12, which publishes the letter that the scholastic inspector of Nuoro wrote on May 7, 1926, and sent to the commissioner of education in Cagliari). This occurred a few years after the above-mentioned reprimand for not having taught the lesson about the Duce.

During the second half of the 1930s, which saw the war in Ethiopia and civil war in Spain, Fascism showed its intolerant soul increasingly openly.

Mariangela was also repeatedly reprimanded because threatening letters, true or false, reported her hostile attitude to the regime and her friendship with various "subversives." She wrote:

One day, the inspector [. . .] called me into his office and in a mysteriously solemn tone of voice told me: "We are constantly receiving anonymous letters that accuse you of having connections with the city's most rabid anti-Fascists. Here is one . . . "

He took a sheet of paper from a folder and read it out loud, quickly mumbling the less important parts and stressing the words of accusation in dramatic tones. After he finished reading it to me, I stood up and said: "Very well, inspector."

Right after this, I learned from a colleague who was secretly anti-Fascist that the inspector himself had written this anonymous letter, one evening when he had stayed late in his office in the company of a teacher who also had a rank in the "militia."

But these anonymous letters were also sent to the Fascist Party federation. Back then, there was a professor [Luigino Deffenu] who was a "federal." He was kind to me because he had studied under my father and remembered him fondly. One day, he sent me a missive by means of the director informing me that the federation was constantly receiving anonymous letters that accused me of being an anti-Fascist at school, of anti-national propaganda, of friendship with "the most rabid anti-Fascists of the province." The "federal" recommended prudence. To show my prudence, the director advised me to mark in my detailed programs the mandatory lessons on Fascist culture that, he had noticed, were missing. "Luckily," he said, "there are a few empty lines." He personally dictated to me the titles of the topics that, needless to say, were never taught. It wasn't the first time I ran up against the formalism of the rules, but accepting this compromise was as distressing to me as though it were the beginning of a capitulation.

By now, the teachers were all card-carriers; nevertheless, in the judgment of the scholastic hierarchy, teachers were classified according to a degree of belief that corresponded to the indications listed in a printed leaflet that supposedly taught the perfect Roman salute and distinguished between "fervid," "lukewarm," or "dubious" Fascists, according to the position of the person's arm. The fervid teachers flaunted their pupils, or rather, their perfectly trained platoons of *Balilla* [boys who were members of the Fascist youth group—translator's note] and *piccole italiane* [the girls]. The lukewarm and dubious Fascists limited themselves to celebrating—ostentatiously or resignedly—the various commemorative holidays that ministerial circulars ordered the scholastic authorities to respect (Maccioni 1988, 53–54).

The war in Africa, which was an excellent pretext to teach the young people about war and racism, was welcomed by all the schoolteachers of Nuoro with great participation and enthusiasm, even when it meant donating their wedding rings to the homeland. Mariangela refused to do so (she had married Raffaello Marchi in 1935), and soon this gesture, too, would have its consequences. She wrote:

In 1936, the war in Africa rekindled imperialistic enthusiasm and the zeal of the spies. One teacher taught her students that "England is a snake" and, in the presence of her students, as she saluted an officer who was leaving for Africa, she sent him off with the request "and bring me back a dozen Negroes' heads."

All the teachers offered their wedding rings: the most zealous ones donated their real "wedding band" and substituted it with a small iron ring, the others donated a ring they had bought at a jeweler's shop for this purpose, but they, too, wore a surrogate on their ring finger. At school, people were already murmuring that I hadn't donated my ring, and some people were lying in wait for me. One colleague, who was worried about my tranquility, rushed into my classroom at the end of the lesson and, after looking around to make sure no one else was in the classroom, told me with great agitation:

"I know you're sorry to give up your ring, we all are . . . Listen to me, I'm not telling you to give away your ring, I gave mine, the real one . . . But you could have the jeweler make a ring just like it and you can donate it. Don't get yourself in trouble, listen to me, don't be stubborn . . . "

The good woman went away, saddened, because she realized that, although I was touched by her consideration, she hadn't achieve the desired result.

48 *Chapter 5*

A lot of people worried about my wedding ring. One evening, during the hour when people strolled down the main street, I was stopped by another colleague, a party official of the women's Fascist movement. She grabbed my left hand, then she grabbed my ring finger, and as she twisted the ring around my finger, she said loudly:

"You will be the first to give your ring to the homeland!" I saw this was an act of provocation and I answered with a laugh: "Don't count on it . . . " (Maccioni 1988, 54–55).

But it was during the Spanish civil war that Mariangela, who by then was under special surveillance, experienced the harshest Fascist repression.

I later found out that many falsehoods were being spread about me; one affirmed that I was in correspondence with the combatants in Spain, with Lussu, with the anti-Fascists in Tunisia, and even "with Russia." In fact, I was doubtless receiving an unspecified amount of rubles from Russia . . . Plus, I was hiding a cache of bombs at home in a storage room . . . (Maccioni 1988, 55).

In April 1937, Mariangela learned from her friend Maura Puggioni in Tunisia that a young man from Nuoro, Giovanni Dettori, a member of the international brigades, had died in Spain. She wrote to her friend Graziella Sechi, the wife of the engineer Dino Giacobbe, who in turn answered her, manifesting his sorrow for the heroic death of young Dettori. Mariangela doesn't recount this, but the letter was delivered to her home just as she was tutoring a sixteen-year-old girl she thought she could trust. Since she was busy with the lesson, instead of reading the letter and destroying it immediately afterward, as she and almost every anti-Fascist under special surveillance did, she decided to read it later, and she hid the letter in her bookcase between two books.

But the girl was evidently one of those many young Fascist spies, an expert at playing both sides for the police. In a report sent by the prefect of Nuoro to the interior minister, she was defined as "a trustworthy person of the local Provincial Fascist Federation, a sixteen-year-old student" (Maccioni 1988, 121–24).[2]

A few hours later, agents entered Mariangela's home and went straight to the letter, which was indisputable proof of her anti-Fascism and, thus, the pretext for a meticulous search of her entire house. They searched for traces of contact between Mariangela and local anti-Fascists, in particular with Emilio Lussu, the anti-Fascist group in Paris, and the anti-Fascists in Tunisia. They didn't arrest her right away, but instead they did so two days later, in the evening, on the street.

A short while later, they also arrested her friend Graziella and the other anti-Fascists of Nuoro.

The above-mentioned report dated April 22 and sent by the prefect of Nuoro to the interior minister is very detailed. Besides Mariangela's incriminating letter, the agents also confiscated three issues of *La Vie Intellectuelle*, a bimonthly journal directed by Marie-Vincent Bernadot, because of its "anti-religious content;" and the book by Léon Blum, *Les Problèmes de la Paix* (Paris: Librairie Stock, Delamain et Boutelleau, 1931), because it "criticizes the politics of Fascist governments regarding disarmament and glorifies the politics of collective security." At the Giacobbe home, they also confiscated the book by Leon Trotsky *La Révolution Allemande et la Bureaucratie Stalinienne*, published in Paris as a supplement to *La Lutte de Classes. Revue Théorique Mensuelle de l'Opposition Communiste*, dated April 15, 1932 (Maccioni 1988, 122).

The report also explains that the sixteen-year-old girl had been working for a while as a spy and had achieved several results:

> The trustworthy person, having introduced herself into Maccioni's milieu, affirmed that Puggioni Maura sent Maccioni news of a political nature, including news about the exile Lussu Emilio. She added that, for political reasons, Maccioni was in contact with the cited Prof. [Efisio] Caria, with the lawyer [Pietro] Mastino, a well-known opponent of the regime, with the lawyer Filippo Satta, and with Mr. and Mrs. Giacobbe (Maccioni 1988, 123).

The prefect concluded by requesting "police confinement" for Maccioni and an injunction "in accordance with the law" for Giacobbe. Surprisingly, Mariangela was able to get off the hook, thanks to the compliance of a police commissioner who was a Fascist, but perhaps not an entirely convinced one, and of a prefect, Achille Martelli, who, although a lukewarm Fascist, had authority, thanks to the gold medal he had earned during World War I. To this regard, Mariangela remembered:

> I was deferred to the internal exile commission. I had already received a letter from the superintendent of studies, announcing that, for political reasons, he had suspended me from teaching.
>
> I presented myself at the internal exile commission with my spirits already prepared for a conviction. Since the specific accusation had proven to be unfounded, the investigation regarded my sentiments. I candidly declared my principles.
>
> This declaration must have seemed bold: when I went to sign the injunction, a police commissioner, a Sicilian [Giuseppe Oddo], who was the secretary of the commission, said to me:
>
> "Several times, while you were talking, I was tempted to step on your foot to make you realize that your imprudence was, forgive me, foolish; but I refrained, thinking that I risked finding myself in your place as the accused."

50   *Chapter 5*

I already had the impression that this commissioner wanted to treat me with consideration and, later, I realized he wasn't a Fascist. During the first days of my life as a prisoner, he had manifested his courtesy with a gesture that was in keeping with the atmosphere of sentimental politeness of *My Prisons*. He accompanied my husband, who had arrived from Rome when he heard I had been arrested and had rushed to police headquarters asking to see me. After obtaining permission, he came to the prison with a magnificent bouquet of flowers for the "prisoner." The head of the prison was strictly against flowers in that place of punishment but he ended up granting the commissioner's request. It was decided that the flowers could be delivered to the visitors room, shown to the prisoner, and then taken away. I knew nothing about this compromise and when, at the end of our conversation, I saw that emblem of springtime being carried away, my consternation must have been quite evident. At that point, the commissioner began to confabulate with the prison warden, who stood there stiff and hostile, aware that, right then, she was the sole custodian and almost the vestal of the "Regulations." In the meantime, I was able to prolong the sight of those flowers and of my husband's face for quite a while.

The commissioner prevailed this time, too, since the prison warden had to accept his proposal that one flower out of the large bouquet be left with me. The commissioner came over, took the bouquet from me gently, chose a splendid red carnation, and with a courteous and complicit smile, which didn't hide childlike emotion, he handed it to me, saying loudly:

"You can keep this one: the responsibility is mine alone."

The Prefect, too, spoke of personal responsibility at the end of the trial, when he dismissed me with these words:

"I could have sent you into internal exile, I could have given you one hundred, twenty, eight years, at least one year of internal exile; however, I am setting you free. But remember that I had to assume full responsibility . . . " (Maccioni 1988, 59–60).

However, the journal *Nuoro Littoria*, a periodical of Nuoro's Fascist federation, didn't lose heart that May 31, 1937, and it returned to its customary Fascist style as it accused Mariangela and Graziella of being "two lesbian Passionarias [sic!]" who, along with another "four outdated fools," "think they are giving themselves airs by flaunting an aversion that is only the outcome of spiritual blindness or mindless stubbornness that denies the light of the sun! Which, naturally, progresses anyway" (Maccioni 1988, 27).

Although she had avoided internal exile, Mariangela was nevertheless temporarily suspended from her teaching duties with an administrative order dated April 22, 1937. She later tried to be reinstated, but on March 22, 1939, the eve of World War II, her suspension became definitive.

She continued to give private lessons, and she helped her mother, who was almost ninety years old, but by then her every action was controlled by the regime. It was a situation of public isolation, similar to that of many other teachers, such as Alda Costa.

In 1939, Mariangela left her home at Vicolo Barisone no. 6, the one the Fascists had searched in 1937, and moved to Via Deffenu. Many people visited her home, where anti-Fascism was still discussed when the Greek classics weren't being recited or read aloud. She continued her anti-Fascist activity in private and had some difficulty with the Badoglio government, as well.

On March 1, 1944, with some pressure from the Allied Control Commission, she was readmitted to service.[3] On April 27, 1945, she was nominated a "member of the Subcommittee to purge the personnel of the elementary school" of Nuoro. She was requested to sign a letter of defense proposed by family members of the scholastic director Carmelo Cottone, who, in 1929, had forced her to teach a lesson about the Duce. She didn't sign it because it could not be signed, but she didn't rub salt into the wound. Cottone, like almost all the other Fascist teachers, continued teaching and ended his career at the school (Maccioni 1988, 32–34).

Angela was disappointed with the schools of the Republic; they were still too similar to Fascist schools and had no intention of changing. She requested "retirement" in September 1953 and died on September 26, 1958.

The author from Nuoro, Salvatore Cambosu, who was also an elementary school teacher, remembered her thus in *Il Ponte*, the journal founded by Piero Calamandrei: "Inside, she had the ancient strength and kindness of the olive tree. She was moved by flowers and animals [. . .]. She believed in God and never said His name in vain, in keeping with the custom of true Sardinians. Until the end, she preached the Christ of the needy, for which she risked being lynched, during an election rally, by churchgoing women, and was saved by working class people, who have remained nameless" (Cambosu 1959, 1331).

NOTES

1. I owe almost all my information about the anti-Fascist teacher from Nuoro to this collection of writings by Mariangela Maccioni and documents about her personal, political, and scholastic experiences; this collection was initially edited by her husband, Raffaello Marchi, and completed by Luisa Selis Delogu after his sudden death, which occurred on April 16, 1981.

2. The transcription of the report sent by the prefect of Nuoro to the interior minister. Direzione generale PS Nuoro, April 22, 1937.

3. See, Letter from the commissioner dated March 9, 1944, in the State Archives of Nuoro, Prefettura, R. Provveditorato agli Studi di Nuoro, March 9, 1944.

Chapter 6

Abigaille Zanetta

A Fighter

The value of a life depends on what you devote it to!

—Abigaille Zanetta

On December 1, 1946, Andrea Tacchinardi wrote in the journal *L'Ora della Scuola* that, like *A Fighter*, Abigaille Zanetta, the Socialist and anti-Fascist schoolteacher, died on March 29, 1945, one month before Italy was liberated:

> One of the founders of the Italian Teachers Union was Abigaille Zanetta, who was nominated with me and three other colleagues to run the new organization. I knew Zanetta personally and even better for her reputation as a terrible . . . "Montagnard." Well, I worked with her for many years in fraternal and trusting friendship, and to me and the other members of the Committee, she was an unparalleled companion thanks to her affability, courtesy, and politeness, and her activity, fervor, and intelligence. I often brought my daughter along with me and Zanetta showed her motherly displays of affection that my daughter still remembers today and that would have certainly amazed her detractors. Her adversaries didn't like her because of the intransigence of her principles, her harsh oratory, her caustic prose that cut into the flesh; she was even less popular with cowards, opportunists, and turncoats, who were frequent back then, too, and whom she mercilessly scourged. And they repaid her with veiled and often petty hostility; in the same way, she was repaid with devotion by the humble people she defended and by the students she loved.

She was born in Suno, in the province of Novara, on May 18, 1875. She was the daughter of Bartolomeo, a notary and municipal secretary with a passion for archeology and an admirer of Garibaldi, and Filomena Neri, who was from a middle-class, Catholic family from Varallo Sesia. Abigaille was the youngest of four siblings; one of her sisters, who died at four and a half

54 *Chapter 6*

years of age the year before Abigaille was born, had her same name. It was an unusual name, which, in the opinion of Angela Stevani Colantoni, derives from the alleged daughter of Nebuchadnezzar and was supposedly given to her due to her father, Bartolomeo's passion for the opera by Verdi, *Nabucco*.[1]

Her parents died prematurely, and Abigaille found herself orphaned at twelve years of age; her relatives were rather closed and traditionalist, and she was solely dependent on the help of her elder sister Giacinta and her sister's husband (Fortichiari and Malatesta 1948, 6). Albeit with difficulty, she was able to receive her teaching degree from the Scuola Normale in Vercelli. In 1894, she taught at a private school in Turin, and then, in 1898, she moved on to the Collège "La Printanière" in Veytaux, Switzerland, on Lake Geneva, where she perfected her culture and awareness in a European context, a crossroads of innovative and international pedagogical methods. She soon made friends with Ide Epplée, the owner of the private school. After returning to Italy the following year, she won a pedagogical teaching examination and obtained a teaching post in Milan that began in January 1901. She moved there with her sister Erminia, who was also a teacher, and lived at Via Ariberto 22. In Milan, Abigaille came into contact with exponents of the progressive Catholic world, with the reformist Socialist world, and, more in general, with the city's cultural milieu. This included the Catholic scientist Temistocle Calzecchi Onesti, thanks to whom Abigaille wrote for the weekly *Il Bene*, using the pseudonym "Atomo Cosciente"; and Vittorio Emanuele Mariani, one of the founders of Milan's workers center and a teachers' representative on the board of the Trade Union that was founded in 1891. Abigaille wrote about *L'Alleanza, La Rassegna settimanale politica, artistica, letteraria per l'istruzione sociale della donna, La Cooperazione* and she started to become a union reference point for topics regarding welfare and the delicate issue of maternity insurance. This was the subject of a speech she gave at the 5th International Congress of Welfare, held in Macerata on August 30, 1909, in which she reminded the State of its responsibilities:

> Now, we believe that maternity is not a female illness but rather the highest function of the human species, the most precious social function, and as such it demands the right to collective and legal protection. Every problem that involves the defense of lives, the growth of productive energies, the overall improvement of sanitary conditions for the people, enters the realm of state law. [. . .] But that is not enough: besides the many moral reasons that every civil and modern spirit recognizes, consider a State that entails its most direct responsibility; that the lives saved for the country's progressive gain are also brought into the mechanism of the nation's life; as a consequence, it feels impelled to include in its budget part of the insurance obligations, half of which, in the law proposal, weigh on the entrepreneurs and half on the female workers (Vecchi 2017, 92).

Only in 1910 did Abigaille decide to join the Socialist Party, in part as a result of her encounters with Anna Kuliscioff. Her political activity increased significantly: she collaborated with the pacifist movement and with the Socialist Women's Group. She oversaw the unionizing of teachers, employees, and rice paddy workers, as well as smaller categories, such as laundry workers and corset-makers. She enthusiastically collaborated with the journal *La Difesa delle Lavoratrici*, where she usually signed her articles "Vera" and wrote a column entitled "Piccole e Grandi Verità [Small and Large Truths]," to which Anna Kuliscioff refers in a letter dated March 19, 1912:

> My dear friend, thank you for the *Truths*, and don't think that the preceding ones have been thrown away. [. . .] I saw in *Avanti!* that you are on the list of candidates for the Ex[ecutive] Com[mission] of the Trade Union and by now there is no point in discussing your acceptance. Of course, it's excellent that one of our comrades is on it, as long as health, time, and the necessary habits for that difficult and complicated environment will help you fulfill the undertaken commitment with good results. I hope so for you, and for us, with all my heart (Vecchi 2017, 120).[2]

Abigaille was firmly opposed to any form of conflict, and during the war in Libya, although she had initially supported the pacifist movement of Ernesto Teodoro Moneta, she dissociated herself from it because he considered that war legitimate, as did many Socialists. From February 17 to May 7, 1911, she featured several times in the journal *La Scuola Popolare*, with a long essay, divided into several articles, entitled "The Education of Young People for a Civilization Without War." Angelo Vecchi published excerpts in the issues dated March 12, 19, and 26:

> We do not want war!
> We do not want it, not because we are sugary philanthropists with their heads in the clouds, or fanatical sectarians, but because we sense how criminal the violation of the right to life is, and the brazen monopoly of that right, in the face of the urgent work of justice, solace, and redemption that lies before us! [. . .]
> The champions of pall-bearing politics try to energize us with prattle about the homeland and national sentiment, to justify the barbaric fact of war! First of all, what is needed is for every person to feel they have a homeland that is wise and loving, that truly safeguards their existence, that truly endeavors to provide hospitality, bread, dignity, and a superior life of the spirit for them!
> Our humble position as school teachers might be one of the most favored for the clinical experience of the spiritual and material state of common people's lives. [. . .]
> How many times have we been pained by the sad spectacle of a child who hides behind his elbow when you maternally approach him with anything but the intention of hurting him, and this because, even though he has overcome

56   *Chapter 6*

that fear, he expects the habitual violence of brutal paternal and maternal actions. [. . .]

We must [. . .] renew our methods: use more spontaneous ways, align ourselves with positive science and apply it like artists; above all, we must (we, who want to instill feelings of fraternity and universal solidarity) abolish systematic coercion, abuse of authority, and violence that generates hate and rebellion (Vecchi 2017, 94–95).

During these years, Abigaille founded a so-called left-wing current of the Socialist Party in Milan with Bruno Fortichiari, Luigi Repossi, and the pharmacist Livio Agostini. Research should be conducted regarding the Socialist society that revolved around the pharmacist Agostini in Milan, at Via Ariberto 19, not far from Abigaille's first home at number 22, and around the law office of Roberto Veratti, at Via Ariberto 21. Throughout the entire Fascist period, Varatti worked with the teacher Salvatore Principato, first in Milan's management committee of Giustizia e Libertà, for which he was arrested in 1933, and then, starting in October 1942, in the MUP (Proletarian Unity Movement) (Cavalli and Strada 1982a, 49; Rossi 2000, 155; Monina 2004, 33–34; Giovana 2005, 224). Lina Merlin, after she arrived in Milan in 1931 following her internal exile in Sardinia, wrote that she, too, had drawn near this society (Merlin 1989, 52–53).

Between 1913 and 1914, Abigaille increased her political activity in associations within the party, and as Anna Kulischioff had hoped, she also joined the executive committee of Milan's Chamber of Labor. Her fight for adult education was equally determined: she collaborated with the Popular University, the Consortium of Popular Libraries, and the Union of Popular Education. She was also on the Committee of the People's Tribute to Giuseppe Verdi, which was chaired by Arrigo Boito. She moved from Via Ariberto to Via Plinio, and her home became a reference point for Milan's left-wing Socialists, as Bruno Fortichiari and Mario Malatesta recall (Fortichiari and Malatesta 1948, 39).

Her work with and for children must also be placed within this framework of political activity, as well as her teaching activity in the schools at Via della Spiga and Via Brunacci, activity that has been slightly neglected by her biographers.

On March 13, 1909, Abigaille wrote an article published in *La Cooperazione Italiana* against the false conscience of a shared morality, in this case against the glorification of a false charity that wanted to prostitute the "dignity" of mankind (certain episodes of Alda Costa come to mind); the article was entitled "Regarding Welfare Pulpits":

Abigaille Zanetta 57

A few days ago, a close schoolmate of mine, who teaches in a village in Lombardy, told me she had assigned this essay to her 2nd grade students: "A poor boy shows up at Carletto's door; what did he ask for? What did kind Carletto do?"

This is the old morality that sanctions begging, prostituting individual and collective dignity; this is the vindication of a lack of foresight, on the one hand; and of the unfruitful dispersion of human aid, on the other!

"Bad idea, my dear!" I exclaimed to my scandalized friend. But no matter how hard I tried to explain my opinion, I was unable to persuade her that she had committed (albeit in good faith) a small act of corruption of the children's souls (Vecchi 2017, 91–92).

Elsewhere, she fought false prejudices and the absence of a critical outlook, such as when she recounted a moral lesson she had learned from her father, Bartolomeo:

There. I remember that my father's Garibaldian strictness could not bear the slightest lack of virility or candor in our behavior as simple, free children. If we were asked anything, for example: "Is the garden gate closed?" we would reply: "I believe so." We were sure we would hear him reply: "Believing and not knowing are one and the same thing, go make sure and then come back." Well, today more than ever, concluding all my experience and deducing the strongest synthetic meaning from my positive and social studies, I can repeat with my father: "Believing and not knowing are one and the same thing!" ("Piccole e grandi verità," in *La Difesa delle Lavoratrici*, February 2, 1913: Vecchi 2017, 96).

All this was like a denunciation of a school that was inadequate: its ministerial programs, the number of students the teachers had to instruct, and the scanty resources that were allocated:

Thus, instead of complaining about people who don't learn, schools must become able to truly compensate for that enormous, proletarian misfortune. If, in a crowded class, we are unable to take care of each child, as dictates the conscience and the science of teachers, and if, in a pathetic rush to carry out the unreasonable teaching programs inflicted on us by those ministerial geniuses, we must leave behind too many students who aren't cultured enough, who aren't prepared for either their exams or a useful life, this wouldn't happen if schools were properly conducted, if the students were, above all, less numerous, so we could get to truly know them, one by one, to educate them, instruct them, and assist them as long as needed.

But it takes lots and lots of money to give people this kind of school! ("Beneficio ancor troppo costo[s]o al proletariato," in *La Difesa delle Lavoratrici*, August 2, 1913: Vecchi 2017, 97).

58   *Chapter 6*

Fortichiari and Malatesta recall a dictation given to female students, perhaps during the First World War:

> Blessed are the kind, just, and good souls, who in this sad hour of war and massacre dream of a future of peace for all their human brothers on Earth! Blessed will be the day when egoism and hate disappear from the world as a cause for fierce dispute, and iron and steel will no longer be used to forge instruments of death but instead plows for the land and machines for free, redemptive labor. Dream this lovely dream of love and peace, oh little girls, for the day you will be women, perhaps the loving mothers of men who will hate each other no more (Fortichiari and Malatesta 1948, 17).

In 1914, Abigaille published two didactic booklets, which integrate the vast bibliography presented by Angelo Vecchi (Vecchi 2017, 139–52). They were published in the series by Vallardi "Museo di Scienza Minima. Letture Illustrate per I Giovinetti," edited by Virginio Carnevali, and both are in the A series, dedicated to "students of the working-class course and to young people already in the work world": no. 13, *L'apiario (sorgenti neglette di agiatezza patria)* [*The apiary (neglected sources of homeland wealth)*] and no. 15, *La seta (umili istinti ed opere magnifiche)* [*Silk (humble instincts and magnificent works)*]. In each case, the intention was to teach arts and crafts that could lead to retraining and, as a result, social redemption. To quote the preface of *L'apiario*:

> *Where I was inspired to write this booklet*
> Would you like to know, young readers? Here: in a village in our Alps, about 1,000 meters above sea level, during a summer holiday that would have been delightful if my spirits hadn't been slightly dampened by the sight of the local inhabitants' excessive struggle to make ends meet.
> The climate and the soil are not generous with their products. Wheat doesn't mature well in the scarce arable soil that is available. All the wealth comes from the forest and livestock farming. But there is little grass for this and sometimes those good mountain dwellers risk their lives to gather a tuft of grass on the edge of a precipice.
> Healthy young men go abroad to carry on a trade in order to escape the poverty of the village; the women and old people remain at home to do every difficult chore. "Beasts of Burden" is the title a modern painter gave to one of his marvelous and compassionate paintings that represents those mountain women exhausted from carrying heavy loads as they descend the mountain paths.[3]
> One day, I was cheered from these sad sights to learn that the delicious honey I was served at the small hotel came from the village and that the beekeeper was an upstanding young woman admired by one and all.
> Was the village about to improve its economic conditions by introducing a new industry?

Abigaille Zanetta 59

Could the lovely mountain flowers, the aromatic herbs, the resin from the trees not only help make these places beautiful and dear to tourists on vacation, but also directly benefit the poor villagers thanks to an industrious insect?

Just so, my readers! And I was inspired to write this booklet about beekeeping to communicate to your souls, as future workers, my own cheerful hope in a more flourishing and joyful future for the Italian people when, through education, through the propagation of science and experience, they will learn to defend themselves from extreme poverty through honest endeavors. Our land, so favored by nature, offers so many opportunities to the intelligent industriousness of her children!

A successful choice of crafts

Eighteen-year-old Rosetta, the village beekeeper, received her certificate a few years ago from the women's Agricultural School at Niguarda, near Milan. She had been sent there to study by a Milanese aunt, to foster the girl's true vocation for study and agriculture. Her health had proven to be too delicate for the life of a worker in indoor laboratories. At the School-Farm, in front of that model beehive, she dreamed her wonderful dream of returning to her beloved hamlet, to her large, needy family, as an expert and to attempt the undertaking we have learned about. Today, that dream is a triumphant reality.

The war years saw Abigaille, who had already assumed a position against the war in Libya, firmly against every form of interventionism, as well as against the so-called active neutralism and any form of support of the war effort. She was an internationalist for peace at the Conferences of Zimmerwald and Kienthal; this led to open dissent with Filippo Turati and, as a result, Abigaille broke off her heretofore good relations with Anna Kuliscioff, radicalizing her internationalist position and moving closer to Costantino Lazzari and Amadeo Bordiga.

With the war underway, a public anti-war stance could easily become a crime, with serious accusations of defeatism and sabotage. A colleague of hers, Pamela De Dionigi née Maj, denounced the teacher Zanetta and gathered testimony that ranged from militancy with subversive forces to having read "L'Avanti!" in class and giving defeatist speeches on streetcars. These accusations joined the more institutional ones, such as having clandestinely circulated Zimmerwald's pacifist manifesto, or distributing clandestine leaflets.

There were even many anonymous accusations within the Teachers Association, which sided almost entirely with interventionism (Vecchi 2017, 52–53).

Abigaille was arrested on March 28, 1918, with Bruno Fortichiari; she was initially taken to San Vittore prison and later transferred to the town of San Demetrio ne' Vestini, in Abruzzo. In June, she was once again transferred to

60   *Chapter 6*

San Vittore, and was definitively released in November "for the nonexistence of the crime."

A note from Milan's police headquarters, dated May 2, 1918, reads:

> In response to the document in question, I add that this office has repeatedly had to deal with the well-known subversive Zanetta Abigaille [. . .]. But despite the investigations, undertaken with full commitment, and the surveillance conducted, we have not been able to gather proof for her conviction, be it for a lack of witnesses, be it because I believe the person in question, cunning and wary, has carried out her actions [. . .] at associations, during meetings, and at gathering places of fellow followers, where it is not easy to find those who could betray her (Vecchi 2017, 124–25).[4]

But in 1918, the police headquarters weren't Fascist yet.

That year, Abigaille resigned from the Teachers Association. For her, and her entire generation of Socialist teachers, the post-war years represented important battles, with the birth in Milan, on April 17–19, 1919, of the Teachers Union. She gave speeches at teachers' assemblies and at public commemorations, such as in 1919, when the factory worker Giovanni Gregotti was killed during a police raid. At a congress in January 1920, she also proposed the creation of an international union. On May 9, she met with Alda Costa in Ferrara. In August, she went to Bordeaux to a conference of France's Teachers Union, in hopes of fostering an internationalist perspective as much as possible. During these same months, Abigaille also looked into the potential development of Esperanto as a shared language of the people, and founded the Proletarian Esperanto Group, presenting it at the Women's National Socialist Convention, which was held in Milan at Palazzo Marino in the Sala dell'Orologio on November 28, 1920 (Vecchi 2017, 58).

During the work conducted over the following months, which resulted in Fortichiari, Bordiga, and Repossi shifting to the nascent Italian Communist Party in January 1921, the teacher Zanetta stayed with the Socialists, despite their contradictions and divisions, perhaps in part because she was too closely linked to the world of schools and the Teachers Union, which was traditionally and firmly tied to Socialism.

But by then, the real problem for everyone was Fascism, which was increasingly aggressive, invasive, and devastating.

On April 13, 1921, a tragic blow was struck to the Teachers Union when the teacher from Pisa Carlo Cammeo was murdered. Exactly one year after his death, Abigaille remembered him in an article—which I permit myself to add to her full and well-known bibliography—in the journal Cammeo had edited, *L'Ora Nostra* of Pisa, in an issue dedicated to his memory. The article

Abigaille Zanetta 61

was full of sincere anti-Fascism, an excellent representation of the moment Italy was experiencing:

Come on, you cut-throats, tell me: *but with reason*, with the dignity of your thought, if you can stand up to such a challenge, without dragging in stupid daggers and savage bombs, tell me, for once, if you think that what the privileged, rich, Italians have done is beautiful, right, civic, patriotic; the exploiters you defend to the detriment of the other Italians, of the poor working people, of this multitude that lies under a haze of ignorance, painful destitution, civic superstition! Come on, defend, if you can, your landowning barons enemies of the alphabet, the vampire hierarchy of hoarders, the industrial lice of the nascent Italian industry that sucked the life out of the mothers of Italy's children in the rice paddies, in the fields, in the spinning factories . . .

And then, come on, you *heroes* (long live civilization!), destroy the house of the organization of those poor people who, for the first time, looked up at the sun in hopes of scientific Marxism (*inexorably* scientific, or boldly moribund): who held tightly to this salvation of collective resistance, shouting out their protest against this recognized, atrocious injustice of the past, the martyrdom of their old folks, the eternal hunger of their children . . . shouting: "Finally, *our arms are* at least *our own.*"

And before this proud and epic shout of resurrected *Work*, a shout that your homicidal borders were unable to stop because it awakened the souls of the oppressed throughout the world as one; you wretched stage mimes of village theatrics, what is this miserable, farcical masquerade as saviors . . . of . . . what? What is it you want to save in Italy's name? The lice? Illiteracy? Pellagra? Tuberculosis? The hunger of your people?

You are against salaries, isn't that so? Against a policy of productive spending? For the war? To you, is Italy the usurers, instead of the workers? The failed bankers?

Are they the harpies of the landowners' properties, these anachronistic shadows reincarnated among the ruins of Italy's medieval fortresses, where owls nest?

And will you bring these glories before the other nations? The lice and the usurers? The illiteracy and Italic arrogance, pellagra and the sharks that die of surfeit . . .

The tragedy . . . is comical! But just as it was born in pain and blood, it will die in pain and blood.

And it will no longer be that of the innocent, of the holy apostles of human justice, of the suffering who gift the pleasure-seekers with wealth and joy through the daily torture of their starving and tired flesh. We have lived, we are ready to die in this and for this sublime human faith.

One year, Cammeo, our Martyr! But what is one year in history, this atrocious, slow, strenuous history of human conflict?

62   *Chapter 6*

One? But today, You are in the enormous throng of Martyrs for the advancement of justice! And, by commemorating you today, we do not intend to remove you from the Multitude of those you have joined by dying for the Idea!

The value of a life depends on what you devote it to!

Our memories surround you, Cammeo, you are surrounded by the heartbroken love of brothers, but your vivid figure that we have evoked radiates a light onto our souls that sparks virile intentions: Memento: We are militants in the class struggle! (*L'Ora Nostra*, April 13, 1922, 1).

At that point, Abigaille had to be careful; she had her mail sent to her in a double envelope and to a different address; she had to dodge Fascist attacks, such as the one that involved her in August 1921 at Laigueglia, in Liguria, where a group of students was attending summer camp. In the meantime, she was progressively moving closer to the party's most intransigent positions and in January 1922, at the 3rd Convention of the Teachers Union, she, along with the doctor Fabrizio Maffi, the brother of the teacher Fabio Maffi, voted in favor of a motion to draw near to the Third International, which was in increasingly open conflict with Turatti's positions.

In August 1924, during the crisis following Matteotti's assassination, Abigaille left the Socialists and joined the Italian Communist Party, whose secretary was Antonio Gramsci; she was immediately given important leadership duties in Milan's chapter.

Even though some teachers chose active, but dissimulated, anti-Fascism at school during those difficult years, Abigaille, animated by her internationalist intentions and motivated by her political role, looked abroad and traveled throughout Europe. In August 1925, she represented Italy in Paris at the 3rd Congress of the Internationale des Travailleurs de l'Enseignement, a vast organization with hundreds of thousands of members and present in at least ten countries, including the Soviet Union. The most famous representative in Paris was Célestin Freinet, a theorist of an educational method founded on cooperation, and who was in good relations with Soviet pedagogists, starting with Lenin's wife, Nadezhda Krupskaya. From Paris, Abigaille continued on in a delegation to Leningrad, Moscow, Riga, and Berlin. She returned to Italy on September 19, 1925, and was supposed to go abroad again, to Vienna, in 1926, to attend the 4th Congress of the Internationale des Travailleurs de l'Enseignement.

In the meantime, she sadly witnessed the internal divisions of the Communist Party following Lenin's death, which occurred in January 1924. She also saw her companion in arms Bruno Fortichiari marginalized from his own party in 1926 because he was against Stalin's rise to power, without any sign of compassionate solidarity, and during such a difficult moment, when the Fascists first arrested him and then sent him into internal exile.

Abigaille Zanetta

These bitter events were of no support when, fortified by the authority of law, Fascism didn't hesitate to expel her from school. In 1926, Abigaille taught at the "Antonio Stoppani" elementary school, and that is where she received an injunction of expulsion from the *podestà* Ernesto Belloni for "insufficient compliance with the government's political directives" according to artcle 1 of the royal law decree, dated December 16, 1926, n. 2123.

The Fascists also fired the teachers Virgilio Bellone, who was the former editor of the weekly *La Battaglia Socialista*, and Attilio Banderali.

On March 4, 1927, she took her leave of her students, leaving the following written words behind:

> After four emotional days, I say goodbye to my students, nothing will ever erase the memory of them, days of marvelous revelations of sentiments, virtue, the vivid power of children's pain, pain which I was only able to stem through the suggestive power of personal, affectionate serenity. The emotional regret of the Families was not the least special note of this separation, which concludes a cycle of 26 years of work in Milan's public Elementary Schools (Vecchi 2017, 106).

Her dismissal was followed a few months later by her arrest, on June 14, 1927. She remained in solitary confinement until the end of August, when the judge communicated to her the accusation that she was a member of the so-called Red Aid, which helped imprisoned and confined companions, and their families. She was acquitted and released on December 14, after six months of preventive detention.

On July 15, she wrote to the prison's directors:

> With regard to the notification and the request contained in the presidential letter I received on the evening of the 13th of the current month, I reply that I have no defense to present and that I present none [. . .].
>
> My culture and the life I have lived have made me a convinced Marxist and there is nothing I can do about it. My life's coherence to the principles in which I believe and which I profess were and are for me a modest norm of personal and civic morality, and I still await public trial on the part of official morality for this reason.
>
> The external manifestations of my thought were those variously allowed me by the political atmosphere which arose in Italy starting in 1910, and from the compatibility, which I spontaneously felt, with my juridical state as a teacher of the Municipality, and I have always been accountable for this (Vecchi 2017, 107–08).

She returned to her home on Via Aselli, where she had moved with her sister Erminia from Via Plinio. She tried to make ends meet through occasional

64   *Chapter 6*

translations and private lessons. Erminia, who retired in 1929, moved in with their other sister, Giacinta, in Borgosesia, starting at least in 1933, and for a while, Abigaille remained alone in Milan. She never broke off her political contacts, even though she was under special surveillance.

Giancarlo Pajetta, the son of her colleague Elvira Berrini Pajetta, turned to her in 1929, when he was trying to make contact with the party after being suspended from his high school for anti-Fascism. In May 1930, so did another colleague, Camilla Ravera, who was trying to reconstruct the internal Communist center, before she was arrested in Arona on July 10, 1930.

During World War II, Abigaille joined her sisters in Borgosesia and, over the years, she came into contact there with the nucleus of partisan fighters led by Vincenzo Moscatelli, known as "Cino," who, according to his daughter Carla, held Abigaille in great consideration. Unfortunately, on April 28, 1945, when Cino Moscatelli entered Milan to salute the city that had been liberated from the Nazis and the Fascists, Abigaille had died at the hospital of Borgosesia less than one month earlier.

NOTES

1. Abigaille, one of the best-known and most active anti-Fascist teachers, is the subject of two recently published and well-researched books, to which I am greatly indebted for this chapter: Stevani Colantoni and Barberini 2016; Vecchi 2017.

2. Letter conserved at the Institute "Parri" in Milan, Fondo A. Zanetta, b. 1, fasc. 1, *Lettere indirizzate ad Abigaille Zanetta*, D-L.

3. This is almost certainly the painting by Teofilo Patini dated 1886 (oil on canvas, 244 x 416 cm) that was conserved for a long time in the Palazzo del Governo at L'Aquila. The painting survived the earthquake in 2009 and was subsequently placed in the Pinacoteca Patiniana at Castel di Sangro. It depicts three women, one standing and clearly pregnant, exhausted by their struggle to gather wood for the winter. It was—and still is—considered an emblematic denunciation of the exploitation of women's work.

4. Source: Institute "Parri" of Milan, Fondo A. Zanetta, b. 2, fasc. 9, Detenzione e confino del 1918, Tribunale di Milano. *Processo penale contro Zanetta Abigaille. Udienza 13.8.1918. Nota della Questura. 2 maggio 1918.*

Chapter 7

Fabio Maffi

The Teacher of Teachers

Do not think that loving your country means hating other people.

—Fabio Maffi

The morning of February 27, 1955, was cold and windy, with gusts of sleet as we accompanied the body of Fabio Maffi to his final resting place. For many eventful years, he had worked alongside the authors of this narration. The crowd that followed the coffin included well-known urban personalities and many comrades in faith of the deceased, who had been a Socialist right from the beginning, a Party member from the start, and he remained faithful to his ideals throughout his life.

He was one of the survivors of a generation that had disappeared by then; he had grown up and studied during the second half of the past century, when it seemed as though one era was ending and another—promising—one was beginning under the auspices of science, whose elating progress heralded a new era, a springtime for the world, propitious to humans and their cohabitation.

Thus, the men who looked to the future were optimists, with faith in themselves and their own power; they believed in the perfectibility of individuals and in the evolution of institutes, certain that the new century carried within itself a better society, founded on justice and human solidarity.

Fabio Maffi was one of those men who invoked new times and fought to remove the obstacles that hindered its birth and success.

This is what Andrea Tacchinardi wrote in a rare booklet, published in Milan by Edizioni Labor in 1956 and entitled *Fabio Maffi. L'uomo e le Opere* [*Fabio Maffi: The Man and His Works*].

He was born on January 13, 1863, in San Zenone Po, a town in the Bassa Pavese area of the Po River Valley, where the Olona River flows into the Po.

66 *Chapter 7*

He was fifty-six years old when Fascism arose, and thus, even though he continued to work assiduously until the end of his days, he had already conducted a large portion of his activity as a teacher and educator, as well as an author for young people.

He could have kept to the sidelines—his work duties did not necessarily put him in direct confrontation with the regime—but he was nonetheless just as active and present as the younger and more exposed people, working with them and advising them.

He was considered a pioneer by one and all. Tacchinardi continued: "The generation to which Fabio Maffi belonged did not fight in vain: if the new generations do not want to perish, they will have to resume the pathway the pioneers have blazed, not out of kindness, perhaps, but out of need. These were the thoughts that his death sparked in some of us, as we sadly followed the coffin."

His father, Francesco, who died in 1912, was a farmer, a clog maker, and, later, the municipal secretary; his mother, Cristina Gobbetti, died in 1918. Fabio had ten brothers and sisters. Quirino was his oldest brother, and Fabio was sent to Lodi with him to earn his teaching diploma; other brothers of his studied medicine: Fabrizio in Pavia; Luigi and Attilio in Turin (Maffi 1939, 12, 19–20, 24, 32, and notes).

The *Risorgimento* spirit was profoundly felt in his family. Fabio proudly recalled that in 1859, their home in San Zenone Po welcomed the patriot from Lodi, Francesco Rossetti, who had been released from the prison of Ljubljana but was sought by the Austrian police. With the help of a trusted boatman, they helped him cross over to Arena Po, in Piedmont, where Giacomo Griziotti was waiting for him (Maffi 1939, 12, note 2).

In 1881, after receiving their qualifications as elementary school teachers, Fabio and his brother Quirino participated in a competitive exam for teaching positions in Massa. They were both hired at the elementary schools and moved there, taking along two younger brothers, Fabrizio and Giotto. In 1884, they moved to Turin, followed by two other brothers, Orazio and Attilio, their sister Felicita, and Contardo, an orphaned cousin (Maffi 1939, 48, note 1). These details are not irrelevant because they help outline a situation and a way of life that was certainly not easy, but compulsory. Their salary was sixty-seven lira a month, and in order to maintain their siblings, they had to at least double the sum through private lessons and other jobs, which forced Fabio and Quirino to work no less than twelve hours a day.

In Turin, both brothers developed their Socialist leanings, even before the Congress was held in Genoa in 1892 that created the Italian Socialist Party.

Quirino died soon after of consumption, on December 23, 1893.

Instead, his younger brother Fabrizio received his degree in medicine in Pavia in 1894 and pursued both a busy profession as a doctor and a long political career in the Socialist Party. A member of Parliament from 1913 to 1926, he was harshly victimized by the Fascists, beaten in Pavia, attacked in Rome, and persecuted after his final speech at the Chamber of Deputies, on May 1, 1926, during which he defended the International Workers' Day, which had been suppressed by Fascism. He was first sentenced to internal exile in Pantelleria and Ustica, and then he was imprisoned for a year and a half at San Vittore, after which he was freed but kept under constant special surveillance. He fled to Switzerland in December 1943, to join his brother Luigi in Ambrì. After the Liberation, he was a member of the National Council, a representative at the Constituent Assembly, and a senator during the first legislation. Like Fabio, he died in 1955 (Detti 1987). For Fabio Maffi, the final decade of the nineteenth century was a period of extremely intense political activity, which he conducted in tandem with his teaching duties and the financial support of his siblings.

Using the popular pseudonym "Biagio Carlantonio," he wrote for the *Grido del Popolo* [*The Cry of the People*], Turin's Socialist weekly journal, and he edited the fortnightly supplement *La Parola dei Poveri* [*The Poor People's Word*].

Between 1895 and 1897, his writings were published in small pamphlets that sold for five cents in Turin at the Libreria Editrice Socialista, which belonged to the *Grido del Popolo*. A few of them were collected under the title *Crumbs of Socialism* (1. *The Weapon of the Vote*; 2. *The Institutions and Morality in Socialism*; 3. *Individualism and Collectivism*; 4. *Socialism and the Good of All*). They examined the most serious political and economic problems of the time with acumen and diligence. With simple language, an avenging spirit, and the ardor of an apostle, the articles were addressed to workers, teachers, and even the middle class, criticizing its corruption before the demands of the common people's rights.

The objectives were the affirmation of social justice and the salvation of all: the exploited and the exploiters. The reasoning was simple, often elementary, but rigorously logical and easy to follow.

Between 1896 and 1897, always for the publishing house Libreria Editrice Socialista of the *Grido del Popolo*, and always using the pseudonym Biagio Carlantonio, Fabio published "Vangelo e Socialismo" [Gospel and Socialism] and "Fra Operaie di Città e Campagna" [Among City and Country Female Workers]; these pamphlets were republished several times in Reggio Emilia (ed. Società Anonima Cooperativa fra Tipografi ed Affini) and in Rome (ed. Luigi Mongini).

In September 1897, he was deferred to the judicial authorities as the author of the propaganda pamphlet "Tra Operaie di Città e di Campagna," which was believed to foment class hate. The investigating judge, with a decree dated December 31, 1897, declared "a nonsuit in the case against Maffi

68   *Chapter 7*

Fabio with regard to the crime of which he is accused because it has not been proven that it was committed by him." But on May 23, 1898, unexpectedly and without warning, the Municipal Council of Turin decided on the teacher's immediate dismissal.

Many people protested, including Cesare Lombroso, who deplored the occurrence in the *Gazzetta del Popolo* since Maffi was a teacher who was "meritorious, renowned for his culture, kindness, and the elevation of his soul; a man to whom the purest conservatives entrust their children for their education, who has not one blemish in his past, not even political, taking upon himself political opinions that differ from those of the majority."

The disciplinary action offered the public prosecutor of the Court of Turin the pretext to arbitrarily reopen the trial and to condemn Maffi to four months and twenty-five days in prison and a fine of seventy-five lira, "for fomenting hate among the classes in a way that endangers public serenity" (Tacchinardi 1956, 18–20).

The sentence was remitted but his dismissal remained effective; only through the good offices of Camillo Prampolini was Maffi hired as the director of a boys' orphanage in Reggio Emilia in the spring of 1902. He remained in that position until 1904, even though on June 8, 1902, he was elected municipal councilor in Turin, and on November 18, 1903, he was readmitted to the schools by the permanent board of education.

He collaborated with the journal *Alleanza Cooperativa*, with the Socialist Party, and with *La Voce dei Maestri*, the organ of Piedmont's Teachers Association.

In 1909, he wrote a small book of educational prose and poetry for schoolchildren entitled *Dal Cuore: Piccole Pagine Educative* [*From the Heart: Small Educational Pages*], which was published by the Cooperativa Editrice Libraria of Milan.

One of these pieces was very popular; entitled "Decalogo di Morale Civile" [Handbook of Civil Morality], it was printed on a single sheet of paper and distributed in thousands of copies in the schools of Sagliano Micca, Reggio Emilia, Finale, Cremona, Rovigo, and, translated into French, Paris and Brussels. It was a true manual of secular and Socialist morality, and in one decade, it became a trusted anti-Fascist guide for many. It is worth quoting in its entirety:

Oh young people, love your school companions, who will be your lifelong companions at Work.

Love Study, which is the bread of the mind; and be grateful to he who gives you this bread—your Teacher—as you are to your Father and your Mother.

Sanctify every day with a useful and good action, with a kind deed, with the fulfillment of your Duty.

Honor Virtue, honor the kindest and wisest people, respect everyone, do not prostrate yourself before anyone.

Do not hate, do not offend, never seek revenge; but defend your Right and do not submit to arrogance.

Avoid all cowardice; be a friend of the weak; love, above all else, that which is right. There is no true Civilization without Justice.

Remember that the goods of life are the fruit of Labor: to enjoy them without doing anything is the same as stealing bread from those who work.

Observe and meditate to know the Truth; do not believe that which disgusts Reason; do not let yourself be deceived and do not deceive others.

Do not think that loving your homeland means hating other people, or dreaming of war, a remnant of barbarism. Those who think this way hate their homeland. Only legitimate defense from subjugation can justify violence, wars.

Instead, hope the blessed day is near when all the human beings, free Citizens of one single Homeland, will live in peace and Justice as good Brothers.

In the fall of 1917, Fabio Maffi once again interrupted his teaching duties and moved to Milan, where he became the director of the Institute of the Destitute and remained there for two years, until July 1919. He then moved on to the National League of Cooperatives, directed by Antonio Vergnanini, as secretary and editor-in-chief of the journal *Cooperazione Italiana*, until 1925, when the Fascists dissolved the League and suppressed the journal.

Fabio was over sixty years old; for him, it was the end of his prospects for the free and direct communication he had pursued until then. He was obliged to adopt an indirect, allusive language to communicate the same concepts, all the while eluding Fascist controls. He collaborated with the journals *I Diritti della Scuola* [*The Rights of Schools*]; *Propaganda*, the newsletter of Milan's pharmaceutical cooperative; and *La Cooperazione*, an Italian language organ of the Swiss union of cooperatives.

During the years that saw the rise of Fascism, he was writing against the prevailing trend, of course. He published three books for young people: *Il Teatrino di Nonno Biagio. Dieci Brevi Commedie per Fanciulli e Bambine* [*Grandfather Biagio's Puppet Show. Ten Short Comedies for Boys and Girls*] (Milan: Vallardi, 1926); *La Fiera di S. Giorgio, e Altri Racconti* [*The Feast Day of Saint George, and Other Tales*] (Turin: Paravia, 1932 and 1934); *La Gora del Molino* [*The Mill Race*], with illustrations by R. Albertarelli (Turin: Paravia, 1935). None of these books makes reference to the Fascist cultural climate; instead, they describe a world founded on solidarity between wealthier children who take white bread to school and children who already work as laborers and eat "black bread." More in general, they talk of comprehension among people, fulfilling one's obligations, and demanding one's own rights, such as when, in the *Teatrino* comedy entitled *Pietà di Bimba* [*A Little*

70   *Chapter 7*

Girl's Compassion], a mother teaches her daughter to respect a blackcap's yearning for freedom.

Going against the indications of the regime, which was progressively adverse to the publication of foreign literature, Maffi translated various classics of nineteenth-century children's literature into Italian from English and, above all, French: Charles Dickens, Hector Malot, Alphonse Daudet, George Sand, Rodolphe Töpffer. His translation of the book by the French anarchist Élisée Reclus, *History of a Brook*,[1] merits special attention.

In 1933, he was involved in a broad-ranging and very ambitious project by a number of friends, Socialist teachers who were working on the *Dizionario Enciclopedico Moderno*, which was initially supposed to be published by the Milanese publishing company La Prora. Besides listing commonly used Italian words, the *Dizionario* was also to be an encyclopedia, ranging from science to history and literature. Above all, it intended to offer knowledge that hadn't been contaminated by the Fascist infection. Inevitably (I consulted the second edition, published in 1938), they had to give extensive space to entries such as "Fascism," "Mussolini," and "Hitler," in part to avoid censorship but also because those were the times. However, the compilers also managed to treat, without reticence or political falsifications, entries such as "anti-Semitism," "Jew," as well as "Lenin," "Trotsky," "Gorky," and "Stalin," not to mention "Bissolati," "Gobetti," and even "Marx" and "Turati." All these entries were explained with a respect for historical accuracy that was not to be taken for granted—and seemed impossible—during the second half of the 1930s. Only the entry "Matteotti" was sacrificed because of his extreme symbolic and anti-Fascist value. They were forced into silence but they nonetheless tried to speak, within the permitted limits, without forcing the regime into a direct confrontation that would have deprived them of any opportunity to further the cultural education of the people, in keeping with Socialism's most authentic project.

All this fully justified the idea behind the *Dizionario Enciclopedico Moderno*, which over the years gained a vast audience of readers and merits a monographic study. Let us read a few excerpts from the second edition, published in 1938:

> *Antisemitism*: [. . .] the pseudo-scientific elaboration of *a*. Conducted primarily in Germany, it made wide use of falsifications (see *The Protocols of the Elders of Zion*). In France, there was an explosion of *a*. at the time of the *Dreyfus Affair*. In Russia, during the Czarist regime and the post-war period, there were several episodes of the widespread massacre of Jews (*pogroms*). After 1933, *a*. became official doctrine in Germany, where a series of measures placed the Jews in a state of moral and legal inferiority, catalyzing intense emigration. [. . .]

Jews: [. . .] Maintained in a condition of serious legal inferiority, forced to live in separate areas (*ghettos*) whose gates were closed at night, sometimes obliged to wear indications on their clothing that were meant to identify them, excluded from liberal professions and in many places also from the possession of land, made the object of violence and massacres, they nonetheless resisted in an extraordinary way. Only small groups of them abjured their religion to save themselves and mixed with other populations. Still today, in many parts of Romania, Poland, etc., bloody assaults (*pogroms*) are conducted against them. Recently, a fierce persecution has begun against them in Germany (See *Antisemitism*). [. . .] Today, they are emerging to a remarkable degree in the sciences, the arts, the liberal professions, and political activity. Their characteristic qualities are their nimble intuition and perseverance. Their greatest contribution to civilization is the monotheistic religion, the first in history, from which the other monotheistic religions derive, as well [. . .].

Lenin Nicola: Pseudonym of Vladimir Ilyich Ulyanov (1879–1924), a theorist of Bolshevism and the head of the Russian Revolution of November 1917. In 1895, he joined the Social-Democrat organization "Emancipation of Labour," was imprisoned and deported to Siberia (1895–1900); he then continued his activity abroad [. . .]. Following the victorious revolution of March 1917, he returned to Russia through German enemy territory and prepared the revolutionary explosion in November that brought the Bolsheviks to power. After this, he became President of the Council of Commissioners of the People of the Soviet Russian Republic, and, after the foundation of the Union (1922), also of the Council of Commissioners of the U.S.S.R., effectively becoming the dictator of that immense country. This is not the place for reflections on the upheavals the Party caused in Russia, or on its individual achievements (See *Bolshevism, Communism, Russian Revolution*, and *Russia*). We will only say that he constantly combined theoretical and practical activity, first revolutionary, then governmental [. . .].

Stalin Giuseppe Vissarionovic: [. . .] effectively took over Lenin's legacy; even though he had no official directive, he strengthened his position in the Party, and consequently in the State, and became dictatorial after his victory over trends that leaned to the right or the left, and the removal of Trotsky and other Bolshevist leaders from the Party. A practical person, *S.* tried to reconcile Communist theory and the revolutionary nature of the regime with the need to stabilize the regime itself, both internally and abroad; hence, the insistence on revolutionary manifestations, whereas a few fields saw a return to ways of life inherent to capitalistic States (See *U.S.S.R.*). An expression of this tendency is the constitution of 1936, the result of a Commission he himself chaired. In 1936–1937, his conflict with other senior leaders flared up again and marked the beginning of a period of repression that is still underway.

72   *Chapter 7*

The publishing house La Prora soon pulled out of the undertaking, considering it too unrealistic. The creators of the *Dizionario* decided to continue on their own and created the publishing house Labor in 1934. The founder of Labor and the originator of the undertaking was Daniele Ercoli (Pagani 1962, 121), who had already written a number of grammar and math anthologies for schools, had first worked at Mondadori, and later co-founded the publishing house La Prora with Giuseppe Locatelli. From a letter dated April 26, 1931, and written by the spy Carlo Del Re to the head of the Fascist police, Arturo Bocchini, we learn that, in Milan, Daniele Ercoli helped distribute clandestine papers for the anti-Fascist group Giustizia e Libertà (Rossi 2000, 200).

He was assisted by the Socialist teachers Luigi Bertana and Andrea Tacchinardi, indirect protagonists on several occasions in this book, and by the assistant director of the municipal library of Milan, Giovanni Bellini (1892–1986), a convinced anti-Fascist who cautiously participated in clandestine activities. He "declined" an invitation "to become a member of the Fascist Party" and believed that "to nip the Fascist adventure in the bud, in 1922 all it would have taken was for the king to confirm the state of siege decreed by the Facta government, which would have resulted in the mobilization of the army and the police" (Bellini 2013, 52–53).

They were soon joined by the Socialist teacher Aurelio Molinari. (To get an idea of his spirit, read Molinari 1924.) Besides Fabio Maffi, his closest collaborators included Aurelio Castoldi, Achille Agazzi, Giovanni Zibordi, Antonio Basso, Carlo Fontana, Lamberto Jori, Carlo Dell'Acqua, and Gustavo Della Frattina.

Andrea Tacchinardi recalled:

> The promoters were catalogers, editors, revisers, illustrators, proofreaders of the work [. . .]. The sections were cheerfully distributed and they passionately set to work. [. . .] Work progressed with difficulty but success was becoming increasingly assured, above all thanks to Ercoli, who directed the propaganda and production. Nevertheless, we needed to work faster. So we looked for collaborators. The first, in chronological order, was Fabio Maffi, to whom we entrusted the revision of the folders that the writers completed every day. This job held great responsibility and required attention, diligence, a sure eye, culture, taste, and a great mastery of the language: talents and qualities he proved to possess to a very high degree. To the point that he effectively became the referee of the small quarrels that inevitably arose among the authors and also among the collaborators, whose number gradually increased. [. . .]
>
> [Fabio Maffi] worked in a small room in his modest apartment in Via Bronzetti 37, packed with dictionaries, encyclopedias, books, texts of every kind that no longer held any secrets for him, and that he sometimes consulted more out of scrupulousness than out of necessity. The folders piled up on his desk in tall stacks. He pulled them out of the stacks one by one; he read them, reread

Fabio Maffi 73

them, and then reduced, added, altered, recomposed, blended those entries of ours, which were sometimes tormented by the desire to include something the limited number of words did not allow. His variations, which were written in tiny yet clear handwriting, were always, or almost always, appropriate, whether they were entries for the dictionary or regarded history, geography, science, art, sport. He had amassed an encyclopedic culture, not through occasional reading but through unflagging study, his whole life long.

It was a great fortune for us to have had him as a fellow worker during those memorable years.

By then, he was over seventy years old; he was pushing eighty but he was an example of resistance and ability to all of us, in a job that exhausted even those who were younger than him (Tacchinardi 1956, 22–25).

He was such a modestly reserved person that his name does not even appear in the list of collaborators. This dignified and industrious discretion, too, was anti-Fascism.

NOTE

1. C. Dickens, *La casa trista. Romanzo*, Milan: Sonzogno, 1925; H. Malot, *Romain Kalbris: avventure d'un piccolo marinaio*, Florence: Salani, 1928 and 1930; A. Daudet, *La Bella Nivernese. Storia d'un vecchio battello e del suo equipaggio*, Milan: Sonzogno, 1928; G. Sand, *La palude del diavolo*, Milan: Treves, 1931; R. Töpffer, *Novelle ginevrine*, Rome: A. F. Formiggini, 1933; A. Daudet, *Racconti del lunedì*, Milan: Signorelli, 1934; A. Daudet, *Tartarino*, Milan: Treves, 1935; A. Daudet, *Tartarino: Tartarino di Tarascona, Tartarino sulle Alpi*, Milan: Garzanti, 1944; É. Reclus, *Storia d'un ruscello*, Turin: Paravia, 1932.

Chapter 8

Carlo Fontana

From Councilor to Mayor of Magenta

He was born with the humanitarian utopia.

—Ciro Fontana

Carlo Fontana, too, helped draft the *Dizionario Enciclopedico Moderno*, printed by the publishing company Labor, and he is listed among the collaborators in the 1938 edition.

He was born in Magenta on March 23, 1890. His father, Francesco Napoleone, was a greengrocer and Carlo was expected to continue in his footsteps; his mother, Luigia Albasini, had other ambitions for him and hoped he would find modest employment at the De Medici match factory, in Magenta. Thus, his degree as an elementary school teacher was a great conquest, in line with his Socialist ideals. From a very young age, he studied by day and worked by night as a delivery boy for the town's baker.

He had a personal aversion to office work. "The idea of locking myself up between four walls and submitting myself to a slow mummification of the body and spirit," he wrote, "gave me a feeling of anguish" (Fontana Carlo 1956, 14). Plus, he was following the grand Socialist project of accomplishing for himself what he dreamed of for everyone: to be free to give a direction to his own life, in line with his personal aptitudes, and not have to succumb like the vanquished to the social and cultural conditions imposed on him by his family of birth. "Are we or are we not free," he asked, "to change the course of our existence through our actions, or does our life run on two rigid rails, which were previously laid by an unknown power?" (Fontana Carlo 1956, 14).

He received his diploma from the Giovanni Gherardini school in Milan in 1912. But he was unable to teach in Magenta because the municipal

76 *Chapter 8*

administration denied him this right due to his declared Socialist ideas, which the local lower and middle classes evidently considered dangerous.

He shared his early idealistic battles with his friend Camillo Formenti, who, in one of his numerous articles, entitled "Il Socialismo Nelle Campagne" [Socialism in the Countryside], published on July 25, 1914, in *La Battaglia Socialista*, an organ of the Provincial Socialist Federation, wrote in an openly anticlerical polemic:

> "Blessed are the poor because theirs is the kingdom of heaven." If your landlord evicts you, bear patience, for he, too, has the right to live and cannot do without money . . . don't you know that it takes gasoline to make cars move? If the master confiscates your cow, be patient, you'll understand, it's his wife's name day, and a pearl necklace, a pair of drop earrings are indispensable . . . , and the woman, come on, she doesn't want to do without, it would be to the detriment of her dignity as a woman of high society. And if the master, when he needs to make you work, pays you one lira and 20 cents a day, you must thank him, because, ultimately, he is always the one who feeds you, who protects you, who looks after you and your family! Without him, you'd starve to death; therefore, gratefully kiss the charitable hand that keeps vigil over you. [. . .] As the priest always says, fear not, paradise is not for the rich, it is all yours, you poor devils!

It was a blunt diatribe, and it was followed up years later, on June 18, 1919, in the same journal, in an article entitled "Religione e Preti" [Religion and Priests]:

> It is the highest malice on the part of our adversaries to pass us off as sworn enemies of religion, when they know that Socialism doesn't deny religious belief, which—when it is interpreted and practiced with faith—is ideal beauty, elevation of the spirit, goodwill. It does not deny religion because our Socialism is also a religion of the weary spirits that yearn for a better future [. . .]. Let the priest stay in his church to mumble Hail Marys [. . .] and no one will pay any attention to him. But when he leaves the sacristy and throws himself into the political arena in defense of a given class or category, then he cannot prevent people from fighting him, unmasking him, locking him—to the extent he deserves—to a pillory! Anticlerical, yes; anti-religious, no!

On August 19, 1913, Carlo Fontana, who was increasingly opposed by the local administrators, wrote from Magenta to Nino Turati, a functionary of Milan's Humanitarian Society, which was founded in 1893 for philanthropic purposes, and illustrated the reality of the community of Magenta:

> In these places, untouched by Socialism or organization, the workers do not comprehend the meaning of certain struggles. Here, we are still in the era of evangelical propaganda. [. . .]

Carlo Fontana 77

As for me, I have done and do what I can, but my adversaries' hate reaches me everywhere. The fact is that they do not only manifest it verbally, but also through material aggression, such as—for example—taking away my sustenance.[1]

He found a position at Boffalora sopra Ticino, thanks to the intercession of a manager at the De Medici company and an uncle of his. Thus, in early 1913, he was assigned a co-ed first grade class with the usual exorbitant number of students that was typical of rural schools: fifty-one boys and forty-three girls (Tunesi, Morani 2016, 93).

He wrote to this regard:

Having refused to renounce principles I considered right, I was thus virtually banished from that doltish and small-minded rustic coterie. After all, there was work for everyone at home and it certainly wasn't a humiliation for me to go back to working as a baker and greengrocer. Except that by then, I also had to deal with the susceptibility of my father and mother's distress, which pained me more than anything else. Add to this the fact that when certain lukewarm friends would meet me in public places, they pretended they didn't see me or wouldn't stop to talk with me for fear of compromising themselves, and you will understand my state of mind at the time. [. . .]

And my purgatory began. I would get up early in the morning and walk my three kilometers through the high snow that was never lacking that year. When I reached Boffalora, I would cross the old bridge over the Naviglio Grande and slip into a courtyard located on the bank of the Naviglio itself. At the back of the courtyard, on the ground floor, there was a large room that had previously been used as a storehouse. This was my classroom. A large column, right in the middle of the room, prevented me from seeing all the students at the same time. Those poor children arrived from the town and the surrounding farms, so numb with cold that it was a pitiful sight. But almost all of them brought not just their schoolbag but a good piece of wood and, throughout the winter, the first task was to light an old stove, which only served to prevent certain death from exposure. [. . .]

Can you imagine this young man, twenty-three years old, as he leaps over the desks and passes over the young children in front to get all the way back to the last ones, to guide their uncertain hands as they write their first vowels and consonants? Can you imagine this impetuous young man, always intent on reining in his temperament, on limiting his reactions, above all in order to avoid frightening those small children, who stared at him with their large eyes, full of serenity and sweetness? (Fontana Carlo 1956, 23, 26–27).

At the Municipal Archive of Boffalora sopra Ticino, Natalia Tunesi and Carlo Morani have examined the yearly report that the teacher Fontana prepared on August 7, 1913, providing information "about the precarious hygienic-sanitary conditions of the classroom, the lack of drinking water, the feeble illumination." In the attached questionnaire, Fontana expressed "his indignant reaction in laconic answers." To the request: "Disadvantages the classroom presents," he sarcastically commented: "Impossible to list them all here." Alongside the questions "Is the didactic material suitable? Is it sufficient?" two curt negations appear, while the discouraged teacher answered the embarrassing question: "What is needed?" with "the eloquent silence of an empty sheet of paper."

With regard to the children, he wrote: "They come to school dirty, tattered, poorly dressed and malnourished, half savage, they are not looked after by their parents, who have to leave the house early for the fields and factories." He noted the "ancient desks, where 5, 6, 7 children have to sit together and from which they cannot get up, unless they climb over the desk or the bench, dirtying and stepping on their classmates," a squalid classroom-storeroom, the absence of adequate didactic material.

"In the face of all this," write Tunesi and Morani, "Fontana's ears ring with the words of an obtuse and conservative managerial class that urged the teachers to 'educate the commoners only as much as required,' with the fairly undisguised goal of hindering their moral and social elevation" (Tunesi, Morani 2016, 93–94).

His method, he wrote, consisted in "instructing by educating and amusing," in "aiming, above all, at practical results," in "trying to make mathematics pleasurable," in "taking advantage of things the students have seen or that have happened to them, having them describe these things and correcting them"; plus educational walks, at least once a month, colored pebbles and cents to teach them how to count. In this way, he was able to promote fifty-nine out of his ninety-four students (Tunesi, Morani 2016, 95).

However, Fontana's activities at Boffalora sopra Ticino weren't limited to teaching children; he also conducted social, medical, and health-care activities, for the children and throughout the entire territory where the school operated: hygiene, propaganda against tuberculosis and malaria, the struggle against the non-completion of compulsory education, solidarity with the demands of other workers and with the more indigent families, sharing life. This was the most direct way to put his project as a Socialist teacher into action.

In the meantime, he joined the National Teachers Association; in view of the hostility he had received from the people of Magenta, he took advantage of the new Daneo-Credaro law (1911) that took control of the elementary schools away from the municipalities and made them directly dependent on the State. He also won a competitive examination in Milan and was sent to Ronchetto sul Naviglio, a district of Buccinasco.

He joined the writing staff of the Socialist newspaper *La Scuola Popolare*, signing himself Torrente on a dozen articles during the two-year period 1915–1916 and, as Carlo Cammeo and many others had done, taking a position of internal opposition within the Association and fostering the constitution of the Teachers Union.

> When the war brutally came to tell us that remaining in that association meant putting ourselves at the service of the State and the master of the proletariat, we could no longer bear such company and left: first morally, at [the congress in] Bologna in April 1916 and, later, officially, to found the union and march alongside the entire proletariat organized on the clear and open pathway of class struggle (Carlo Fontana, "Scuole e proletariato (II): I maestri col proletariato," in *La Battaglia Socialista*, June 19, 1920).

A convinced pacifist, he was called to arms on April 29, 1916. To this regard, his son Ciro wrote:

> He was born with the humanitarian utopia. A pioneer of Socialism in the area around Magenta [. . .], he preached non-violence and brought it down upon himself. A burning anti-militarist, he did his duty at the front. "Italy is on Monte Grappa!" Filippo Turati had said, and, to my father, whatever the lawyer from Canzo said was gospel.
>
> He preached Christianity and was sent from the front to Genoa, where he was committed to a military hospital and caught the "Spanish flu," after an anonymous letter denounced him as a "dangerous anarchist." One of the proudest moments of his life was when he shouted "whore!" at Mussolini during the memorable assembly in Milan, when Mussolini, already the "Duce *in nuce*," was expelled from the Socialist Party and, all of a sudden, switched from the proudest anti-interventionism to the most ardent warmongering.
>
> A friend of Filippo Corridoni, an angelic soul, he spent entire nights debating with him. Corridoni claimed that the war of 1915–1918 would be the final war and for this reason they had to fight.
>
> Corridoni heroically lost his life in the trenches of the Frasche, and he, at least, was spared the bitter and tragic disappointment of his comrades in faith who remained in the world (Fontana Ciro 1981, 8–9).

Despite the war, during the two-year period 1916–1917, Carlo married his young colleague Domenica Bubani in a civil ceremony on October 7, 1916; his son Ciro was born on October 24, 1917. In Magenta, like everywhere in Italy, while monuments to the Unknown Soldier and memorial chapels to the fallen were being built, reality revealed all of the war's contradictions: death, permanent disabilities, poverty, destitution in contrast to speculation, deep lacerations of the social fabric. Carlo Fontana wrote passionately:

80 — Chapter 8

There are only two names on the list of contributors to the famous monument to the infantryman. [. . .] And the others? And all the numerous local squires, the finest patriots, where have they all gone? Where has it vanished to, the Homeland's gratitude to the glorious, to the heroic defenders of yon gentlemen's wallets? A large committee busied itself tapping money from those whose only contribution to the war had been chatter and lies and fibs, to the detriment of the people who are thrice-over good, who went to be killed at the front. The war, the homeland, gratitude toward those who lost their lives? Lies, lies. The war was grand while it lasted and while the men were away, off to be killed for their filthy interests. But now the party is over. Now the men have returned and their eyes are open and they remember and they hate. It was a terrible lesson but it has produced its results. And those people who applaud the "beautiful war" for the "grandest Italy" have repudiated it and thrown it onto the dung heap. And the promised sign of appreciation for the victims of their enormous crime has been forgotten, they have perjured themselves. Cowards, cowards, cowards! (Carlo Fontana, "Magenta," in *La Battaglia Socialista*, July 3, 1920).

As in many other cities in northern Italy, the Socialist Party gradually came fully into its own in Magenta, too. Camillo Formenti and Carlo Fontana were its two main reference points, starting with the first strikes in 1914 and until the sweeping electoral victory on October 10, 1920, which voted Camillo Formenti in as mayor. The councilors included Brenno Cavallari for finance, the food administration board, and the board of health, personnel, and the registrar; Ambrogio Olgiati for public works; and Carlo Fontana, who was also elected provincial councilor, for public education.

The new council began to transform Magenta, giving its support to workers organizations, the Chamber of Labor, the Labor Union, and membership in the League of Socialist Municipalities; it also provided money for the town's new band, the Proletarian Musical Corps, which, as opposed to other bands, played at every service the municipality requested (Tunesi, Morani 2016, 71–80).[2] They next addressed the tax burden, guaranteeing free medical examinations to the underprivileged; raising taxes on rooms, terrains, and buildings; and doubling business taxes for various companies. They maintained the special tax for civil assistance that had been created in 1916, when the war was in full swing. They decided to abolish the tax on livestock, which "weighed entirely on farmers," who possessed, "to a large degree, only one animal, designated as an indispensable work instrument."

As for the shops, they had the municipal officers collect "a sample of the paper [. . .] used to wrap food in the delicatessens and grocery stores." They found that, in almost every shop, the paper weighed more than required by the sanitary regulations and the offenders were fined. They did the same thing with samples of milk to check whether it had been diluted with water.

Carlo Fontana

They also took measures to rectify local unemployment and, on the initiative of Carlo Fontana, promoted the education of children and adults.

Evening and holiday classes were inaugurated, financial support was provided to the community library, a subsidy of ten thousand lira was given to support education, and the People's University was founded for adults, to "foster the moral elevation that is so useful in achieving their just aspirations."

As a council member, Carlo Fontana did everything he could to increase the heating in classrooms, to refurbish the electrical system, and to provide subsidies to the most indigent students.

On the other hand, he rejected the request to "bless" the school and convinced the council to invite teachers to "abstain from reciting prayers and other religious manifestations in school"; classrooms were made available for after-school religious education, for the children of families who requested it.

The entire administration declared itself contrary to manifestations that were "clearly aimed at military glorification," including the commemoration of the battle of June 4, 1859, whose municipal financing was abolished. This is what the council deliberated on December 19, 1920:

> First of all, the Mayor in no way intends to seem to be lacking in respect toward those who died in battle, deaths that are as sacred as the deaths of all those who have fallen for an idea, and he declares that the present administration, a genuine representative of workers, has no interest in this manifestation, nor in any others that, in view of their nature, are clearly aimed at military glorification. At the same time, he believes that this duty should logically and coherently be the responsibility of the middle class. Furthermore, he will strive to be a moderator among the working classes of Magenta because every manifestation, regardless of its color, should be respected. At the same time, he affirms the intangible right of the administration to not be provoked in the fulfillment of its mandate.

Perhaps they went a bit too far when they ordered that various pictures depicting "portraits of the Royal family" be removed from the walls because they were considered "too cumbersome."

But this was not the only reason why the prefect of Milan, the senator Alfredo Lusignoli, decided to dismiss the Municipal Council of Magenta on November 12, 1921, placing it under receivership and suspending the majority of its resolutions.

To Carlo Fontana, there was only one motivation; by then, the Fascist threat was clearly behind it, as were the small- and medium-sized merchants and shopkeepers, including the ones the councilor Brenno Cavallari had forced to weigh their paper and not dilute the milk:

> The reason is intuitive, it is the same one that acted against hundreds and hundreds of our Municipalities. We do not know if the Fascist parties in other

82 *Chapter 8*

towns are full of shopkeepers; the one in Magenta is, for sure (Carlo Fontana, "Insurrezione di esercenti," in *La Battaglia Socialista*, July 23, 1921).

[. ..] the administrator comrades [were] banished from the town hall by the arrogance of the worst faction that exists in the world, the merchants—and it has a nature so malign and ruthless, that after food is hungrier than before[3]—with the help of the senator Lusignoli, so that from the balcony of the municipal building the Italian flag still waved. And it was a great celebration for each one of these sharks! (Carlo Fontana, "Le difficoltà del bilancio del comune," in *La Battaglia Socialista*, August 6, 1921).

Brenno Cavallari, with his firm Socialist faith, was the director of the new Reunited Workers Board, which was founded in March 1920. It was, as Fontana wrote, the "Socialist soul" of the town. He also ran the production and consumer cooperative "L'Alleanza," which was laying the foundation for change in Magenta, with the goal of safeguarding the purchasing power of salaries and monitoring the shopkeepers, creating outlets for foodstuffs at controlled prices.

Both Fontana and Cavallari knew, as De Amicis wrote in *Primo Maggio* [*The First of May*] that "there is no morality that can resist the prolonged test of need" (De Amicis 1996, 694), and that in order to educate the people, dignified living conditions had to be provided for children and their families. Their collaboration became assiduous and inevitable.

Less than one hundred years after these events, Italy seems to have forgotten these so-called red councils, which were swept away in the space of two years by Fascism but which elaborated extremely advanced programs for the regulation of fiscal pressure; the defense of rights, above all the right to education, even for adults; the municipalization of services; the development of public works; limiting unemployment; and providing assistance to the needy. They wanted to prevent the so-called proletariat from being the only class that paid for the cost of the war, which they had not sought and did not want, but had paid for with the sacrifice of too many lives.

It was not a dream;—was an ongoing revolution, which Fascism violently overturned and canceled, with the support of a portion of the upper and middle classes and many small merchants.

When the Municipal Council was renewed, the Socialists won once again and on March 19, 1922, Cesare Fontana, Carlo's brother, was elected mayor (Carlo Fontana, "Domenica abbiamo vinto!," in *La Battaglia Socialista*, March 25, 1922). But it would not last long.

Already in December 1920, the Fasci of Combat was constituted in Magenta, and its first targets were Formenti, Fontana, and Cavallari. Above all, as Fontana wrote, Brenno Cavallari's Alleanza Cooperativa represented a threat for the shopkeepers:

Carlo Fontana 83

Their sleep is not tranquil, and until they manage to destroy it, they will know no peace [. . .]. And if the shopkeepers don't manage to do it . . . , the remedy is easily found: a Fascist—sorry, a punitive—expedition. The Alleanza has placed a white banner (please note, a white one) up high across a street, letting citizens know that shoes and other merchandise are sold there at a good price. But the Fascists don't like white, either, and they paint it red-white-green and moreover they search for the comrade Cavallari for an "explanation." The truth is that the merchants want to be the masters, and in order to do this, they become Fascists. And in the name of the Homeland (poor Homeland, how many crimes are committed in your name!), the shopkeepers blackmail the citizens (Carlo Fontana, "Insurrezione di esercenti," in *La Battaglia Socialista*, July 23, 1921).

In August 1921, the local chapter of the newborn Italian Communist Party was burned down, followed by an attack on the Chamber of Labor and the cooperative L'Alleanza.

The Fascists arrived on the evening of Sunday, July 22, 1922, in one car and four trucks, commanded by the leader of the *squadrismo* of Casale Monferrato, Giovanni Passarone. They entered town around 10:45 p.m. A group of *squadristi* headed toward the cooperative's headquarters; another one went in the direction of the three outlets located on Via Pretorio, on Via 4 Giugno, and on Via Manzoni: they knocked down the doors with reinforced clubs and axes, set the rooms on fire, and destroyed and ransacked the merchandise. Seven people were stabbed. They destroyed everything. Even the prefect of Milan, Alfredo Lusignoli, called the enterprise "barbaric" (De Felice 1965, 264), but needless to say, the legal authorities only pretended to pursue the guilty parties. Following an oft-repeated script, the usual suspects were brought in and then freed.

Brenno Cavallari, who was trying to put the destroyed cooperative back on its feet, became the prime target of the Fascists. He often had to wait for the intervention of the Carabinieri to escape Fascist violence.

Carlo Fontana remembers him as a "mild, good, and courteous man, incapable of the slightest vulgarity" (Carlo Fontana, "Magenta. La nostra vittoria elettorale," in *La Battaglia Socialista*, February 4, 1922). He was bombarded with threatening letters, anonymous ones, of course, and threats of every kind. Fontana remembers that he returned to Magenta a few days after the Fascist devastation, under the protection of the police and the Carabinieri, while hundreds of Fascists threatened him, "vomiting insults at him at the top of their lungs" (Carlo Fontana, "Intimidazioni e minacce fasciste," *La Battaglia Socialista*, October 14, 1922). His eyeglasses were slightly fogged over as he walked firmly down the street, the street to the train station that, following the Liberation, was named after him by Carlo Fontana, who had

84 *Chapter 8*

become mayor. I don't think many people walking down this street today can sense the tragic atmosphere of those final terrible days of freedom.

Brenno Cavallari's fate was sealed: he survived the Fascist violence in July 1922, but he didn't live to see the Liberation of Italy. On July 12, 1944, he was shot near the Fossoli camp with sixty-six other political prisoners.

On August 17, 1922, the Socialist council chaired by Cesare Fontana resigned, and in just a few months Fascism set its new rules. In September 1923, they shut down the journal *La Battaglia Socialista*, for which Fontana and Formenti had written with such political passion.

But things weren't silent. His son Ciro wrote:

To me, a child, Fascism was summarized by my father's face, bruised and marked by Fascist "attentions" when, starting in '19, he would return home from Socialist rallies, often making us spend distressing nights.

He didn't join the Communist Party during the secession of '21 because he thought they might want to impose Socialism with force, instead of with persuasion. Well!

One time, it was summer, he was walking down a street, with his hat in hand. A squad of Blackshirts passed by; they were led by a band playing "Giovinezza, Giovinezza" out of tune. A few thugs began to shout at the passersby "off with your hat!" And my father ostentatiously clapped it down on his head. You can imagine the consequences.

Another time, in May 1931, he was one of the promoters of a manifestation of solidarity for Arturo Toscanini, after the famous "slaps" in Bologna. "Hurrah for Toscanini" echoed throughout the gallery at the Scala, where, by the way, you could say I spent my childhood and adolescence with my parents, all three of us angry music lovers (Fontana Ciro 1981, 9).

A few evenings after the episode of the "hurrah for Toscanini!," Carlo was once again stopped at a concert at the Scala for having manifested indignation at the sound of the Fascist hymn *Giovinezza*. He was roughed up and shoved around, a few tufts of his beard were pulled out, and one of his eardrums was broken, after which he was conducted to police headquarters. He got off lightly, perhaps thanks to a policeman who was the father of one of his students, just like another student of his saved him from being arrested years later, when his great and unforgettable comrade in Civil Resistance was imprisoned in Milan: Salvatore Principato, executed by a firing squad on August 10, 1944 (Fontana Ciro 1981, 10).

An as-yet-unpublished memorial by Marcella Chiorri, Salvatore's wife, notes with regard to the first twenty years:

Fascism, which advanced desperately, had destroyed many of our illusions, and my husband often returned home agitated and bruised. We both knew the people for whom we had fought ever since we were schoolchildren [. . .]. Back then, my direct contacts were Professor [Ugo Guido] Mondolfo, whose books we studied, whose story we knew, and with whom we shared the anxieties of the times, at school, through his worthy companion, Signora Lavinia Mondolfo, my teacher. I later heard my husband talk a lot about [Giuseppe] Faravelli, [Andrea] Tacchinardi, the teacher [Alessandro] Piazza, the teacher Fontana, and many of his colleagues whom I gradually came to know.[4]

This friendship with Fontana lasted throughout all the difficult years of the dictatorship and Nazi occupation, starting when Salvatore Principato became the Socialist representative in the Milanese committee of Giustizia e Libertà (Giovana 2005, 224), and also later, when the CLN [National Liberation Committee] school was founded; until his arrest in July 1944, Principato was the coordinator of the Socialist group (Cavalli and Strada 1982a, 72, 91). Fontana worked by his side.

Another great friend of Fontana's during the dark years when Fascism was in power was Paolo Pini, the "doctor of the poor," whose great kindness Fontana remembers:

All you had to do was follow him around in his everyday life, in his daily work. His work began very early in the morning, when he would run to the homes of the sick, to the hospitals, to the nursing homes, in the city and further afield. After a very frugal breakfast, his work recommenced at his modest studio at Porta Magenta. Those who went there for the first time, and only knew Pini by fame, were slightly disappointed, and sometimes irritated. Oh that endless wait in those very modest rooms, surrounded by the most assorted people! But finally Pini called [. . .]. The patient felt the need to stay with him. It is as though he were subjugated by those magnetic eyes that, luminous and serene, stared at him from under the thick arch of his eyebrows. Pini asked questions and, slowly but surely, the patient made his confession, bared himself, abandoned himself to that beneficent power that cured the soul, even before the body. And he left with new hope, murmuring: a saint! Between one visit and the next, he would have a quick chat with a comrade, there, in that small kitchen surrounded by reagents, test tubes, and all sorts of medicine. It was getting late. He heated up a small saucepan of soup or some coffee and milk on a burner. Pini couldn't permit himself the luxury of a regular dinner: his patients were waiting for him and his visits began again and continued into the night. [. . .] Where did all of our Pini's altruism come from? Certainly from his nature as a good man, but also from his Socialist faith. He was a convinced Socialist; a steadfast supporter of the rights of workers, whom he defended in the organizations, whom he represented in the administration of the Municipality and the Province. [. . .] He was consumed by the great dream of human redemption, which can only occur if the curse that weighs on human toil is removed, if we begin to liberate the modern slaves of machines (Tunesi, Morani 2016, 50–51).[5]

86   *Chapter 8*

For Carlo Fontana, this was the beginning of the difficult pathway of conspiracy, opposition to the regime, civil resistance, which had to be manifested in every small, daily gesture, starting with teaching, which strove to ignore Fascist pseudo-history and offer students alternative values, without blatantly violating the regime's increasingly restrictive provisions.

For example, they were allowed to talk about the *Risorgimento*—this was permitted under Fascism—and they had to do so by instilling in the young people a love for the freedom of thought, opinion, and action. And this could be done by reading and interpreting Dante, Foscolo, and Mazzini.

One of the favorite readings of anti-Fascist teachers was *The Parliament* by Giosue Carducci, which took inspiration from the republican ideals of the Lombard free commune against the foreign usurper Frederick I. Carlo Fontana, too, held a lesson on this subject; it still exists.

In an exercise of *Recitation*, conserved in his archive and datable to 1937, he wrote for the young people "First and fundamental article: do not recite before perfectly understanding the meaning of the words, you must try to penetrate their spirit" (Tunesi, Morani 2016, 150). This, too, was anti-Fascism, whereas instead, Fascism was empty rhetoric, the deformation of the meaning of words and history.

During the years of the dictatorship, he adopted the pseudonym Don Alvaro, and no longer Torrente because he had to set aside his youthful ardor; by then, he identified with the character Verdi had invented, with the knowledge that he, too, had to contend with "the force of destiny."

Fontana also dedicated himself to writing, above all dramatic works, poetry, as well as texts in dialect and didactic verses. What emerged were literary tales that are clearly anti-Fascist in spirit, such as the Don Quixote who appears in his "individual drama of a man who rejects the vulgarity and sordidness of reality and seeks refuge in madness, as the supreme affirmation of truth" (Fontana Ciro 1981, 158). Basically, it is the Don Quixote by Miguel de Unamuno (De Unamuno 1913).

And thus, Fontana's Don Quixote recites, in a typewritten manuscript conserved in his archive:

> Ungrateful humanity . . .
> ungrateful and cowardly . . .
> cowardly with those who oppress and trample it
> sad with the good people who want its redemption! [. . .]
> I fight for a Holy Idea,
> nor do I care about the living who are dead (Tunesi, Morani 2016, 158).

Of all of Fontana's writings, I want to examine the script of the ballet *Pinocchio*, set to music by Guido Ragni, a collaborator of Toscanini. The ballet was performed at the Scala of Milan on March 18, 1943, starring Olga Amati, one of the theater's young and promising ballerinas. A typewritten copy of the script is conserved in Fontana's private archive, as well. It was very well received by the public, much less so by the critics, who went so far as to call its vision mute and even "colorless and ponderous" ("Il Popolo d'Italia," March 19, 1943). But instead, a few Fascists praised the Italianicity of the performance, as opposed to Walt Disney's mangling attempt ("Il Regime Fascista," March 19, 1943). But Fontana wanted to valorize aspects of the Risorgimento and the nineteenth century, as well as a widespread sense of the love for freedom, paying much attention to Pinocchio's escape from the evil puppeteer Mangiafuoco.

The text concludes with Geppetto's reflection:

> Naturally,
> he who is without brain and heart
> is nothing other than a sad puppeteer.
> The homeland wants
> her children to be full of ardor
> So they will grow frank and strong
> and ready for strife
> but may their companions always be
> their heart and their reason.
> In this way, the family and the nation
> will rise to high goals.
> Remember this, my son! . . .
> Now, come here, embrace me!
> Nothing out of the ordinary, if World War II and Fascist war propaganda hadn't been in full swing.

During those same years, Carlo Fontana, too, joined the ranks of the Socialist and openly anti-Fascist teachers who participated in the editorial projects of the publishing house Labor. These included Daniele Ercoli, Fabio Maffi, Andrea Tacchinardi, Aurelio Castoldi, and many others.

Fontana also collaborated on the previously mentioned *Dizionario Enciclopedico Moderno* and, starting with the second edition in 1940, on the *Enciclopedia del Ragazzo Italiano*, another editorial initiative that was coordinated by Aurelio Castoldi and Giuseppe Latronico and, as we will see, aimed to introduce young people to Italian culture and history but avoid Fascist contamination.

He secretly continued his clandestine political activity with a number of them and worked with his wife to distribute *Avanti!*, as their son Ciro

88 *Chapter 8*

remembers (Fontana Ciro 1981, 39–40) and as Carlo himself wrote in a note entitled *Autobiografia* that is conserved in his archive:

> With the Second World War, I clandestinely recommenced my political activity, avoiding arrest by pure chance because my name was illegibly written on a piece of paper listing the names of the "Committee of Socialist teachers," which had been confiscated from a young man who had been told to summon us to a meeting, following the arrest of the group's major exponent, Salvatore Principato, who was later shot in Piazzale Loreto. In those circumstances, another dear comrade, the teacher Alessandro Piazza, was also arrested. I oversaw partisan activity in the area of the Ticino and the reconstruction of the Socialist Party in Magenta (Tunesi, Morani 2016, 158).

And thus, after the fall of Fascism, the administrative elections of 1946 voted Carlo Fontana in as mayor of Magenta and he remained in office for a decade. He retraced the years of his life under Fascism and couldn't help remembering "the affectionate solidarity of my dear friend Ercoli and the dear friends who constituted my family at [the publishing house] Labor" (Tunesi, Morani 2016, 168).

He died in Magenta on June 29, 1959, with the knowledge of having espoused and conducted to the fullest the battles of his many traveling companions who were tragically lost to Fascist violence, from Brenno Cavallari to Salvatore Principato.

NOTES

1. Handwritten document, Historical archive of the Società Umanitaria di Milano, f. cc. 10: *Organizzazione operaia a Magenta. 26 luglio 1913–16 settembre 1913.*

2. All the information provided here regarding the activities of the Formenti council is quoted from the book written by Tunesi, Morani 2016, 71–75; the authors examined all of the Council's resolutions in the historical archive of the Municipality of Magenta, listing the resolution of every initiative in a footnote, Tunesi, Morani 2016, 80.

3. It is almost superfluous to remind readers that the quote is from Dante: *Inferno* I, vv. 97–99.

4. Typewritten manuscript conserved at the Chiorri-Principato-Castoldi Archive.

5. From a typewritten manuscript by Carlo Fontana entitled *Un premio di bontà*, conserved at the private archive of Carlo Fontana and published in Tunesi, Morani 2016, 50–51.

Chapter 9

Aurelio Castoldi

From the Typographers Union to the Publishing House Labor

To educate the people for a free and equal society.

—Aurelio Castoldi

On May 15, 1946, one year after the Liberation of Italy, a dispatch from a chapter of the Socialist party in Milan provided a thumbnail sketch of the teacher Aurelio Castoldi:

> Sincere and serene, extremely kind, an eclectic scholar and sentimental poet, he seems to be straight out of the pages of *Heart* by Edmondo De Amicis.
>
> Like all long-standing Socialists, he is the sworn enemy of all theories of hate and violence but he despises any form of cowardice.
>
> Aurelio Castoldi has dedicated his entire life to teaching, to the education of young people. When he talks, when he writes, it is as though he were at his teacher's pulpit; he is a teacher in the most complete and noble sense of the term.
>
> He is an advocate of proletarian unity, in which he pursues a very pure ideal of human redemption (*Voce socialista. bollettino della Sezione socialista del Psi di P. Romana-Vigentina*, May 15, 1946, 2).

He was born in Genoa on April 8, 1892, but he lived in Pavia until 1925, when he moved to Milan. His father, Gaetano, was born in Pavia on March 22, 1856, and died on August 2, 1913; he worked as a tanner and was the secretary of Pavia's workers association, founded on March 9, 1873.[1] He married his second wife, Virginia Apollonia Bottoni, in 1884, and together they had seven children, Giulia, Giovanni, Aurelio, Ines, Carmela, Giuseppe, and Raffaello, plus Serafino, his son from his first marriage. Several of these children are the protagonists, under different names, of the novel *Fratelli*,

90   *Chapter 9*

in which Aurelio recounts their difficult childhood in Pavia (Castoldi A., *Fratelli. Romanzo*, preface by G. Latronico, illustrations by R. Bandirali, Milan: Arti grafiche Ponti & C., 1940).[2] Their mother died at a very young age, on May 22, 1905, and Gaetano had to raise the children on his own; he was unable to offer them the comforts they needed to continue their studies, excepting night school. Thus, already as a child, Aurelio was forced to earn a living during his free time from school; his first job was hawking newspapers, and he later became an apprentice at a printing house. As a typographer, following in the footsteps of his Socialist father, he participated actively in union protest marches and in the social life of the early 1900s. Starting in July 1910 and until the spring of 1912, he wrote articles for the Milan-based *Il Lavoratore del Libro*. He was eighteen years old, and the spirit of his articles reflected his age; his attitude was clearly polemic, sometimes anticlerical, and always in defense of the rights of male and female workers, which required adopting a class conscience:

> You, who, together with thousands and thousands of comrades, have fought for the achievement of workers' rights against capital, why are you straying from the organization and have unconsciously sided against it? Your flight is inexplicable: you say you see everything black, and you flee: why do you flee? If you see everything black, sound it out, search, sniff around, and if your investigations lead you to a deplorable discovery, protest. Yes, protest, if you are correct, you have the right to, because only faith and solidarity can make us strong and let us prevail.
>
> Colleagues in flight, return to the Federation! Yours will be the precious supervision that will put it back on its rails when it tries to depart from them (Castoldi A., "La fuga," *Il Lavoratore del Libro*, September 10, 1910, 6).

And more:

> All you have to do is take a quick look at Pavia's typographical situation to convince yourself how far they are from the rebellious spirit and Garibaldian tradition that foreigners praise. [. . .] Democratic and Garibaldian tradition, of course! San Siro, the city's patron saint, watches over and rules all! (Castoldi A., "La città delle cento torri," *Il Lavoratore del Libro*, May 25, 1911, 2).

As a typographer, with partisan spirit he manifested his resentment against the Catholic printing school that belonged to the Private Institute Artigianelli (Chierico and Resegotti 2013):

> It is shameful that the *Private Institute Artigianelli* belongs to anti-clerical Pavia. This institute, which brazenly calls itself *Pious*, is instead a workshop that exploits minors. It passes itself off as a Private Institute and prints public works and gets work from the printing houses when their workers are on

Aurelio Castoldi 91

strike. It is a true strikebreaking factory. Work is conducted there in defiance of the laws regulating child labor, and nobody cares. In view of the name it bears, *Typographic School*, it should train skilled workers; instead, it tosses out ignoramuses who don't know anything about their craft and, moreover, whose heads are full of religious notions and reactionary ideas, which induces them to become scabs (Castoldi A., "La città delle cento torri," *Il Lavoratore del Libro*, May 25, 1911, 2).

Elsewhere, he revealed his internationalist fervor by inviting typographers to adopt the red flag as their banner instead of the Italian flag:

We must pit the red flag against the red, white, and green flag that is raised by the warmongers and patriots of the *let us arm ourselves and off you go!* Let the red flag be the symbol of workers who are organized throughout the world, to show our enemies how great the feeling of solidarity and love is inside us, to the point that we don't even use our national colors to contrast the differences in caste.

We must not raise the colors of the bourgeois homeland, which denies work to many laborers and forces them to emigrate to foreign lands.

Our homeland is the entire world: we who own nothing, here where we were born, have nothing to defend, if not the melancholy memory of the things that are dear to us and the people we love.

I would be happy if these few lines of mine made a difference, and that at least the typographers, who are in the vanguard of the workers' organization, understood the error they commit by inaugurating the Italian flag as their symbol. Let this be a lesson to all those chapters and groups that do not yet have a flag, and to those who have one and will soon be renewing it.

If an international congress of workers will be held, let me simply point out the poor figure that will be cut by all those multicolored flags, marking the differences of nationality and race, in the midst of so many people who talk of one idea alone, as though we were one big family. Thus, always forward, comrade workers, together for a shared ideal and with the red flag unfurled in the sunlight!

The workers organization must not have the same flag as the masters' organization because the abyss that separates us from them is too deep.

The *red shirts* used to fight on the battlefields to conquer a homeland, not as it was but the way their imaginative minds as sentimental poets and warriors dreamed it should be; in like manner, now the *red flag* of the united workers—who strive for a new homeland that is bigger, more beautiful, more just—must wave in the sun and blaze with light (Castoldi A., "L'internazionale dei lavoratori," *Il Lavoratore del Libro*, November 25, 1911, 2).

On another occasion, he resolutely defended working women:

The entrance of women into the Federation would in no way hinder the ongoing agitation to wrest a beneficial law from the Government; on the contrary, I am sure that since they are the most affected, they would rekindle it with their help, which is enthusiastic, supportive, and, let's admit it, more sincere than ours.

Looking at the history of past turmoil, we find infinite examples that reveal women's superiority over us.

Who does not remember the spirit of sacrifice of those poor mothers of Argentano, who, in order to prolong their strike, entrusted their children to distant female comrades so they wouldn't starve to death! And during the unforgettable strike in Parma, the heroism of the women who threw themselves into the streets with their children in their arms, to prevent the cavalry from initiating a bloody conflict with the strikers; and the courage of the other women who, during the strike of Vercelli's rice paddy workers, lay down on the train tracks to keep a train full of scabs from departing! [. . .]

Women are considered inferior because we don't pay attention to them, [. . .] we deny them our support and prohibit them from emancipating themselves. But it is not by ignoring the condition of working women that we will resolve the question that concerns us today.

Instead, let us open the Federation's doors to our female fellow workers; let us involve women in political and economic issues, and we will always see them in the vanguard, strong, self-assured, rebellious, as they fearlessly march toward that society of free and equal people for which we must all fight in concord. And as we fight, let us remember that the symbol of the revolution is represented by a woman walking toward the city of light, crushing in her passage the amalgam of exploiters of every color who infest humanity (Castoldi A., "Discutendo sulla questione femminile," *Il Lavoratore del Libro*, June 25, 1911, 3).

In general, he fought favoritism and strike-breaking, which he called a "gangrenous scourge that infiltrates every initiative, ruining the future of those who are truly deserving" (Castoldi A., "Sull'insegnamento della composizione meccanica," *Il Lavoratore del Libro*, March 10, 1912, 2; Castoldi A., "Dalli al crumiro!," *Il Lavoratore del Libro*, March 25, 1912, 3). Lastly, a critical article of his about how the first of May was transformed from the workers' holiday, in the sense of an international demand for workers' rights, into an opportunity for a pleasant outing. He wrote this article on May 1, 1912, and it was one of the first commentaries on this dangerous custom (Antonioli 1988, 150–52):

Our Federation is one May Day older, this is true: but how sad May Day is this year! It brings with it two frightful nightmares that stands out in black against a red background: *Unemployment* and *increased quotas*.

Unemployment and increased quotas, what horrible words! The latter term is the direct consequence of the first, and together, the two go arm-in-arm like twins.

Aurelio Castoldi 93

What was the starting point of the nature of these two phenomena? The war, some say. No . . . Colleagues employed by newspapers who work overtime in defiance of the tariffs, others rectify. No . . . no . . .

There is no point in investigating the origin. There is unemployment and there are increased quotas, and those who want to remain federated must bear the consequences.

But if it really is the war's fault, why didn't the workers prevent this? Why? . . . Because there is ignorance and thoughtlessness among workers.

This year, May Day must adopt a new form of struggle. Custom has transformed the revolutionary tradition of May Day into an outing with a picnic. That must not happen this year. There are too many serious problems to resolve and every worker must arm himself with earnest resolutions. To fight the war means to destroy ignorance; to combat strike-breaking means to educate the workers' conscience (Castoldi A., "Chiacchiere di 1° Maggio," *Il Lavoratore del Libro*, April 25–May 1, 1912, 2).[3]

Aurelio Castoldi's personal and political experiences unfolded parallel to those of Carlo Fontana, who started out as a baker's errand boy and became a teacher. He continued to work as a typographer until World War I forced him to leave for the front. He remained at the front for three years and six months, from 1915 until 1918, and even though he was openly non-interventionist, he earned a War Merit Cross.

After returning to civilian life, he was finally able to pursue his two major projects, which, to him, were closely linked: realizing the Socialist utopia to educate the masses and earning his license to teach at school, at which point he left his job as a typographer and became a teacher.

During the years 1919–1924, which saw the rise of Fascism, he was a protagonist in the political and cultural life of Pavia. He wrote frequently for *La Plebe. Organo della Federazione Provinciale Socialista Pavese*, often signing his articles with the acronym "Acas." He was a candidate at the elections held on October 31, 1920, he was one of the protagonists of the great Socialist victory, and he was elected to the municipal council with 3,202 votes. On November 2, *La Plebe* wrote with regard to the "Election Day":

Despite the vile weather, a workers march, with red flags in the lead, was immediately improvised and, singing our hymns, went to the corner of the Demetrio, from whose balcony the comrades Ercole and Minuti gave short speeches. [. . .] The procession continued on to Palazzo Mezzabarba, where the red flag was immediately hoisted, to the rapture of the crowd. From the balcony, Ercole, Montemartini, Malagugini, Canevari, and Ghinaglia spoke briefly, glorifying the Socialist triumph and emphasizing the great example of civil and political education the victorious people had displayed.

94   *Chapter 9*

The new Council, composed of thirty-two Socialists and only eight representatives of the other political bloc, elected Alcide Malagugni mayor on November 15 (Castoldi M. 2018, 16–26). This is what *La Plebe* wrote on November 18:

> On Monday evening, a flood of people (a true crowd of workers, many thousands and a few hundred, as the "Provincia Pavese" seems to have seen or wanted to see) accompanied the new councilors as they took office at Mezzabarba, and waited in the vast piazza in front of town hall to salute and applaud the Socialist Mayor. [. . .] The newly-elected Mayor stood up to thank them. At first, he was pale and his voice trembled with emotion but he then gathered his strength and, as he recalled past struggles and the recent victory, his soul vibrated along with everyone else's. He noted that the third anniversary of the great Russian revolution would be taking place in those days and, from his position, he sent the best wishes of Pavia's workers to the many people who were still struggling. To the applause of all those present, he also recalled the great Socialist success of proletarian Milan and in the council chamber, he repeated what the president had already shouted: *hooray for Socialism!*

The minutes of that Municipal Council's meetings are all conserved in Pavia, at the "Bonetta" civic library. The Council's activity can be followed month by month, and a number of important speeches given by the teacher Castoldi can also be found.

I will quote only one, which he gave at the meeting on December 13, 1920, addressing the need to control the price of milk and bread:

> The councilor *Castoldi*, also in the name of the absent colleague Griziotti [Prof. Benvenuto], requests information about the significant increase in the price of milk that has occurred on two occasions within a short space of time.
>
> The *President* declares he is happy to respond, in part to dispel the impression that has spread among the population that the increase was decided by the present council. [. . .] He adds that the Council is planning on opening two municipal dairies, which certainly cannot lower the price of milk, but which will provide whole milk and not diluted milk. To this regard, we will increase our surveillance of the independent dairies; but this surveillance must also be conducted by the consumers, whose cooperation we request for an effective defense.
>
> The councilor *Castoldi* declares his satisfaction and calls attention to the problem of the price of bread, for it seems impossible that the middle class cannot find a better way to fill the holes in the budget than by raising the price of bread, whereas, given the present prosperity, it would seem more obvious to hit the wealthy. It is said: do not play with fire; today, this should be paraphrased: do not play with bread. He concludes by presenting the following order of business:

"The Municipal Council, while proudly protesting against the project to raise the price of bread—that tends to make the proletariat pay the debts of the war, instead of the middle class—applauds the battle engaged in the Chamber by the Socialist parliamentary group, to whom it sends the greatest solidarity and the most fervid wishes for victory." Signed Castoldi.

The President, also in name of the Council, accepts his order of business and believes he would renege on his Socialist ideals if he did not invite the Council to approve it. And the Council approves by a show of hands, with 29 votes in favor, 8 opposed.

Starting in 1920, Aurelio Castoldi was the secretary of the Popular University of Pavia, chaired by the well-known pupil of Carducci, Giorgio Rossi, who at the time was the town's superintendent of education (*L'Università popolare di Pavia* 1925; Castoldi M. 2016, 149–67). Castoldi also kept a periodical column in *La Plebe*, which lets us partially reconstruct the university's activities. It was inaugurated on March 8, 1920, at 8:30 p.m. at Palazzo Olevano in Via Mazzini with a lesson by the hon. Luigi Montemartini. Lessons were held on Tuesdays and Fridays; the membership card cost two lira and could be purchased where the lessons were held. The lessons lasted roughly an hour and a half.[4] On February 19, 1921, a members meeting was held to approve the proposals.[5] The university's entire story deserves to be reconstructed in full, since it fervently followed the Council's activity and continued, in a more low-key manner, its cultural project even after 1922, an example of the Socialist concept of adult education. The lessons ranged from history, literature, science, and economy to more practical and contingent matters, such as occupational illnesses, alcoholism, home economics, labor law, and cooperation. Recreational activities were also organized, with tours of historical palazzi and educational trips. The Popular University of Pavia is one of the universities that has yet to be studied, but its history is similar to that of many other popular universities, which were established during those years in various cities throughout Italy (Rosada 1975).

As mentioned, during those years, Aurelio wrote frequently for *La Plebe* using the pseudonym "Acas": political polemics; a request for education for the proletariat, to make them aware and able to stand up to the middle class; even a description of the Popular University's activities.[6]

One of these articles, entitled "Istruzione" and published on October 9, 1920, illustrates the degree to which the redemption of humanity, through the permanent education of children and adults, was Aurelio's primary project his whole life long, his "very pure ideal of human redemption":

The worker who becomes a Socialist refines himself and is pervaded by a feeling of beauty and the desire to know. Socialism, which is a school of freedom and education, regenerates the people it welcomes to its breast and makes them

96   *Chapter 9*

strong and good. This strength and this goodness frighten the middle class, which possesses, among other things, brute strength and, in its egoism, is deaf to the appeals of those who suffer.

But the duty to educate themselves belongs not only to Socialists, but to all workers.

Once, when workers labored ten, twelve, and even more hours a day, the demand for education was an impossible request. No longer. The splendid conquest of eight hours has made the people's education possible.

Thus, during the moments of rest from their economic struggles, workers should dedicate themselves to the culture of the mind by attending popular universities, libraries, conferences, in short, by participating at the institutions of popular culture where, without spending a penny, they can acquire amusing and useful notions they would never have dreamed of learning for so little money and with such a minimal effort of will. By educating themselves, the proletariat will gain greater energy for their labor struggles, they will recognize the legitimacy of their rights even more, they will learn to better love their families and fellow workers, and, lastly, they will do a good service to themselves, to their beloved, and, above all, to the cause of the class to which they belong.

If education is at the basis of all progress and the best weapon of every revolution, the education of the proletariat will mean the end of the middle class, and thus, will represent the termination of exploitation, the resurrection of the humble, Socialism. *Educate yourselves because we'll need all your intelligence.*[7] May the workers understand the importance of this appeal and believe they are on the threshold of becoming not only the administrators of the Municipalities and the Provinces, but the arbiters of the world's destinies.

Unfortunately, while Castoldi was striving to make all this happen and was writing these ideas in *La Plebe*, Fascism was violently asserting itself in Pavia, as well.

On April 19, 1921, a number of Socialist students at the university were attacked, including Roberto Veratti, who would play an important role in Milan in the struggle against Fascism, representing the Socialists in the Committee of National Liberation for Northern Italy. On April 20, Fabrizio Maffi, Fabio Maffi's brother, was attacked, slapped, punched, beaten, and risked being thrown from the balcony of the Caffè Demetrio, where he was dining (it was only the first of a series of increasingly violent attacks against him). The next day, on the evening of April 21, the young medical student Ferruccio Ghinaglia was killed on the street. One of the young men with him that day was Aurelio's younger brother, Raffaello, who, with Ghinaglia, was one of the founders of Pavia's Communist Party (Ferrario 1969, 109).[8] Aurelio, too, was attacked by the Fascists and forced to drink castor oil. Matteotti remembered an attack against Malagugini, as well (Matteotti 1983, 249).

Aurelio Castoldi

On October 29, 1922, the Council resigned, with an official letter to the prefect signed by the entire group of Socialist councilors.[9]

But just as Fascism was forcing the combative Socialist councilor Aurelio Castoldi into silence, the future teacher was preparing to obtain his teaching license and begin his much-desired career, which began in April 1924 (he was thirty-two years old) at the elementary schools of Chignolo Po, continued throughout Italy's Fascist era and until 1939 in Milan, at the Vittorino da Feltre elementary school in Via Polesine, with a brief interlude at the Pasquale Sottocorno school in Rogoredo (1926–1930), and then at the elementary school on Via Giulio Romano until 1949.

The years of incipient Fascism also coincided with the birth of two children for Aurelio, who had married Maria Ida Busca in 1919: Maggiorina (1921) and Alcide (1923).

From that moment on, much of his activity shifted to the school, where he distinguished himself by completing the curriculum without bowing to Fascist culture, for which he was occasionally reprimanded in inspection reports. But on the whole, the teachers' evaluations were positive.

Between 1926 and 1927, in Pavia, the editor Abele Boerchio, an anti-Fascist Republican and, later, the editor of the daily *La Provincia Pavese*, published a number of plays for children, inspired by egalitarian and Socialist principles, similar to the ones written by his friend Fabio Maffi: *La festa per la dote della scuola. Disposizioni ministeriali—Commediole—Dialoghi—Monologhi— Brevi discorsi*, with a preface by Prof. Comm. G. Rossi R. Commissioner of Education, 1926; *Piccole attrici. Teatro educativo per le Classi elementari femminili*, 1927; *Piccoli attori. Teatro educativo per le Classi elementari maschili*, 1927. The following is a short, emblematic monologue, "È Bello Studiare!" [It's Nice to Study!], that presents the Popular University for adults to children (*Piccoli attori*, 77–79):

That evening, I was more listless than ever. I opened a book and drowsily closed my eyes; I picked up a pen and dipped the point of the holder into the ink instead of the nib; I opened my mouth to recite the lesson and yawned. Then my father's voice roused me. (*Imitating father's voice*): "You lazybones!" I kept quiet. (*Same voice as above*) "You deserve to be punished!" I was already preparing to get into the usual position when, instead, my father said to me: (*Same voice as above*) "Fetch your cap because I'm taking you out with me!" It was just what I needed and I happily went out with him. We walked for a while; and then my father led me into a lovely palazzo where lots of people were gathered in a large room. But what odd people they were! Workers of all ages, mothers with their children, young ladies, employees, elderly retired teachers, students, teenagers, young female workers, and even soldiers. All these people were speaking in a low voice and were gathered as though they were waiting for a show to begin. I was dying to know what was going on. "Is it the cinematographer?" I asked my

98   *Chapter 9*

father. And my father, silent. "What are we waiting for? A magician, an impersonator?" No reply. After a while, a man entered. Everybody stood up respectfully; then, he motioned with his hand and they sat back down; nobody said a word. The man began to talk and I was enchanted to observe how carefully and with what pleasure they listened to his words. Then I started to listen, too; and to my great amazement, I realized he was talking almost like my teacher at school, and that he was saying more or less the same things. That's when I realized my father had taken me to a school. But what silence and what attention! I was stunned. All those people—most of them were workers who had left their workshops a few hours earlier—were attending school with a composure that would be the envy of any classroom of youngsters; they listened to the lesson with joy, and instead of getting tired, it was as though they were reinvigorated by the teacher's words. I ended up enjoying myself; I began to listen and became more and more interested.

Everyone was sorry when the lesson ended; and then they all began to applaud and thank their teacher. That good man was so pleased!

When we were back out on the street, I asked my father: "What school is that?" And my father replied: "It's the Popular University; it's the school of everyone; it's the place where you learn to love studying and improve yourself. May the memory of what you have seen this evening make you love studying and School!"

Ever since that evening, I am ashamed to be a lazybones; and when boredom overwhelms me, I think of those workers, those old folks, those mothers. And I study, and I study, and I study. And I enjoy it; and I realize that it's nice to study! Yessiree! It's really nice to study! . . . I hadn't realized it before . . . because I had never studied!

Between March and May 1933, Aurelio collaborated with *Topolino*, published by Edizioni Nerbini in Florence (*Il cavaliere e il buffone*, a. II, March 4, 1933, 10, 5–6; *Marzo*, March 25, 1933, 13, 4; *Gira, gira somarello*, May 27, 1933, 22, 6). During the 1930s, he also published two novels with the Milanese publishing house La Prora: *Paesi di bimbi. Romanzo. E le commediole: Il miglior carnevale, Il personaggio misterioso, Il dottor purgante* (1931) and *Volpone. Romanzo* (illustrated by Italo Giovanni Mattoni, n.d. [but between 1931 and 1933]).[10]

Up until this point, there was nothing that could directly disturb Fascist sensitivities, except for the fact that it represented a world that was completely foreign to them.

In 1937, Castoldi published a short theatrical operetta entitled *Romoletto. Operetta in un atto*, with music by E[milio] Mazza, in the publishing house La Prora's series "Prime Gemme. Bibliotechina per la Fanciullezza."

That Roman-sounding name, *Romoletto*, dated 1937, called to mind the two most famous members of the Fascist youth group Opera Nazionale Balilla, who appeared in the comic book *Corriere dei Piccoli*, in the comic strip drawn by Bruno Angoletta, accompanied by the usual octosyllabic rhyming couplets. The strip was featured on an irregular basis from December 8, 1935, until May 9, 1937, during the war in Ethiopia. The two boys, Romolino and Romoletto, always managed to get the better of the Ethiopian enemy (Mignemi 1984, 58). Their code of conduct and all their stories were an implicit lesson in racism and the logic of the stronger subjugating the weak.

The Ethiopians were always rather unintelligent and ready to fall into the traps set for them by the two insensitive and merciless Balilla boys, who were nonetheless rendered appealing to young readers. When Romolino and Romoletto were still appearing in *Corriere dei Piccoli* and helping to "civilize" barbarous Ethiopia, Aurelio Castoldi published his *Romoletto*, set in the Public Gardens of Via Palestro in Milan, on the occasion of the Carnival of 1937.

The operetta is a true celebration. Everything comes to life onstage, even inanimate objects. There is a confetti choir, streamers running here and there in every direction with "long strips of red and green paper on their white dresses," primulas, daisies, violets, stars in the planetarium, and even Spring.

Romoletto, who commands a small platoon and is dressed like a warrior, picks a small bouquet of flowers for his mother and saves a child who has fallen into the lake, but in doing so, he loses his helmet and musket. He only conserves his bouquet of flowers, and it all concludes under a shower of streamers and red-white-and-blue confetti, as a choir sings the praises of the "young hero"—a true antagonist of the two Balilla boys in *Corriere dei Piccoli*—who implicitly rejects the racist and imperialistic war that just ended and the art of deception and subjugation of the stronger over the weak. He triumphs in a world ruled by peace, unity, and universal harmony, in which helmets and muskets are nothing more than a grotesque carnival costume and can be heedlessly thrown away, when it's a matter of accomplishing the only true and heroic action possible: a gesture of solidarity.

The commission for the reclamation of books had been active for one year; its purpose, and I quote, was to "adapt, on the one hand, literature and art, and, on the other, the culture of the multitude and of young people, to the aspirations of the new Italian soul and the necessities of Fascist ethics" (Boero and De Luca 1995, 172).

Few people might have noticed the intense allusiveness of this apparently innocent comedy for children, but someone certainly did, because the 1939 *Annual Informative Report to the R. Commissioner of Education of Milan* suddenly became very critical of the teacher Aurelio Castoldi, whose honesty and professionalism had always been praised and appreciated until then:

100   *Chapter 9*

The teacher's flat personality also influences the industriousness of the class [. . .]. I do not find it appropriate for this teacher, in the future, to be entrusted with tasks that call for a sense of responsibility. The didactic performance is weak.

On the report, the following is written just to the left: "*The teacher's activities in integrative initiatives*: Talents for school and Patronage: theatricals, with scarce results" and above, in red: "does not belong to the N[ational] F[ascist] P[arty]" (Castoldi M. 2003, 65–71).

That year, Aurelio Castoldi also changed schools, from Via Polesine to Via Giulio Romano, even though the former school was closer to his home at Via Mompiani 10. It wasn't until April 25, 1945, that he was able to publish something for children again: his third novel, *Gianni Olal. Romanzo per Ragazzi* (Castoldi A. 1945), which could be defined as the full rendering of his Socialist and anti-Fascist spirit.

Gianni Olal is eleven years old. He has an expressive face, dark eyes and hair, he is tall, slender, and attends fifth grade. His family isn't wealthy, but great stability reigns at home. The workers in the household are his father and his sister, Lisetta, who is a salesgirl in a department store downtown, where she works in the women's hosiery department. In the meantime, she also attends school on her days off: she learns to sew, knit, embroider, cook, keep the house clean, and even cultivate flowers. Mr. Olal is an operative in a workshop that has a large number of workers, where you can hear "the rumble of motors, the thrumming of belts, the screeching of machines." We don't know the names of his mother and father. They live in an unspecified city, located on a river and serviced by streetcars. Gianni's father frequents a club that is inspired by the values of Socialism and where workers, employees, and students gather on Sunday. Gianni is still too young to take an active part, but when he grows up, he dreams of becoming a member, like his father and the mechanic Mario Veri, a nimble and robust young man with an open and intelligent face.

The club's entire program can be synthesized as the interaction of three concepts: nature, work, and solidarity. Nature offers common goods that should be enjoyed equally by all, in a condition of general well-being; work is the means by which these goods are enjoyed, as well as the means for learning how to enjoy them properly. And in fact, as Mario Veri explains to young Gianni, work, "through its results, also produces ideas." Only through work can people aspire to that higher awareness that ennobles outward behavior. In fact, to work means to make oneself useful to others and to society; work catalyzes an awareness of altruism as a founding ethic of human existence. Every member of the club must intervene "whenever possible, where there is a wrong to right, an abuse to fight, where justice must triumph."

These simple principles animate the behavior and determine every action of the protagonist, Gianni, who never ceases to put his intelligence and generosity at the service of others (Castoldi M. 2002).

It was a true Socialist novel for young people, and this is one of the reasons Aurelio was unable to publish it before 1945, just like the scholastic anthology he wrote in collaboration with his daughter Maggiorina, *Voci di Bontà*: reading lessons for the five elementary classes, with the cover and illustrations by the painter Mariani (Milan: Edizioni Centauro, 1946, 5 vol.). But, during the Fascist period, his great initiative—besides his Socialist propaganda in Milan, when he distributed the clandestine journal *Avanti!* in the Romana-Vigentina area (Cavalli and Strada 1982a, 88)[11]—was joining the group of Socialist teachers at the publishing house Labor, collaborating with Daniele Ercoli, Andrea Tacchinardi, Fabio Maffi, and Carlo Fontana in editing the *Dizionario Enciclopedico Moderno* and, above all, working on the *Enciclopedia del Ragazzo Italiano*, which was entirely devised and structured along new learning strategies, and on which he worked with the didactic editor Giuseppe Latronico.

Initially, the encyclopedia was supposed to comprise six volumes and an index; eight editions were published between 1938 and the early 1970s. Castoldi is listed as the typographical director, Latronico as the editorial director.

The project's insight lay in the way it handled its relationship with Fascism. Fascism existed and this was very explicitly declared (this is important) in the sections "Nel Segno del Littorio) ["In the Sign of the Fasces"] and "Realizzazioni Fasciste" ["Fascist Achievements"], but it remained confined within those two sections, without damaging or contaminating the rest of the work's structure in the slightest. Collaborators included Fascists such as Franco Ciarlantini, Vittorio D'Aste, Luigi Emanuele Gianturco, and Arturo Marescalchi. But the initiative's intelligence lay in the way it maintained, as much as possible, zones that were free of Fascist infection, and the more easily recognizable they were, the more dangerous they became. In my opinion, the pages dedicated to "The People of Israel" are exemplary because, even after 1938, they remained free of any racial prejudice (I, 129–32; IV, 181–84). Nor are there misleading opinions regarding the Bolshevik Revolution of 1917, for example, or the government of the Soviet republics of the time, in the entry dedicated to Russia as the U.S.S.R. (V, 159–60). Perhaps that was as much and as well as could be done during those years, if they wanted to have an effect on society and not only through clandestine propaganda. After the Liberation, they published the fifth edition and limited themselves to eliminating the Fascist entries.

It would be worthwhile studying this *Enciclopedia*, too, with a greater awareness of the editors and the way they compromised with the regime,

102   *Chapter 9*

and bearing in mind the unquestionable anti-Fascist coherence of its primary authors: Castoldi, a Socialist; Daniele Ercoli, a member of Giustizia e Liberta; and Latronico, a Republican and follower of Gobetti. The teacher Salvatore Principato was well aware of this; in part to conceal some of his clandestine activities, he helped sell volumes of the encyclopedia retail.

It is interesting to flip through the sections *Moral and Civic Education* and *Chronicle of School Life* from Castoldi's class register for the year 1945–1946, a fourth-grade class of boys. The register is conserved in Milan at the elementary school on Via Giulio Romano, and it reveals his joy at finally being able to teach civic education and his dedication to a Socialist idea that never waned for a moment:

> *September–October*. Discussions and initiatives to organize the collective life of the class [. . .] *November*. The duties of one's country. I particularly insist on moral education. After much denial of moral goods, it is our duty to insist on education. *December*. The need for laws in social life. This year, too, the school has no heating: we feel the cold. But any suffering is slight compared to the tremendous cold of war. *February*. Solidarity and assistance. The duties of the citizen in relation to the country's moral and economic reconstruction. *March*. The upcoming administrative elections. The municipal administration: the councilors, the council: the mayor and councilors. *April*. Examples of social life. The duty to participate in political life. Political electoral law and the Constituent. Holiday for the administrative elections. During the preceding days, I explained the elections and the municipal administration to the students. *May*. May first. Labor Day is justly ensured by the school, as well. Notions on the referendum, the monarchy, and the republic. *June*. 7. Lessons begin again after a week's interruption for the political elections and the referendum. During previous dedicated lessons, I spoke to the students about the Constituent Assembly, the monarchy, and the republic. 11. Vacation to celebrate the advent of the Italian Republic.

In 1949, Aurelio Castoldi left school and dedicated all his time to the publishing house Labor, initiating a third phase of his intricate existence as a typographer, politician, teacher of adult education, elementary teacher, author of children's books, and editor. He was able to navigate—but also to oppose—Fascism, in the conviction of giving his all for the education of the people, an indispensable premise for the creation of that "society of the free and equal," as he wrote in 1947, "to which we Socialists aspire and for which we fight" (Castoldi A. 1947).

NOTES

1. There are very few documents conserved to this regard. His signature as secretary appears in a leaflet inviting people to a Socialist gathering on November 28, 1880, and in a related letter, conserved at the Archive of the Democratic Workers Society in Chiavenna (SO): Carteggio per numero di protocollo, b. 16, fasc. 212, *Festa sociale*, n. 205 (1880 novembre 4), consistenza cc. 2; fasc. 223 *Festa sociale generale*, n. 216 (1880 novembre 23), consistenza cc. 2.

2. In the novel, Giovanni (1889–1942), the oldest brother, is Pietro Cesàri; Aurelio is Marco; Carmela is Eugenia; Giuseppe is Menico; Raffaello, called Ello, is Gino. No characters correspond to Serafino; Giulia, the oldest sister; or Ines, who was born on March 7, 1894, and died prematurely in Pavia on April 6, 1923.

3. In this same journal, by the same author: *Come gli antichi romani*, July 25, 1910, 7; *Raccomandazioni . . . deplorevoli*, September 10, 1910, 6; *Un brano di romanzo*, March 25, 1911, 6.

4. See *La Plebe*, March 6, 1920, 3; January 1, 1921, 3; January 15, 1921, 3; January 29, 1921, 1, in which Prof. G. [Gaspare?] Antonietti declares he is encouraged by the "illustrious comrades Prof. Alcide Malagugini and Acas" in creating a provincial body with headquarters in Pavia for the culture of workers; February 5, 1921, 3.

5. See *La Plebe*, February 19, 1921, 3.

6. A few of the titles: *Ai giovani che si congedano*, October 18, 1919; *Le elezioni e la Russia*, November 1, 1919; *Pipì* [this is how the exponents of the Popular Party were jokingly called], November 8, 1919; *Senza partito (bozzetto elettorale)*, November 15, 1919; *Il significato della battaglia*, September 11, 1920; *L'occupazione. Dialogo d'attualità*, September 11, 1920; *Lenin*, September 18, 1920; *Istruzione*, October 9, 1920; *Il fallimento*, October 16, 1920; *La violenza*, October 23, 1920; *Due novembre*, October 28, 1920; *La concentrazione Pro Pavia*, October 28, 1920; *Mentre suonava il campanone*, November 6, 1920; *Milano*, November 12, 1920; *E l'Università Popolare?*, January 1, 1921; *Sapere e bontà*, January 15, 1921; *L'Università Popolare a Pavia*, January 15, 1921; *Questioni annonarie*, January 22, 1921; *Università popolare. Palpiti di solidarietà umana in un Poeta del Risorgimento* [Giuseppe Giusti], January 29, 1921; *Università popolare. La lezione del prof. Lenzoni*, February 12, 1921; *Università popolare. I moti del '21. La formazione della Terra*, February 19, 1921; *Nuovi spacci comunali. Università popolare*, February 26, 1921; *Perché il blocco fu sconfitto a Pavia*, May 21, 1921; *Università popolare*, May 29, 1921.

7. A well-known quote by Antonio Gramsci, in *L'Ordine Nuovo*, a. I, May 1, 1919, 1: "Educate yourselves because we'll need all your intelligence. Stir yourselves because we'll need all your enthusiasm. Organize yourselves because we'll need all your strength."

8. See "La furia fascista scatenata sulla nostra Città. L'on Maffi vilmente aggredito [. . .] Un efferato delitto fascista. Il compagno Ghinaglia assassinato [. . .] Studenti socialisti aggrediti," in *La Plebe*, April 23, 1921; Ferrario 1969, 109: "The traces of other *Communist* exponents were soon lost: this was the case of *Raffaele* [Raffaello] *Castoldi*, a close friend of Ghinaglia, Contardi, Massa, Savoia, and Calvi, all members of the federation's first directorate."

104 *Chapter 9*

9. To this regard, for an opposite perspective, read Bianchi 2004, 330, which also publishes the letter of resignation written by the council and the Socialist councilors.

10. Because in the endpaper, *Paesi di bimbi* is quoted as already published, and a copy exists in the Chiorri Principato Castoldi Archive with a signed dedication dated September 28, 1933. Both novels were then republished in a single volume: *Le avventure di Poldino e Oziosetto. Nuova edizione dei romanzi Paesi di bimbi e Volpone*, Milan: La Prora, 1945; *Paesi di bimbi*, posthumous, Milan: Casa Editrice L'Ariete, 1967.

11. Cavalli and Strada 1982a, 88: "The journals were stored in various areas in the sector. The group of activists was very numerous and the organization was divided per territorial group; responsibility for it alternated: Barberi, Barlassina, Bianchi, the teacher Castoldi."

Chapter 10

Giuseppe Latronico
Director of Studies and Gobetti's Friend

"Che l'inse! che l'inse!" And Balilla's shout echoed from contrada to contrada.

—Giuseppe Latronico

We know that Giuseppe Latronico was the director of studies at the Tito Speri elementary school during the 1930s. Research conducted to date does not reveal head-on confrontations with the Fascist regime, nor was he persecuted or reported.

Nonetheless, the few available indications in his biography clearly lead us to the milieu of anti-Fascist culture and awareness.

Barbara Allason, in her book *Memorie di un'antifascista 1919–1940*, remembers that he and his brother Ettore were collaborators for the journal *Il Caffè*, directed by Riccardo Bauer in 1924. Even though his articles never appeared with his name on the byline, Ettore's name does appear as one of the writers ("Mezzogiorno e fascismo," *Il Caffè*, October 15, 1924, 8, p. 4) (Allason 1946, 23). Ettore was also the author of "Lettera dalla Basilicata," which Gobetti published in April 1925 in *La Rivoluzione Liberale* and dealt with particularism, Southern Italy, and the lack of political awareness in Lucania.

Giuseppe was born in Basilicata in 1895.

His mother's family was of modest economic means and he was destined to the "profession" of farming, but his elementary teacher recommended to his family that he continue his studies. Thanks to the scholarships he received, he made it all the way to university but was unable to continue his studies any further and dedicated himself to teaching. At a very young age, he wrote for local newspapers and became a friend of Giustino Fortunato. He went to Milan and

106 *Chapter 10*

won the competitive exam for elementary schools; a few years later, he won the competitive exam to become a director of studies, a position he was almost not assigned because he was not a member of the Fascist party. The year was 1924 (Callegari 1991, 128–29).

Through his correspondence, we know for sure that, during the 1920s, he was in contact with Romolo Murri[1] and Piero Gobetti, whom he often met in Milan on Thursdays since he helped distribute his books. Two letters and two postcards he sent to Piero Gobetti have been conserved; they are dated October 17, 1922; December 17, 1923; March 21, 1924; and November 29, 1924, respectively.[2] In the first, Latronico urges the editor from Turin to send the invoices for the distribution in Milanese bookstores of the book by Ubaldo Formentini, *Collaborazionismo* (Turin: Ed. La Rivoluzione Liberale, 1922) because, he wrote, "the booksellers have received the copies; but they told me they will not display them in their shop windows unless they receive the invoices." The letter then lists the booksellers: "Baldini no. 10 copies/ Sonzogno 6/ Hoepli 6/ Casiroli (Corso Vitt. Eman.) 6/ Paravia 6 copies/ Carrara 6 copies/ Bocca 10." Latronico adds, "As soon as I receive them, I will take them to those concerned and I hope to convince them to immediately display the book in their shop window and very much in the fore."[3]

The next letter, dated December 17, 1923, reveals Giuseppe Latronico's collaboration with the journals *La Parola e il Libro. Mensile della Università Popolare e delle Biblioteche Popolari Milanesi*, edited by Ettore Fabietti, and *Lo Sculture e il Marmo. Pubblicazione per gli Interessi Artistici e Commerciali*; this collaboration confirms his clear interest in the world of art (see G. Latronico, *La scultura alla XV Biennale di Venezia*, Milan: "Lo scultore," n.d. [1926]; *Uno scultore della maternità e dell'infanzia. Eugenio Pellini*, Lecco: Edizioni di cultura (via Gran Sasso 5), tipo-litografia Fratelli Grassi, n.d.; *Luigi Zago da Villafranca. Pittore*, Milan: Galleria Italiana d'Arte, 1943). Latronico wrote to Gobetti:

> When you send books to Fabietti's journal "La Parola e il Libro" for review, please have them delivered directly to me. For a while now, I have been writing many of the reviews for that magazine and I am responsible for controlling all the reviews that are published. The books you send to that magazine's editorial staff are taken by the first person who passes by and, almost always, neither the book, nor the review, are ever seen again. If you send them directly to me, you can be sure that you will read a thorough review for every book. Agreed? You will be satisfied and I, too, will be satisfied because, in this way, I will be able to follow your activity as an editor and author more assiduously.
>
> Have the book about Casorati (Gobetti 1923) sent to me. I can review it soon in "La Parola e il Libro" and *at length* in the journal "Lo sculture e il Marmo." I will also be able to send you many of the excerpts from the review since this

Giuseppe Latronico 107

latter journal has the good habit of sending me excerpts of the reviews that are longer than one column.[4]

During the War of Liberation, he was in contact with Ferruccio Parri, Mario Paggi, Antonio Basso (Basso A. 1987), Tristano Codignola, and Piero Calamandrei. "He was very close to Salvatore Principato. They lived in the same house at Via Gran Sasso 5. He joined the Action Party" (Callegari 1991, 129).

Marcella Chiorri, Salvatore's wife, wrote in an unpublished memoir: "On the upper floor of my house [Milan, Via Gran Sasso 5, third floor, overlooking the street, right-hand staircase] lived another teacher, Fulvio Benedetti, who followed the anti-Fascist Popular Catholic movement, and below lived the Director Latronico Giuseppe, who was also a sworn anti-Fascist."[5]

In 1946, Latronico wrote the entry "Fabian Society" in the *Dizionario di cultura politica* by Antonio Basso, printed in Milan, a fundamental reference for Milan's anti-Fascist culture in the immediate postwar period (Basso A. 1946, 257–28).

What remains to be understood is how the anti-Fascism of the multifaceted editor from Lucania translated into cultural activities. We know nothing about his direct relationship with young people but much of what he wrote for children remains; for example, he was one of the collaborators on the series *La Scala d'Oro*, published by Utet (Rebellato 2016).[6]

In June 1961, Severino Pagani, who, at the time, was the delegated vice president of the Italian Publishers Association, spoke at a conference in Turin about young people's literature. He recalled the dark years of Fascism, when the regime conditioned people to "absolute dedication to Fascist doctrine and ethics" and abolished any authentic reference "to the past." Pagani proudly laid claim to having personally proposed to Giorgio Cavallotti, the editor at Utet during the early 1930s, the publication of a series for young people "inspired by total freedom of thought in every field, and with independent choices in every genre of literature and art, both Italian and foreign": *La Scala d'Oro*, edited by Vincenzo Errante and Fernando Palazzi (Pagani 1962, 118–19). The first edition of the encyclopedia was an important editorial and financial undertaking: ninety-two volumes divided into eight series, each series dedicated to a children's age group, from six to thirteen years of age. At that moment—the year was 1932—to be free meant to look freely at the past in order to remain unscathed by the official propaganda of the regime. In 1934, the otherwise ubiquitous topics of *War* and *Fascism* were relegated to one single volume of the encyclopedia—separate from the others and valid for the entire series—in which Leo Pollini explained the concepts to young people.

108   Chapter 10

All one had to do was not purchase that particular volume and *La Scala d'Oro* could be read without encountering the language—above all, but also the clichés—of Mussolini's rhetoric.

Pagani confirmed that the underlying intention of the series was to offer itself as an example of "liberal Italian culture," which did not let itself be "conquered and dominated by Fascist coarseness" (Boero and De Luca 1995, 206–27).

Besides the editors of the series, there were also other, more famous, and much-studied contributors of clear anti-Fascist and Republican tradition, such as Mary Tibaldi Chiesa, or authors of Jewish tradition and culture, such as Eugenio Treves and Giuseppe Morpurgo, who was later included on the list of "authors who are unwelcome in Italy" (Fava 2004, 219–29; Lollo 2003, 175–80; Boero and De Luca 1995, 207).

Giuseppe Latronico's contribution to *La Scala d'Oro* consisted in five volumes: for six-year-old children, *Il libro d'oro del fanciullo Episodi storici* [*The Child's Book of Gold. Historical Episodes*] (1932); for seven-year-olds, *I passatempi del giovedì. Giuochi, aneddoti, filastrocche e indovinelli* [*Thursday's Pastimes. Games, Anecdotes, Nursery Rhymes, and Riddles*] (1932); for children aged nine, *Il libro dei treni. Aneddoti, notizie, impressioni, ricordi* [*The Book of Trains. Anecdotes, News, Impressions, Memories*] (1935); for ten-year-olds, *Il libro delle ore gioconde. Giuochi e passatempi* [*The Book of Carefree Hours. Games and Pastimes*] (1936); for eleven-year-old children, he rewrote *La vita avventurosa di Lazzarino di Tormes* [*The Adventurous Life of Lazzarino di Tormes*] (1933), in which the life of the vagabond and crafty picaro, eternally hungry and at the service of his numerous masters, had little to do with the life that Fascism had designated for the young Balilla.

Latronico steered in two directions: games and anecdotes. Games, in the sense of free hobbies, were the negation of the paramilitary training forced on young Fascists; they were an instrument to train the mind and set the imagination free. Children needed to be distracted from the rampant and obsessive Fascist rhetoric of the 1930s (the colonies, the war, the gymnastic parades), and one can't help noticing how Latronico's "hobbies" and "carefree hours" were conceived to this end. Obviously, neither *I passatempi del giovedì*, nor *Il libro delle ore gioconde* contain references or allusions to Fascism. Even the game of finding *Five-letter historical names* included the wife of Menelik (Taytu) and the Istrian martyr of World War I (Sauro), but nothing more than that. There were also Fascist martyrs whose names had five letters, starting with Giovanni Berta, who was stabbed and thrown into the Arno River in 1921, and to whom the *squadristi* had dedicated a popular song, *Hanno ammazzato Giovanni Berta*. When Latronico teaches children how to construct figures with toothpicks and matches, he has them make houses, chairs, animals, and ballerinas, but no Fasces (and it could have easily been constructed) (Latronico 1936, 20, 24–34). Other examples abound: puzzles, charades, rebuses, riddles, anagrams, double meanings, games of math, board games, etc. Neither the Duce nor Fascism. The children are free to play.

Elsewhere, Latronico makes use of anecdotes, sometimes historical, sometimes legendary, sometimes with reference to technical and scientific knowledge, such as the highly popular *Libro dei treni*. Although there is not even the remotest reference to Fascism, there are veiled racist comments describing the arrival of the railroad "among the truculent cannibals" of the African tribes (Latronico 1935, 61): perhaps a venal sin for a book published in 1935, at the time of Fascist propaganda for the war in Ethiopia, but one that reveals a surreptitious inclination for racism that has always been present in even the most illuminated liberal culture in Italy.

His text for *La Scala d'Oro* that deserves most attention, in the perspective of dissent from the regime, is *Il libro d'oro del fanciullo*, a collection of twelve historical and legendary anecdotes that narrate some of the best-known events in Italian and European history. The first, entitled *L'elmo di Scipio* [*Scipio's Helmet*], recounts the story of the great general of ancient Rome and concludes with the first four verses of the future national anthem of the Republic. The last story is entitled *La bandiera* [*The Flag*] and it recounts the feat of a young Venetian patriot who rescues the national flag so it won't fall into the hands of the Austrians. The sixth anecdote, and thus in the center of the book and not just typographically, recounts the story of *Balilla*, the young and legendary hero from Genoa, who was an idol of the republic, Mazzini, and pre-Fascist Italy, and who here maintains his Risorgimento characteristics intact, even though a few years earlier, the ruling regime had radically transformed him into the emblematic and grotesque figure of the young Fascist. The Opera Nazionale Balilla had been founded in 1926, and, starting at eight years of age, all boys were required to undergo paramilitary training, with uniform and musket. Perhaps it was right to tell them the true story of Balilla: not a small soldier of the Duce but a free young person, an enemy of oppression and arrogance. Of these idols of clear Mazzinian influence, I would say, others celebrate courage carried to the point of self-sacrifice in defense of one's own faith and ideals: the seven Maccabean brothers, a young Christian martyr, Joan of Arc, Thomas More. Other stories reconstruct anecdotes from the childhood of famous exponents of culture and art, but without Fascist manipulation, such as Ludovico Antonio Muratori, Antonio Canova, Giovanni Dupré, Massimo D'Azeglio, all the way to Giuseppe Garibaldi. All the stories feature pleasant illustrations by Carlo Nicco and use a vocabulary and syntax that, in every detail, contradicted the rhetoric of the party in power.

At the time, some people called the book antiquated and unsuitable to interpret the spirit of the new times, but it was actually a very sophisticated attempt to construct an alternative educational model; not by chance, it was

110   *Chapter 10*

printed by Utet, even during the postwar period and up until 1970. The only variations are the covers and the title pages. The cover of the 1932 edition features an illustration of the story of Giovanni Dupré's childhood, a boy embracing his mother; the 1957 edition features the Archangel Michael addressing Joan of Arc and the title page depicts the young Christian martyr with a cross in the background.

Giuseppe Latronico did not stop there. He undertook other ventures, large and small.[7] In 1936, he and Fernando Palazzi published *Chicchi d'oro. La storia narrata ai ragazzi attraverso l'aneddoto* [*Grains of Gold. History Told to Children Through Anecdotes*] (Milan: Ceschina).[8] Two hundred and ninety historical figures, from the Spartan Lycurgus to King Albert I of Belgium, recounted through short and little-known anecdotes about their lives, once again without the slightest concession to the regime's cultural politics. There are only a few members of the House of Savoy, and Vittorio Emanuele III does not appear. Instead, there are Umberto I, Queen Margherita, and Emanuele Filiberto, the Duke of Aosta, who nonetheless disappear in the editions printed after 1946, leaving only Carlo Alberto and Vittorio Emanuele II.

During the years of the war, Latronico, Bruno Paolo Arcangeli, and the Istituto Editoriale Cisalpino were involved in preparing a grammar book of the Italian language; entitled *Lingua d'oggi*, its first edition was printed in July 1943. I will leave an analysis of the book to linguists and will limit myself to pointing out that, once again, there is absolutely no reference to Fascism, not even when the topic is the homeland and the unity of the language. Also, the courtesy with which various thorny questions of linguistic identity are addressed, such as the use of *lei* and *voi*. The authors do not intervene in the first person and instead let two illustrious contributors, Fabio Tombari and Alfredo Panzini, do the talking. It precedes the playful pages written by Fabio Tombari entitled *La Cena dei Pronomi* [*The Dinner of the Pronouns*], dated 1939, which recount that Tu, Lei, and Voi were invited to dinner by Mr. Language and the great success of Voi, "familiar and authoritative," over Tu, "superficial and intrusive," and over Lei, "old, ambiguous, and servile."[9] But right afterward, a note by Alfredo Panzini explains that "only in ancient Italian was *voi* used as a sign of respect, as is still the custom in the countryside, where the children use the *voi* form with their parents," whereas over three centuries ago, "people started using *lei*" (Latronico and Arcangeli 1943, 142–43). There was a thirty-year age difference between Panzini (1862–1939) and Tombari (1899–1989), and all diachrony was intentionally avoided; on the contrary, Panzini follows Tombari and not vice versa. All it takes is this expedient and *lei* has the upper hand over *voi*, the censors are eluded, and Fascism kept in check.

One of Latronico's books that is of great interest to us is *Periscopio*, in part because it was published—always by the Istituto Editoriale Cisalpino—on

October 15, 1941, during the war and when the seas were populated by submarines. Latronico's submarine was only an exploratory submarine, and his periscope was the periscope of awareness: a pretext so that two boys, guided by an old sailor, can go in search of scientific, historical, technical, and geographical knowledge. *Periscopio* is a small encyclopedia for children, constructed through stories. Thus, there is also war, but only through the fascination this event has always had on young people:

> Around seven years of age, boys feel like warriors, just like girls already feel like mothers. Weapons are to boys what dolls are to girls. And there is no remedy. [. . .] Instinctively, weapons are power, reassurance, security, and power; they are glory. With a wooden sword at his side, or with a lead pistol tucked into his belt, the boy already has self-confidence, just like a man with a revolver in his pocket (Latronico 1941, 88–89).

There are a few concessions to Italy's autocratic politics of the previous twenty years, for example, tobacco farming and woodworking, but Mussolini and Fascism are never named (Latronico 1941, 209, 217, 220). The example of Latronico, an introverted teacher and author who has yet to be studied, in part because he cannot be placed in the Catholic or Socialist tradition, is useful food for thought in order to understand what Civic Resistance meant at school and the efforts that were made to propose alternative models to Fascism. Thus, not a-Fascist but anti-Fascist, even though they did not intend to directly challenge the regime, as was the case with the encyclopedias published by Labor, and which Latronico, with Aurelio Castoldi, created and compiled.

On November 8, 1944, learning of the death in Como of the pharmacist Amilcare Chiorri (October 25, 1944), the father-in-law of his friend and colleague Salvatore Principato, who had been shot by a firing squad in Milan in Piazzale Loreto the previous August 10, Giuseppe Latronico wrote from Lecco to Marcella, Amilcare's daughter and Salvatore's widow, expressing all his pain and explicitly communicating his horror over the tragedy of the present times:[10]

> Dear Madam,
> only today, by chance, did we learn of the new bereavement that has struck you and your family. According to what we have been told, the announcement appeared in the "Corriere" a few days ago, we completely overlooked it.
> You cannot imagine how much sorrow the news has caused us all; you cannot imagine the anguished trepidation with which we think of you and Titti.[11] The blow that has already struck you is one of the most terrible that can be imagined. To deprive you, now, of the comfort of your very kind father is a new cruelty of destiny: a cruelty as inexplicable and ungenerous as the first.

112 *Chapter 10*

Unfortunately, these years of upheaval are reconciling us to seeing lightening strike the most noble and powerful oak trees, to seeing tragedy jolt the most beautiful, the most generous, the tallest houses. But this observation can neither diminish the horror nor alleviate the pain.

You must be strong; for your sake and for Titti's, you must strengthen your ability to resist, in the memory of the great shadows that watch over you, as noble and solicitous as they were during their earthly life.

With my mother, my sisters, and my brothers, I am close to you and Titti, my heart is distressed by their same sorrow.

Yours,

Giuseppe Latronico

Latronico passed away in 1981. He had neither a wife nor children, neither a parish nor party comrades who could recount his story as an energetic, honest, coherent, and always discreet anti-Fascist.

NOTES

1. Some of the letters he wrote to Romolo Murri, written between June 1919 and November 1920, are conserved at the Fondazione Romolo Murri. Centro studi per la storia del modernismo—Università di Urbino, Archivio Romolo Murri, *Corrispondenza di varia natura*.

2. Conserved at the Centro Studi Piero Gobetti in Turin, Fondo Piero Gobetti, serie 3, 9. *Corrispondenza, altri a Piero Gobetti*.

3. The letter is written *recto/verso* on stationery headed "Comitato lombardo per i soldati mutilati in guerra./ Istituti di rieducazione professionale./ Scuole degli impieghi/ Gorla 1°."

4. The letter is written *recto/verso* on stationery headed "Scientia."

5. The typewritten manuscript is conserved at the Chiorri Principato Castoldi Archive.

6. Rebellato (2016), however, does not dwell on the figure of Giuseppe Latronico.

7. An in-depth study should be conducted of the project carried out in Milan during the 1930s by the series "Profili di scrittori per l'infanzia," published by A. Milesi & Figli, in connection with the journal *Il Risveglio Scolastico. Rivista quindicinale di cultura e di preparazione ai concorsi magistrali e direttivi*. Giuseppe Latronico wrote the first issue, *Fernando Palazzi* (1935), and the fourth, *Riccardo Balsamo Crivelli* (1936), two small books that are very useful from a bio-bibliographical point of view, and as an analysis.

8. The date 1937 appears on the title page, but the colophon reads "Finished printing on October 26, 1936-XIV with characters from the Enrico Zerboni printing house in Milan, Via Carlo Poerio 13."

9. The text is taken from *Antilei*, edited by A. Gravelli, a special edition of "Antieuropa. Rassegna mensile di azione e pensiero della giovinezza rivoluzionaria fascista," Rome: Nuova Europa, 1939.

10. Typewritten letter conserved in the Chiorri Principato Castoldi Archive.

11. Concettina Principato, the daughter of Salvatore and Marcella Chiorri, regarding whom, see Principato 2010.

Chapter 11

Anna Botto and the Three Rosaries

From Vigevano to Ravensbrück

Many times, life is harsher and more bitter
for the good than for the evil.

—Anna Botto

1944. August 21. [. . .] There is a poor woman, a teacher from Vigevano, her name is Botto and she doesn't leave my side for a moment; she tells me about herself, about the serious charges of anti-Fascist propaganda hanging over her, and she never stops talking for a moment, as though she is obsessed by something frightful, and in the short respites she walks up and down with a rosary in hand, moving her lips in prayer, as though she no longer knows where to turn for help. I try to make her understand that it's not good to talk so much, that it takes serenity and prudence to keep from losing her way but I know it's useless: maybe all the anguish of a premonition lies within that desperate anxiety of hers.

1944. August 25. [. . .] A few minutes ago, the guard rushed in, telling me in an agitated voice that she had just received an order to gather up the belongings of that poor teacher from Vigevano, who was called in for an interrogation this morning and hadn't come back upstairs. Instead, they were making her leave right away.

The woman, naive or not, seemed to want to make me think they were sending her home; I looked at her, amazed: "Don't you understand," I told her, "that they are sending her to Germany?"

Before the guard gathered up that small bundle, I looked at it, too, to see if there was anything compromising in it: a few personal objects, a missal full of sacred images, a rosary. I held them for a few instants in my hands, like people do, with an absent and lost gaze, those poor, beloved, and familiar

116   *Chapter 11*

things—solitary and dull—that the dead leave behind them when the coffin has
just gone out the front door.

This is what Bianca Ceva wrote, remembering her encounter with the teacher
Anna Botto in Pavia's prison on Via Romagnosi during the last days of
August 1944 (Ceva 1954, 92, 99–100).

Anna Botto was anxious because she realized that not only would she not
return home but, above all, that she had been betrayed.

She was born in Alessandria to Giuseppe and Giovanna Ortica on
December 31, 1895. She received her teaching degree on August 7, 1915,
from the Teachers' Institute, run by Salesian nuns in Nizza Monferrato. She
taught in Villata Novarese, then in Masio, in the province of Alessandria, in
Anzano del Parco, and in Cucciago, in the province of Como. After winning
a competitive exam, in 1926 she taught in the province of Pavia in Langosco,
Robbio, Palestro, for four years, and lastly, starting on October 1, 1940, in
Vigevano, at the "Regina Margherita" elementary school (Anna Botto n.d.).

Her personal file offers significant evidence—commendations and informative reports—that the teacher considered teaching a mission of compassionate solidarity that went well beyond the time spent in class. She was
guided by a profound belief in the Catholic religion that fully confirms the
reminiscence Bianca Ceva has left us. In Palestro, she directed the helio-
therapy summer camp on the banks of the Sesia River, "enthusiastically
conducting truly praiseworthy activity in after-school instruction, as well."
In Langosco, they noted "the synergy between the teacher and her students,
due to the teacher's open personality and the generosity with which she
cares for all her students (note: various needy students who live far away are
welcomed, for free, of course, at midday at the teacher's home, where they
always find a plate of soup and . . . more)" (1933). And again: "The teacher
is serious, active, keen, intelligent, with an exuberant personality, impulsive,
generous. Cultured, with an aptitude for fulfilling directive duties" (1934);
"a young woman of excellent moral and civic behavior, beloved in town and
by her students for the generosity she brings into every good work, an open,
sincere, and vivacious personality" (1938) (Anna Botto n.d., 3–5).[1]

In Rome, on March 27, 1946, on the occasion of an initial commemoration, the director Carlo Fossati added other details before the committee for
political victims: "After having visited Padre Pio at San Giovanni Rotondo to
ask him to pray for a factory worker suffering from tuberculosis in Vigevano,
she gave the man his blood. Always in Vigevano, she greatly helped children
recovered at the Pio Istituto Derelitti: she would often take some of them
home to give them clothing and feed them" (Anna Botto n.d., 5–6).

After September 8, 1943, at forty-seven years of age and after twenty-seven
years of teaching, her choices could only have been in line with those she had

Anna Botto and the Three Rosaries 117

made her whole life long: solidarity, generosity, dedication to others and, above all, to those in difficulty. Her convergence with the Resistance was inevitable.

In Vigevano, she lived at Via del Littorio 11 (today, Via del Popolo), as can be seen in a report dated November 6, 1943, prepared by the leader of Vigevano's "Fasci of Combat" for the head of the province, denouncing a group of men and women who were particularly active in helping Englishmen in hiding, offering them "food and clothing," finding them "accommodations in Vigevano and surroundings," sending them to Milan, "where, it is said, a Committee arranges for said prisoners to be sent abroad." Besides Anna Botto, the report named another elementary school teacher, Angela Manzi; the greengrocer Giuseppe Peretti; the Silva sisters, who were jewelers; and the priest Don Cereghino (Guderzo 2002, 9).[2] The topic has not been researched in detail, but many English soldiers who fled the prison camps were helped by the Italian Resistance, around Cremona, around Pavia, and especially in the Lomellina countryside, around Bergamo and Milan. Anna Botto is remembered as part of a group of women who, in Bergamo, "successfully organized the escape of prisoners held in the camp known as the Grumellina." This group included "Adriana Locatelli, Laura Bianchini, Carla and Mila Malvestiti" (*Le donne nel Parlamento della Repubblica dalla Consulta alla VII Legislatura* n.d., 18), who were some of the most representative Catholic partisan fighters. Laura Bianchini was later elected to the Constituent Assembly for the Christian Democrats, among the Social Christians of Giuseppe Dossetti. Just like Adriana Locatelli helped an entire group of soldiers in Bergamo (Amorth and Antonicelli 1966, 621), Anna Botto, in her own home and with the help of a trusted doctor, helped a sick English soldier whose leg was turning gangrenous (Belli 1998, 21).

Anna had been active in the Resistance ever since the first clandestine committees were formed. On October 21, 1943, she wrote the epitaph that was distributed after Giovanni Leoni, a surveyor at the city's technical office, was executed in the castle of Vigevano. He was shot in retaliation for the killing of the young Fascist Mario Toso the evening before. We can still read the epitaph, which was among the papers seized at the end of the war from an agent at the Fascist investigative political office, Giovanni Carbone, and is now deposited in the CLN Fund of the municipal historical archive:

> German bullets
> decreed that Giovanni Leoni
> was to be a victim of retaliation.
> Your daughters cry to you,
> father, stay near us
> lead us by the hand

118 *Chapter 11*

alleviate our solitude.
May those who consigned you to the enemy
know no peace.
The family in tears
the heartbroken friends
Vigevano distraught
await the inexorable hour
of justice
that will call the sacrificed
to the glory of the strong.

A few months later, on April 3, 1944, the young Catholic partisan fighter Carlo Alberto Crespi was shot near the cemetery of Varallo. The son of a well-known paper industrialist from Vigevano, he had been arrested the previous March 18 at Campertogno, along with lieutenant Pier Celestino Berardelli.

Anna Botto was once again a protagonist when she made a clamorous gesture and took her "regimented" fourth-grade female students to the mass for the soul of the young partisan who had been killed. She also accompanied three of her students to the Crespi house, so that "each girl" could receive "a photograph of the executed man," explaining that he was a "young man who was shot by the Fascists." The gesture was not hushed up, and Anna Botto, who by then had been under special surveillance by the investigative political office for a while, was unable to avoid arrest. This occurred in early May 1944, and she was denounced to the special court for the defense of the State (Guderzo 2002, 231).[3]

Assunta Bocca, who was in fourth grade in 1944, was interviewed by Vigevano's journal *l'Informatore* in April 2018, and she recalled that the arrest took place right at school:

The classroom was on the second floor, the second to the right. The principal's name was Fossati. I saw some men accompanied by two German soldiers come up the stairs. Their uniforms were very familiar to me. They used to force my father to cultivate cucumbers on our land. They ate lots of cucumbers and every so often they would arrive with wooden crates; they made us wash the crates and they wanted them back full. That day, at school, the girl who shared the desk with me was absent, they came in. Professor Fossati was crying, he was like a statue made of salt.

The article continued, summarizing the interview:

The two soldiers, carrying machine guns and wearing boots up to their knees ("for two years I would jerk awake at the sound of boots"), grab 48-year-old

Anna Botto and the Three Rosaries 119

Anna Botto by the arms and drag her outside, while she, holding a rosary she pulled out of her pocket, tells "her" girls to be neat, to respect the teacher who would come to take her place (the teacher Garberini, a good woman but never truly loved by her students), and not to worry about her. "I'll only be gone for a short while," she said (Maniaci 2018, 18).

After reading this article, I went to search for her deskmate, the girl who had been absent that day. Her name is Danilla Gaviglio, she was born on November 14, 1934, and we chatted for two hours at her home on May 28, 2018. She clearly remembered the time their teacher took the entire class to the funeral mass of the partisan Carlo Alberto Crespi ("she took all of us to the funeral mass") and when she and two other girls went directly to the Crespi home to offer their condolences. She also remembered how much the mother of the dead young man suffered: "We realized it was a very difficult moment."

We spoke about life in the classroom and what emerged, above all, was the teacher's profound religiousness: "She often took us to mass," "She was always on the side of religion," "She would say: 'you must never refuse to help someone who isn't well,'" "She was a devotee of Padre Pio, every year she went there . . . "

One of the classroom readings Danilla remembered was *Heart* by De Amicis; above all, she remembered the absolute lack of references to Fascism and Mussolini, in their discussions, in their essays, in their dictations: "Mussolini was never mentioned," "I didn't even really know what Fascism was, we didn't talk about it, either at home or at school," "our fathers came from Socialism, my father certainly wasn't a Fascist, at home we had a photograph of Matteotti on the wall, but I don't think he thought my teacher was linked to the Resistance. In any case, he trusted her a lot."

Danilla also remembered:

When there were parades, Fascist rallies, we didn't participate, we stayed in the classroom, we never wore the uniforms; she didn't force us to, she said, "If you want to attend, go right ahead but I won't accompany you." She couldn't forbid us to go, but the teacher who took her place never made us wear them, either. Her name was Garberini. It was hard to take her place. Maybe the principal urged her to be less uncompromising, during the last months we saw him less and less in class. She got along very well with the principal. I don't think the principal knew. I think he encouraged her to be more careful. You never knew which side the families were on.

Our teacher was resolute, but very sweet and always smiling; she didn't sulk, she was a very energetic person, she didn't talk with her colleagues, she couldn't resist being with children.

120   *Chapter 11*

One day, one of my schoolmates told me she had seen our teacher down by
the Ticino river near the quarry; I told my father and he said: "You didn't see
anything."

I was her student in third grade and in second grade. My parents sent me to
her in the afternoon to do my homework because they trusted her. I went every
afternoon. She would smile at me, she let me drink hot chocolate. She lived
alone, I never knew anything about her family. One day, I found a note that said
"I'll be right back," I sat down on the steps, it was two-thirty; when my mother
got home from work and came to get me, I had been waiting there all afternoon.
I went to the teacher's house for another two or three months. One day the note
wasn't there but I found it lying under the door, where it had fallen. I never saw
her again. Only recently, a lady who lived on the same landing as the teacher and
who was also her landlady told me that one day the teacher had hidden at her
place. She left her home in a hurry because she had been warned by someone.
She ran away so fast that she left her laundry soaking. She spent about ten days
hiding at her neighbor's house.

Danilla's notebook also has a dedication her teacher wrote alongside a large
yellow cross:

March 4, 1944. You are good, Danilla, and you deserve to be happy; but many
times, life is harsher and more bitter for the good than for the evil . . . Danilla,
at the foot of Christ's Cross, you will find light and consolation. Pray with all
your heart and you will always find comfort for new courage! Your teacher,
Anna Botto.

She was released from prison on May 19 but was arrested again on July 5,
after one of the many missions the partisan fighters entrusted to her, a mission Anna carried out, even though she was under close surveillance by then.
This was the arrest behind the "I'll be right back" note that Danilla mentioned to me.

This was the start of Anna Botto's acute crisis: she knew her behavior was
often quite provoking, not crazy, as the Fascist captain of the UPI [Union of
Italian Provinces] Enrico Rebolino sustained, nor "incredibly naive," as the
historian Giulio Guderzo affirmed (Guderzo 2002, 231).

Rebolino took advantage of Anna's good faith, as well as that of other
anti-Fascists with whom she collaborated. He used a young, twenty-year-old
woman from Liguria, Laura Simona Berio, one of the many girls the Fascist
police arrested because they thought she was marginally involved in con-
spiratorial activity, or only suspected of it; but she was also unscrupulous and
easily converted to double-crossing others and collaborationism. This is the
type of spy we met in Nuoro in the office of Mariangela Maccioni and who
could be found in Milan and many other Italian cities.

Anna Botto and the Three Rosaries 121

Laura met Anna Botto in prison, and it was easy for the young woman to gain her trust and confidence. Anna was aware of the imminent risk of her deportation to Germany, and Laura offered to help her. She asked for a note to the industrialist Crespi in order to find her a lawyer, and she asked Anna for the name of the shop owner to whom she had entrusted her savings. Everybody, not just Anna, thought Laura was in good faith, and it was easy for the young woman to weave her net, into which many anti-Fascists from Pavia and Vigevano fell: the industrialist Guglielmo Scapolla and his son Nino, who was an accountant employed in Milan at the Cassa di Risparmio and a close collaborator of Ferruccio Parri; the doctor Ernesto Gragnani, who was a council member at the prefecture, and his wife, Maria Luisa Canera; the entire Pettenghi family: Mario, his wife, Rosa Gaiaschi, and their son, Ugo; fifty-two-year-old Carlo Bertoni, a factory worker at SNIA; forty-five-year-old Pietro Gatti, a factory worker at Necchi. The only one who managed to hide was Nino Scapolla, but he was arrested two months later in Milan. They were all deported to Germany with Anna Botto. The only ones who returned were Ugo Pettenghi, Rosa Gaiaschi Pettenghi, and Maria Luisa Canera Gragnani (Guderzo 2002, 232–33).

Rosa Gaiaschi Pettenghi left very blunt and detailed testimony of Laura Simona Berio's treachery. Berio was taken to trial and found guilty; others have remained borderline, perhaps forever. Rosa remembered that Laura, "in order to follow one of her lovers to Pavia, reported her husband, who was a partisan, and had him arrested." "One morning," she wrote, "we saw her leave the courtyard between two republican guards, she looked extremely distressed. Three days later, she came to us and told us they had released her after a long interrogation and repeated beatings, she even showed us some bruises on her shoulders and arms (marks she had made herself with carbon paper)." Rosa's son Ugo was a partisan fighter by then in the Oltrepò region, in part to escape from the Fascists. Berio was considered increasingly unreliable, and he made her think he had gone to visit some relatives in the countryside. One day, Ugo unexpectedly returned home, wrote Rosa:

Berio came to us all distraught to warn us that she had gone to the Muti barracks, as she did every day to sign and prove she was in the city, and while she was waiting for the commander Rebolini [sic], she saw an arrest warrant for Ugo Pettenghi on his desk. "Thank goodness," she said, "the boy isn't at home!" How could we not believe such concern, such apprehension? Was it me? Was it my husband? I don't remember, all I remember is that we were so scared that we exclaimed: "But Ugo is here, he was with the partisans and he returned unexpectedly." I woke my son up and urged him to go hide in the attic of the engineer M. [. . .], our next-door-neighbor. After Ugo left, Berio, too, went away. She went to the porter and asked him to let her back into her room because she didn't

122   *Chapter 11*

feel she had the courage to see such a young man, a boy, being taken away. From her window, she told some henchmen, who were down in the street, how my son was dressed and where they would probably find him. In an instant, two machine guns were set up in Piazza Petrarca, two in the courtyard, one aimed at my home and one at the apartment of the engineer M. [. . .] One week later, my husband and I were also arrested.[4]

This was Laura Simona Berio: the spy who was behind the arrest of the entire group that Anna Botto belonged to, and who betrayed Anna herself in prison; Anna was anything but naive but, like all the others, she fell into the trap of a skillful and unscrupulous informer.

Anna Botto's premonition of all this and her tragic and growing awareness of having been betrayed help explain her confused state of mind and desperation—described by Bianca Ceva—when the two women met in prison in August 1944. It seems that, before her final interrogation, Berio also gave her two pills to stupefy her, pretending instead that they would give her more strength to face the Fascists.

For a few days, the brave, determined, and sensitive teacher from Vigevano, who was capable of sublime gestures beyond any opportunism or self-interest, became that "poor woman" who was destined to die in the concentration camp of Ravensbrück. She was transferred with the others to San Vittore prison in Milan on August 31, then deported by bus to the transit camp in Bolzano on September 20.

But nothing undermined her temperament, either at San Vittore nor in Bolzano. As Rosa Gaiaschi Pettenghi recalled in an interview she gave to a fifth-grade class at the "Regina Margherita" elementary school in Vigevano on May 28, 1973:

> At San Vittore, she [Botto] was in a communal room; instead, I was in isolation. Sometimes she'd try to evade the surveillance of the Germans and would knock at my door, a small window would open and she would pass me a piece of bread, a bunch of grapes, a pear, various things . . . She did without things that belonged to her in order to distribute them to others; then, on September 20, 1944, at night, around 11 p.m., in a downpour, they loaded us onto a bus and took us to Bolzano, to the city's concentration camp. We stayed there for eight or ten days, then I was chosen to go to Merano to work, as we awaited our departure for Germany. Anna Botto offered to go in my place because my husband and son were also in prison in Bolzano. She said, "I am alone and I'll go instead of you," she didn't know what awaited her but, as always, she sacrificed herself for others (Anna Botto n.d., 12–14).

Anna Botto and the Three Rosaries 123

She also managed to send a final greeting from Merano: an illustrated post-card to her colleague and friend in Vigevano, Giuseppina Sartorio Tollis (Anna Botto n.d., 10).

On October 7, they left Bolzano: the men for Dachau, the women for Ravensbrück on transport no. 91. Besides Anna, there were Maria Luisa Canera Gragnani, Rosa Gaiaschi Pettenghi, Livia Rossi Borsi, and Maria Sillini, all of whom returned and left important testimony.

In 1979, Livia Rossi Borsi (on January 13) and Maria Sillini (on February 21) wrote from Genoa to the professor Noemi Tognaga Gregorio in Vigevano.

Livia: I met Anna in Bolzano: she was a very good person, I remember her well; I had left three children at home, an elderly father, and an older sister, and I asked Anna Botto to help me write a letter to my parish priest, who was near my home.

She dictated the letter to me and told me, "You write better than I do, and I'm a teacher," because I hadn't made any mistakes.

We left together for Germany on October 10 [actually, 7], 1944, in stock cars, crowded together like animals, one week later we arrived in Ravensbrück; we were assigned to block 17 in quarantine. Four of us slept together per bunk bed, we were full of fleas and lice.

Every morning, we got up at four; roll call was outside, under the rain and the snow and, then, after returning from roll call, we had to remove the lice otherwise we were punished.

At the end of November, nine of us left for a work camp, there was also Rosa Pettenghi and I never found out anything about my companions at Ravensbrück (Anna Botto n. d., 21–7).

Maria: I met and clearly remember poor, dear Anna Botto, a work and barracks companion in the damned Ravensbrück camp. During the first months, we gave each other courage, hoping the war would end soon, but then we all became more and more demoralized, day after day. Poor Anna, in the beginning, she talked gladly; she made plans for when she would return home but then she began to feel sick and this worried her, rightly so. She began to talk very little, she often cried and her sadness was terrible. And we had to work; there was always a rifle aimed at us and the cudgel, unfortunately, fell on our poor bones.

We dug the earth with shovels, we loaded it onto trucks or onto carts we had to pull ourselves. Anna, poor thing, couldn't take it anymore; she was reduced to skin and bones and couldn't pluck up her courage any longer. She wanted to go to that camp where they said you didn't have to work anymore (subject to a medical examination). I spoke with a French doctor who was a prisoner and she told me it was better to stay put since nobody returned from that camp because of the mistreatment and because they starved you to death. I told this to dear Anna but by then she seemed to understand very little; and she said: "I'll go, I'll

124   *Chapter 11*

get better, and then I'll have them bring me back here, wait for me and you'll see how well I'll use the shovel."

Unfortunately [. . .] nobody returned from there and if, at the end of the war, some were still there, they were killed and God knows how! [. . .]

In the beginning, dear Anna spoke about school, her friends, she intended to recount her sad experiences when she returned home. [. . .] I am eighty-three years old, when I remember the camp and the companions who were victims of those villains, I become so agitated that I can't help trembling.

The memories of Maria Luisa Canera Gragnani are much more brutal; she recounts that, at the end of October 1944:

after only twenty days in quarantine, the teacher Botto from Vigevano began to show signs of mental imbalance. We didn't see her anymore at the morning roll call. We found out from a "red bracelet," a "Lager Polizei," that a "Transport" had been conducted that night and that its destination was the gas chamber-crematorium. And the same thing happened to Antonia [Frigerio], the secretary of the lawyer [Luciano] Elmo from Milan, who right from the start had shown premonitory signs of alienation (Canera 1980, 10).

I also include two testimonies by Rosa Gaiaschi Pettenghi. She gave the first one to Alessandra Ferraresi:

They put Anna Botto in the nearby shack. But we saw her every morning when she went to wash herself. [. . .] Canera also went to the nearby shack, along with Anna Baldisserotto from Milan and Anna Botto. Anna Botto was worn out. She kept saying: "I can't take anymore, I can't manage to go to roll call every morning; I can't manage to walk all the way there." Since they had asked us who wanted to go to the sick ward to knit, she accepted right away, even though I advised her against it because you couldn't expect the Germans to have a kind heart. After a few days, not even a week that she was there, we met at the *Wasser*, at the toilets, and I said to her, "Anna, how are you doing?" She stared at me and she began to sing: "We'll return in May with lots of roses." She had gone crazy. When I wasn't at Ravensbrück anymore, I asked about her, they told me that the block of the invalids, the crazy people, had been destroyed with flame-throwers (*I deportati pavesi nei lager nazisti* 1981, 93–95).

The second testimony is a follow-up to what she recounted to the students of a fifth-grade class at the "Regina Margherita" elementary school in Vigevano. Rosa recalled that, on the train that was taking them to Ravensbrück, Anna "did nothing but talk about her students, about her school, about when she would return, what she would tell her students. She didn't even talk about her relatives, only about her students;" and at Ravensbrück: "she would make any sacrifice, just so she could pray. She gathered some pieces of wood and twigs and she made herself a rosary; all day long, all she did was pray, pray, pray. Sometimes I would tell her: 'Anna, stop it! You'll wear yourself out!' And she would reply: 'But no . . . Let's pray, let's pray . . . You'll see, you'll see that we'll return.' Unfortunately . . . " (Anna Botto n. d., 14, 20).

NOTES

1. The following are quoted, in consecutive order: *Nota di encomio del direttore didattico C. Fossati del 15 luglio 1940*; *Verbale di visita del 23 maggio 1933*; *Rapporto informativo del direttore didattico G. Ciocca del 3 luglio 1934*; *Verbale di visita del 9 dicembre 1938 del direttore didattico C. Fossati.*

2. Document conserved at the Istituto Pavese per la Storia della Resistenza e dell'Età Contemporanea, Fondo Turri, c. 1, fasc. *Prigionieri di guerra.*

3. See "Verbale di denuncia della nominata Botto Anna fu Giuseppe e di Ortica Giovanna, nata ad Alessandria il 31.12.1895, residente a Vigevano, Via del Littorio n. 11, di professione insegnante, per propaganda sovversiva e favoreggiamento di prigionieri inglesi," in Istituto Pavese per la Storia della Resistenza e dell'Età Contemporanea, Fondo Turri, cartella 2, fasc. *Denuncie al Tribunale Speciale per la difesa dello Stato*, sottofasc. *Botto Anna, antifascista.*

4. *Laura Simona Berio: delatrice. Testimonianza di Rosa Pettenghi*, in Archivio Fondazione Memoria della Deportazione, Fondo Aned, *Ricerche sulla deportazione femminile*, b. 257, fasc. 15.

Chapter 12

Salvatore Principato

Setting an Example as a Form of Civic Education

To know how to give your life for someone or something . . .

—Reginaldo Orlandini

In October 1931, the Socialist schoolteacher Salvatore Principato was one of the primary contacts of the anti-Fascist movement Giustizia e Libertà in Milan.

During those same months, a rift developed between Rodolfo Morandi and Carlo Rosselli. On September 26, 1931, Morandi published an article in the Zurich edition of *Avanti!* entitled "The Italian Revolution Will Have to Be a Socialist Revolution." It was based on the belief that, since Fascism had "ripened a revolutionary situation in Italy," this revolutionary situation would have to be "dealt with by the parties upon the fall of the regime." It declared that, since the "middle class [. . .], under the terror of social upheaval has, in the most general way, abjured all democratic faith," allowing and fostering the rise of Fascism, "the day after Fascism" would "inevitably" consign "the country to a Socialist revolution." This, because "the Italian middle class has categorically lost its material and moral power," which alone could have "effected, with luck, a democratic restoration in the country" (Merli 1975, 171–73).[1] In the meantime, he wrote to Carlo Rosselli that it had become impossible "to forgo the classist approach—classist not in the historical or sociological sense!—of political struggle" (Merli 1975, 175). Rosselli replied that "when founding GL two years ago," they had begun with the fundamental premise that "the battle against Fascism could not and must not be conducted on a platform of class." To Rosselli, those who thought differently put themselves "outside GL, the contradiction not permitting it" (Agosti 1971, 152).[2]

127

128 *Chapter 12*

In a letter dated October 9, 1931, to an unspecified recipient (Merli 1975, 156, asterisked note), just as Rodolfo Morandi was distancing himself from the movement, he identified Salvatore Principato, calling him by the pseud-onym "Socrate" (a name we now know was familiar to the Fascist police, as well), as one of the figures of reference who could be counted on in Milan:

> I once again questioned Socrate at length and urged him to accept the respon-sibilities we'd like to give him. He emphatically replied that he absolutely does not have the time to deal with them. That he cannot do more than what he has done to date, and he asked me to tell you so in precisely these terms. So here we are in an impasse. I hope Italo can come on Sunday. I will give you confirma-tion tomorrow. Today, I made an agreement with our friends in T[urin] to send them a quantity of A[vanti!]. Instead, there's no point in you sending zinc plates of the posters to the workers. They wouldn't be printed, Negretto has probably told you about the matter of the wine (Merli 1975, 174).[3]

Between 1930 and 1931, many members of Giustizia e Libertà were arrested and found guilty in Italy, including Ernesto Rossi, Riccardo Bauer, and Ferruccio Parri; as a result, the entire Milanese organization was weakened. For a few months, the figure of reference was Giuseppe Faravelli, who, although he had managed to avoid identification and arrest, was nonetheless increasingly besieged by the police, above all after the young Belgian profes-sor Léo Moulin was arrested. Moulin, who had decided to go to Italy to fight in the name of freedom but was not fully aware of the delicacy of the under-taking, had convinced Giovanni Bassanesi, who lived in Belgium, to entrust him with some propaganda material that Moulin brought to Italy in the false bottom of a trunk. He was immediately arrested, as were the two members of Giustizia e Libertà to whom he had been sent: Vittorio Albasini Scrosati and Bruno Maffi, both of whom were condemned to two years in prison by the Special Court (Ferro 1985, 98). Faravelli escaped arrest a second time in this police raid, as well, but his position was totally compromised.

Salvatore, along with Alfredo Bonazzi, Romeo Ballabio, Alberto Benzoni, and Roberto Veratti, organized his escape on April 28, 1931. Faravelli went first to Lugano and then to France, after initially throwing his pursuers off by heading toward Sondrio.

Salvatore's wife, Marcella Chiorri, wrote about this in *Critica* Sociale:

> I met Faravelli one afternoon at my home and when he left, my husband told my daughter, who was about six or seven years old, "Remember, you never saw that gentleman!" It was like an ideal consignment and the little girl took it to heart, for the entire Fascist period.
>
> I remember a few important details, for example, organizing Faravelli's expa-triation to France, and contacting him by means of secret notes.

Salvatore Principato 129

For his expatriation, very secret gatherings and meetings were held at my home. One evening, our friend Ballabio, from Parabiago, came over; he locked himself up with my husband in his study and they remained there a long time. When he came out, my husband told me he would be leaving the next day with a few friends to go on a trip to Sondrio.

That trip was a smokescreen because the friends split up into two groups, one of which was to get Faravelli out of the country, and the other was supposed to distract attention from this attempt by attracting attention to themselves as though they were responsible for the escape.

My husband belonged to this second group. Silence was the rule back then, and I never asked who the others were and what roads they would take. My husband and his group returned that evening and I was only told that everything had gone well.

Faravelli directed Milan's Resistance from Paris. Using invisible ink, he wrote to Cagnoli,[4] who lived at Via San Gregorio no. 6, giving him all the instructions for reorganizing the Socialist groups, and we were supposed to reply in the same way, providing all the information at our disposal. I was the one who went back and forth to Cagnoli's house with the excuse that I was visiting his sick mother. Cagnoli would give me the letters. At home, I deciphered the invisible ink and then took them back to Cagnoli, who prepared the replies. I went to collect them and then, with my husband's help, I transcribed them, always in invisible ink, and took them back to Cagnoli, who sent them on, writing very commonplace greetings over them.

All this because my handwriting was clear and easy to read. We always did this work at night, when my daughter was sleeping. In fact, she never noticed anything (Chiorri Principato 1977, 36).

After Faravelli escaped, the reference point of the Milanese Socialist group inside Giustizia e Libertà was Alfredo Bonazzi, who was born in 1865 and was employed at the Società Anonima Fonderia Milanese di Acciaio "Vanzetti." The meetings were always held at Via San Gregorio 6. The group's base was Attilio Antelmi's printing house at Via Santa Sofia 31, where the trusty Ambrogio Broggi worked as a typographer.

Alfredo Bonazzi and Romeo Ballabio kept in contact with Faravelli; they sent him letters written in invisible ink by Marcella, whose handwriting was neat and, above all, not easily identifiable by the Fascist police.

The movement's places of reference were the apartment at Via San Gregorio 6, the printing house at Via Santa Sofia 31, and the Banca Popolare at Piazza Crispi, where both the Socialist Alberto Benzoni and the Catholics Pietro Malvestiti and Armando Rodolfi worked.

All this explains Principato's reluctance to take on those new, undefinable duties Morandi had proposed. He was in good relations with Rosselli, although substantially in agreement with Morandi's position, but he was forced to direct—on a daily basis and with few collaborators—a Milanese

130   *Chapter 12*

anti-Fascist front that was constantly threatened by internal conflict and, above all, by informers and increasingly capillary investigations conducted by the Fascist police headquarters.

Clandestine operations had to be conducted with increasing caution and masterfully concealed. On the one hand, they had to pretend the organization wasn't as strong as it actually was; on the other, they had to broaden the movement's base and political support as far as possible, also within the Catholic, working-class sphere.

This was, in fact, the strategy of the Socialist and Republican groups that were active in Milan and Genoa after Faravelli's escape.

In 1932, the distribution of clandestine press publications was organized in a capillary fashion in Italy, in particular the journals *Giustizia e Libertà* and *La Libertà*, as they tried to increase the movement's connections in Italy and abroad. A program was published for a post-Fascist Italy based on "freedom," "justice," "essentially on the working classes," and "deep economic-political transformation." The new Italian republic would arise from a Constituent Assembly elected by universal franchise and would be founded on "broad autonomy"; substantial agrarian reform; a "reorganization" linked to central planning; the "socialization" of businesses, but not the competitive ones, which would be under "autonomous management"; the "control" of the workers in the major workplaces; and on other social and structural reforms (Garosci 1973, I, 223–29; Giovana 2005, 237–42).

The archive of Milan's police headquarters conserves a great number of reports regarding the distribution of clandestine papers, confirmation of the great activity of the groups—above all Socialist—that were present in 1932 in Lombardy's capital.

On February 26, 1932, the director of public security, Arturo Bocchini, wrote from Rome to the prefect of Milan to share his growing worry over the "introduction into the kingdom by mail [of] numerous anti-Fascist *Giustizia e Libertà* leaflets, preferably hidden among foreign newspapers, most of which from Germany and a few from England and France." The leaflets were addressed to officers, soldiers, "railway workers, sailors, port workers, tram drivers, chauffeurs," factory workers, unemployed people, in order to conduct truly capillary propaganda of information about the movement's programs and what the regime was concealing. Reports arrived frequently at police headquarters, and the police commissioner Bruno regularly informed the prefect. Thus, on March 21, 1932, he reported that six pages of *Giustizia e Libertà* had been found in a German newspaper that was sent on October 17–18, 1931, to the offices of the Credito Italiano bank at Piazza Cordusio, and that five other inserts had been found in another German newspaper in Piazza Duomo at the Cobianchi daytime hotel. On April 2, he reported a number of white envelopes, 15 x 12.5 cm in size, from Stockholm, containing the "noted pamphlets." On May 13, a commissioner of public security advised the prefect that the Giustizia e Libertà pamphlet entitled *Consigli sulla Tattica* [*Advice on Tactics*] was "sent from Berlin hidden among the pages of the 'official bulletin' of the German Touring Club [. . .] edited in Munich"; on June 4, a zealous thirty-year-old Fascist named Lodovico Terruzzi, from Concorezzo, found three "subversive Giustizia e Libertà" leaflets at five o'clock in the morning, and the equally zealous lieutenant of the Carabinieri Spotorno made sure the prefect was informed. On June 8, the cameraman at the Odeon cinema, Roberto Regazzoni, delivered nine subversive pamphlets, always entitled *Giustizia e Libertà*, that were found near the projection room and "contained biased news about the present political-economic-National situation and incited the social classes against Fascism." Nor was there a lack of reports from spies in France, as confirmed in a handwritten letter by—once again—Bocchini to the prefect, written from Rome on June 18 and informing him that "it is reported that the known exile Carlo Rosselli has recently purchased a few thousand old, illustrated naval magazines in order to insert propaganda leaflets and brochures of *Giustizia e Libertà* inside them and send them to people residing in the Kingdom." Subversive press also passed by way of Tunis and Tripoli; in October, it was discovered that envelopes, "commercial-type, ash gray, with typewritten addresses," were being sent from there and that they contained, once again, "subversive publications of *Giustizia e Libertà*." On December 7, Bocchini was informed that the familiar *Notebooks of Giustizia e Libertà* were being sent from Germany and Austria, this time "disguised with a cover bearing the writing *The Fascist Homeland. Journal of Fascist Culture for Italians Abroad* and embossed with the emblem of the Fasces."[5]

Equally capillary was the diffusion of the newspaper *La Libertà*, which was also printed by Concentrazione Antifascista in Paris. The numerous reports sent to police headquarters reveal that the magazine arrived in Italy from all over the world, in an obvious attempt to elude all controls: on February 18, 1932, the commissioner Bruno seized a copy that came from "Australia in a sealed white envelope 14 x 8 cm"; on June 13, the Ministry of the Interior reported it arrived from "Brussels in a turquoise envelope size fifteen by eleven with 'Sindacat de recherches industrielles pour la Belgique et la Hollande S.A.' stamped on the left-hand side."[6]

In short, the Fascist police, above all in Milan, was literally besieged by active, intense, and consistently surprising propaganda.

Some of the publications were addressed directly to selected recipients; some of them were collected by the contact people within the movement, primarily in Milan and Genoa, and then redistributed and in some cases reprinted.

132   *Chapter 12*

Salvatore Principato's name recurs in the reports of the general inspector of Public Security, Francesco Nudi, as a key exponent of the anti-Fascist movement in Milan, above all in running the clandestine press and the project with Alfredo Bonazzi for a political "magazine" of Socialist inspiration, "which would be printed in Milan." His name and his pseudonym "Socrate" were reported to police headquarters by various informers who had infiltrated the movement, in particular in the reports by a certain "Silvino" or "Silvio."[7]

As Marcella Chiorri Principato wrote:

One day, my husband introduced me to someone, a certain Villa, at my home and told me he was a very trustworthy fellow and that his task was to bring printed material and correspondence across the Swiss and French borders because he often went back and forth between our country and those ones on personal business. He used a suitcase with a false bottom. [. . .] In January and February 1933, an anti-Fascist leaflet was launched by the popular Catholic movement in collaboration with the Socialist movement. It was entitled "Dio e Popolo" and it spread like wildfire and was quite a sensation.

The OVRA [the secret police—translator's note] already had its ears pricked, or perhaps it had been well informed by a zealous agent; it began to follow the movements of the group, which thought it was quite safe. It probably followed that fellow Villa, at least that's what was said later on.[8]

One of the recurring methods of the spies was to let themselves be followed, all the while pretending they didn't know they were being followed.

On several occasions, Marcella urged her husband to mistrust that fellow Villa, and she was right. Carlo Villa had, in fact, become a skillful whistle-blowing "traveling salesman," a former "unitary Socialist" who had been the editor of the weekly *Il Lavoro Bresciano* and was arrested in 1929, when "a medal with the effigy of Matteotti" was found in his home. Mauro Canali wrote that Carlo Villa, "exploiting his blood ties with [Guido] Miglioli, managed to gain the respect of the opposition abroad in Canton Ticino, which revolved around Pacciardi."

He was a real estate agent and this facilitated his contacts with Lugano (Canali 2004, 329).[9] There are good reasons for agreeing with Domenico Zucàro that Carlo Villa was, in fact, "Silvino" (Zucàro 1988, 399).

The fact remains that on March 19, 1933, Salvatore was arrested and sent to the Special Court along with Alberto Benzoni, Alfredo Bonazzi, Ambrogio Broggi, Aristide Cagnoli, Ugo Cavani, Luciano Magrini, Roberto Veratti, the fugitive Faravelli, and the Catholic exponents of the Guelphic movement, including Gioacchino Malavasi and Pietro Malvestiti, as well as the Socialist group from Genoa.

The records of the trial include the information provided by the young maid Cristina Morelli, who worked at the Principato household helping Salvatore's mother, Concetta, who was gravely ill and bedridden. Miss Morelli declared that, in the Principato apartment, she had seen a copy of the anti-Fascist newspaper *La Libertà*, with "writing in red," and another, smaller publication entitled *Giustizia e Libertà* and that she had handed this latter paper over to her boyfriend, Mario Cellario, a Blackshirt in the Oberdan Group.[10] Salvatore managed to clear his name, and he was acquitted for "not having committed the crime." He was freed on June 8, but he remained under Fascist police surveillance.

As opposed to other anti-Fascist elementary school teachers, Principato kept his political activity as separate as possible from his teaching duties; he avoided revealing his ideas at school, in order to continue teaching and stay in contact with the young people so he could contribute to their education. He was very prudent and reluctant to attract attention through sensational gestures. He made himself clearly understood by his students, both young and old (he also taught at night school), but he dissimulated with the regime, thanks in part to the collaboration of obliging directors of studies: Maurizio Mataloni in Vimercate, and Piero Bianchi at the Leonardo da Vinci elementary school in Milan.

When he moved to Lombardy, in the fall of 1912, Salvatore had recently graduated as an elementary school teacher in Sicily, in Piazza Armerina, where he was born on April 29, 1892. He was the son of Concetto (1851–1924) and of Concetta Rausa (1863–1933), and he descended from an ancient family of Norman origin from Piazza Armerina (Villari 1987, 343, 389, 554).

In the early 1900s, the new humanitarian, Republican, and Socialist demands were stirring up particularly active political ferment in Piazza Armerina. At the printing house of Adolfo Pansini, the editor Tropea, from Catania, had printed the first books by Napoleone Colajanni *Il socialismo* (1884) and the investigation *L'alcoolismo sue conseguenze morali e sue cause* (1887). In 1903, Mario Sturzo, an anti-Fascist who inspired his younger brother Luigi, the founder of the Popular Party, became the bishop of Piazza Armerina and maintained this role until his death in 1941.

Salvatore was a Socialist ever since his student days; he was accused of being an "agitator" during a trial following a popular uprising in the Sicilian town on November 22–23, 1911, against the transportation company of Nunzio Russo, who had control over the carriages used to transport farm workers into the countryside, thereby preventing the creation of a modern public service. A carriage was dragged into the piazza and demolished; another one was burned. Among the names of the young "agitators" on trial was "Principato Salvatore son of Concetto—nineteen years old—from P. Armerina." Thanks to the solidarity of the people who testified in their favor, they were all acquitted with a sentence pronounced by the Royal Court House of Piazza Armerina on June 12, 1912. During the trial, a certain

134   *Chapter 12*

Carpinello declared that he had seen Salvatore Principato "holding a lit match, but far away from the carriage"; the person who wrote the sentence of acquittal commented that "said act lends itself to various interpretations, including innocent ones."[11]

To Salvatore, moving to the north represented an opportunity to be closer to the more active centers of Italian Socialism. He began his activity as a teacher in Vimercate, first at the private school Tommaseo and then at municipal schools, where he remained in service from 1913 until 1919—thus, during the war years, when he fought on the Karst Plateau.

At Vimercate, he became friends with various Socialist teachers, including Novemi Ferrari, from Emilia; the two Sicilians Pappalardo and Riccobene; and with the director of studies Maurizio Alfredo Mataloni. His daughter Concettina recalls in an autobiographical note:

> Mataloni's son, Jenner, was the superintendent at the Scala, where, at the start of every performance, *Giovinezza* had to be played and, obviously, the public had to stand up. My parents said that one evening, the father, who had been invited to a performance by his son, didn't stand up, which caused a scandal and father and son never spoke again (Principato 2010, 18–19).

We know that Jenner Mataloni was one of the most active Fascists in Milan throughout the entire Fascist period; he supported the racial laws and was the superintendent of the Teatro alla Scala from 1932 to 1942.

Maurizio died at sixty-five years of age on October 13, 1937.

Even though he was against the war and proudly non-interventionist, Salvatore fought in three campaigns as an infantryman, and experienced the contradictions of the conflict firsthand. One of the first to be called up, he insisted on becoming an infantryman in the trenches, a companion of those who were facing the greatest discomforts. He soon found himself fighting on the Karst Plateau with the 247th Infantry Regiment. On May 31, 1917, during the battle of Mount Vodice, one of the most terrible and decisive offensives on the Isonzo River, Salvatore took fifteen Austrians prisoner, accomplishing the double undertaking of saving the lives of fifteen men, whom an interested power forced him to consider the enemy, and at the same time of serving his homeland, in which—despite everything—he still believed, in memory of his Risorgimento and Garibaldian ideals.[12] For this, he received a silver medal for military valor, of which he was always proud. He also earned the gratitude of one of those soldiers, who gave him a pocket watch, which Salvatore carefully conserved his whole life long, one of his most precious belongings. His daughter Concettina remembers that, one time, it fell into the sea in Sferracavallo, Sicily, and he asked a deep-sea diver to retrieve it for him (Principato 2010, 16).

For the rest of his life, he adopted the conduct he had learned in emergency situations in the trenches: in an emergency, search for the best solution in order to avoid betraying one's own principles, at all cost, always preferring action over any form of abstract ideology or theoretical formulations.

After returning to civilian life, he began teaching in Vimercate again and then in Milan, as a permanent staff member. After three years of suburban schools in the Turro neighborhood and on Via Comasina, from 1922 to 1924 he taught at the elementary school on Via Giulio Romano, from 1924 to 1933 at the Tito Speri school on Viale Lombardia and Via Sacchini, and starting in October 1933, without interruption, at the Leonardo da Vinci elementary school at Piazza Leonardo da Vinci.

At the school on Via Giulio Romano, he met the young schoolteacher Marcella Chiorri, the daughter of Amilcare, who owned the pharmacy located at Via Giulio Romano 1. Their love lasted their whole life long, in a communion of Socialist ideals and values. They married in 1923, and on March 6, 1924, their only daughter, Concettina, was born.

As he was beginning his clandestine political activity in the Socialist group of Giustizia e Libertà, Salvatore dedicated himself to his teaching profession with great diligence, as he sought to make his students understand how clearly Fascist propaganda was betraying the ideal of the homeland that had animated the Risorgimento.

That patriotism, which had signified defending their own land and fighting oppression and corruption, had turned into shoddy nationalism, a war against political, social, ethnic, religious, and cultural differences: a premise for an imperialistic war, able to overturn every principle of human dignity. Without openly saying so, he had to make them understand that the pride, courage, and great sense of civilization that had animated Garibaldi's Redshirts had been substituted by the arrogance, cockiness, and hypocrisy of Mussolini's Blackshirts in a process that was destined to profoundly pollute the civic conscience of Italians.

To Salvatore, they had to rebel against this, using intelligence, persuasion, words, and, above all, their example. Herein lay his lesson as a teacher of elementary school children. To make them understand that another way of life was possible.

All it took was a reference to the values of the fathers of the *Risorgimento* during the Five Days of Milan; or the values of solidarity, without underscoring social differences, even though they existed (profoundly) among the children, above all when Salvatore went to teach at the Leonardo da Vinci elementary school in Milan.

And all it took was a dictation about respect for the elderly, their wisdom and their experience, as, all around, squads of Fascists arrogantly sang to the empty shout of "youth, youth."

136   *Chapter 12*

The journalist Alfredo Barberis, who was Principato's student from 1940 to 1942, wrote that he doesn't remember one single time when the "teacher [. . .] read one of the many Mussolinian slogans that abounded in primary school textbooks" and only once did he oblige his students "to memorize a poem that celebrated the splendor of the Duce" (Barberis 2012, 196–97).

Elsewhere, Barberis wrote that,

> At the assemblies, when the other teachers showed up wearing orbace cloth (that is, the Fascist uniform), [Principato] would wear an old, blue double-breasted suit that was shiny from being ironed: in his lapel shone the badge of the silver medal for valor he had earned during the First World War. He was an example of courage, a challenge to Fascist conformism. But his entire teaching was anti-Fascist: he avoided all forms of rhetoric, he tried to tell us as little as possible about Mussolini, he forced himself to teach a sense of civil and democratic life to the young children who had been rendered stupid by massive propaganda (even the primer was studded with A-avant-gardists, M-mothers who ironed the Fascist U-uniform of their D-daughter . . .).[13]

During the war, the only black item of clothing Principato wore was his tie, as a sign of constant mourning for all the innocent victims, including his wife, Marcella's brother, Filippo Chiorri, a lieutenant who went missing in action on the eastern front in Albania on December 13, 1940, during the battle of Progonat.

Elserino Piol, a student of Principato's between 1940 and 1942, remembers:

> When the subject was history, the characters weren't only described for what they were, they were compared to the reality we were experiencing. Even to us young students, the meaning was clear of sentences such as: 'People like this are hard to find nowadays,' referring to a historical character of high moral caliber, and the reference was obviously to those who commanded us back then. A certain amount of caution was necessary, but Principato, at least the way I remember him, managed to send all of us clear messages: within the limits of our abilities, he wanted us to begin to think and reason.

The engineer Gino Troncon, born on August 22, 1925, and a student of his in 1935–1936, remembers that Principato, who still suffered from backaches after his experiences in the trenches, told his class:

> Children, you must know that I fought the War of '15–'18 and the mud and the water in the trenches have left me with severe backaches, so every now and then I have to take a walk to alleviate the pain. I'm going into the hallway now to walk a bit. What I ask is that you keep quiet and not make a racket. [. . .] There were about forty-three of us high-spirited children. We remained in the most educated and respectful silence until he reentered the classroom.

Salvatore Principato 137

And the chemist Giangiacomo Nathansohn, born on May 22, 1927, a student during the years 1936–1937:

> He was a true teacher, every day he gave a short dictation on various topics: recurring themes were respect for one's parents and for the elderly, and solidarity for the derelicts. [. . .] When Fascist party officials came to visit the "Leonardo da Vinci" school, which was considered a model school, the principal Piero Bianchi and almost all the other teachers wore the black shirt, Principato wore a gray-green shirt and the light blue ribbon of the silver medal he had earned during the war of '15–'18 stood out against his dark jacket.

Another student at the Leonardo da Vinci school during 1936–1938, Nicola Prezioso, remembers that, to Principato

> the first and the last didn't exist: everybody had to arrive, everybody had to be accompanied along their educational pathway, independently of their economic and social conditions, but also, in a certain sense, of their abilities. To him, education was truly the right of all. [. . .] We never found out about his political ideas, his opposition to Fascism. And what could we children have understood about that? I only remember his rigor, his love for the homeland, but at the same time, his rejection of every form of empty rhetoric. His moral lesson lay in examples, behavior.

His friend Gian Luigi Ponti, a famous Milanese banker, remembers Principato's "constantly serene face," his "calm and sweet voice," "his words that were always inspired by conscious benevolence." Some of his students remembered his tall, imposing figure, his firm and precise way of speaking, his neatness, elegance, and—an odd but significant detail—the absence of any Sicilian accent during the lessons.

Nino Ferrari, an accountant and the son of the teacher Novemi Ferrari, remembers his unflagging interest in the human and social problems of workers, offering words of advice and confidence, as well as some of his union and political arguments: "The events of 1922 must never happen again," "We must create a union that is unitary and obligatory for all . . . and those who don't join the union will not be able to benefit from the improvements in contracts, salaries, and norms that are brought about by the workers' struggles. . . . "[14]

During the second half of the 1930s, the Principato family often went on vacation to Lizzano in Belvedere, in the Tuscan-Emilian Apennines; they were the guests of Ulisse Orlandini, whose son, Luigi Reginaldo, was born on December 6, 1916, and was already a Dominican friar. The friar would never forget the teacher. They shared the utopia of a better world and the desire to fight injustice. The war separated them forever. But his whole life long,

138   *Chapter 12*

Father Luigi Reginaldo Orlandini treasured Principato's example; during the summer of 1944, he didn't hesitate to collaborate with the partisans who were active in the mountains above Bologna.

Pier Giorgio Ardeni wrote that, during that period "a few Dominican Fathers from Bologna had been evacuated to Lizzano" and that "Father Reginaldo Orlandini, a young man from Lizzano, often went into town for food for the community and had also become the trusted letter carrier of many partisans who took advantage of his trips to send news to their families." In that same book, we also learn that Ulisse was killed at sixty-eight years of age on November 7, 1944, when a "live bomb" exploded (Ardeni 2016, 134, 293).

In 1946, Reginaldo left to become a missionary in Brazil, where he remained for thirty years. He died in Bologna on March 31, 2006. In 1974, he wrote a letter from Brazil to Salvatore's daughter, Concettina, in which, as a missionary friar, he remembered her father's teachings, "a true teacher of the real and essential things of life," one of the few teachers who instilled in his mind and heart "a valid idea of the world." The letter concludes this way:

> I am proud of having been his admirer, and even more, his pupil. In my mind, his violent and unjust death is wrapped in the mystery of the incredible; it was nonetheless a sign of the times and a more profound mystery in which we see that the best are sacrificed, to the shame of the cowards and a lesson to the blind, who don't want to see, but also for the salvation of the humble and the innocent! This is why his image is magnified inside me and it is so vivid that I think it will not wane until we see each other again. [. . .] You have always been present in my mind, even more so than in my album of family memories where, below a few photographs that show you among the green chestnut trees of Piancerè, I wrote in my own hand back then: *Flores apparuerunt in terra nostra!* Just so and . . . in Latin: which today gives a very special flavor to the event. I don't remember how old I was: I was young, you all were adolescents, all equally dreamers, smiling confidently at the lie that was unfolding before us . . . and my life has been what I dreamed of. If today, there is an unregretted nostalgia in my life, it is of becoming someone someday, that saint who is potentially in all of us and who will reveal himself in the act of supreme sacrifice: to know how to give one's life for someone or for something . . . as your father did, my teacher (Castoldi M. 2007a).

Reintegrated into daytime teaching, after thirteen years of service he was excluded from night school, even though he had every right, through seniority and merit of service. The documents that are still conserved today in his personal file at the Leonardo da Vinci school record that the teacher in question "does not provide unfailing certainty that he fully obeys the directives of the Regime," and "not only is he not a member of the PNF, his name does

Salvatore Principato 139

not even appear among the members of the Fascist School Association." His numerous appeals were in vain.

He was under increasing surveillance by the Fascist police. His daughter, Concettina, remembers, "When we went on vacation to Lizzano, the Carabinieri always came to visit us and greeted us politely." A friend of hers back then, Angela Badini, remembers the same (Principato 2010, 25). This also happened each time Salvatore left Milan. Gianfranco Rollini, a fifth-grade student of Principato's between 1941 and 1942, remembers that the teacher made them read many books by Salgari, often spoke about the Great War and the *Risorgimento*, and took them on an outing to Lugano. On this occasion, Rollini threw a piece of paper out the window; the teacher stopped the bus, identified the culprit, and sent him back two hundred meters to pick up the piece of paper.

The clarity of this memory makes it a reliable one; it also gives the impression that Principato was able to cross the border for one day, perhaps to communicate with a political exile.

The 1930s were also marked by Principato's contact with the group of teachers who actively collaborated with the publishing house Labor, starting with Andrea Tacchinardi, Carlo Fontana, and Giuseppe Latronico, who, as mentioned, lived in the same building at Via Gran Sasso 5 and had been his director of studies for a period.

His friendship was longer-standing with the Socialist Ines Saracchi, who was the principal of the "Santa Caterina da Siena" school and offered major logistical support to Milan's Resistance (Principato 2010, 17, 21). Another friend was Alberto Franchino, a compatriot and schoolmate in Piazza Armerina; he was born in 1896 and was the director of studies at the elementary school on Via Giulio Romano during the German occupation, providing a valid cover during that period for the teacher Castoldi, who moved there after 1938.[15] Principato also worked to help, hide, and find work for refugees and those, like Lina Merlin, most likely, who returned from internal exile in economic difficulty and needed adequate cover. The teacher Angelo Taschera, who had been a colleague of Salvatore's at the Leonardo da Vinci school, remembered him in an interview with Paolo Zonca that was published in *La Repubblica* on April 28, 2004:

> I remember the teacher Salvatore Principato as though he were still here with us now: we were friends, he helped my brother-in-law find a job as an accountant at Caproni after he returned from internal exile, and he found me a job giving private lessons when the Leonardo closed because they were bombing Milan (Zonca 2004).

140   *Chapter 12*

In order to carry out all these activities, plus the clandestine propaganda, he needed a series of different covers; thus, besides selling retail copies of the *Enciclopedia* and the *Dizionario* of his friends at the publishing house Labor, he was also an insurance broker for INA. In 1939, he purchased, and registered in his wife's name, joint ownership of the company F.I.A.M.M.A. (Fabbrica Insegne Arredi Mobili Metallo Affini, equipment for shop windows), headquartered in Milan, at Via Cusani 10. It soon became a cover for the distribution of Socialist and anti-Fascist propaganda, and also had a clandestine printing shop (Principato 2010, 23, 31–32).

During the 1940s, anti-Fascist activity struggled more and more to relaunch its activity. One evening in October 1942, Salvatore participated with his friend Roberto Veratti, Ottaviano Pieraccini, Domenico Viotto, and other Socialists at a meeting in Milan, at the home of Ivan Matteo Lombardo on Via Tantardini, to found a new Socialist formation, the MUP, the Movement of Proletarian Unity, whose goal was to bring together all the Socialists (ex-Reformers and ex-Maximalists) into one single organization (Monina 2004, 19, 34, 127).

Salvatore then became a member of the 33rd Matteotti Brigade (Cavalli and Strada 1982b, 58–62) with his trusted former student Giuseppe Ferrarini, a shoemaker at Via Gran Sasso 7 and on Via Pecchio, and later joined the school's National Liberation Committee.

In 1944, he was working in close contact with Prof. Quintino Di Vona, who was executed by firing squad at Inzago, in the province of Milan, on September 7, 1944; with the chauffeur Dario Barni, who was killed in a shootout with Fascists at Santa Maria della Versa, in the Oltrepò Pavese, on September 18; with Maria Arata, who was deported to Ravensbrück, survived, and remembered him in her memoirs along with Giuseppe Ferrarini (Arata Massariello 1979, 18); and with Mino Micheli, a Socialist hairdresser who was deported to, and survived, Mauthausen (Micheli 1967). Mino Micheli's shop was located in Milan on Via Saverio Mercadante, almost on the corner of Corso Buenos Aires. Mino's brother, Onorino, worked with him as a barber. Interviewed in 1985, when he was a patient at the Pio Albergo Trivulzio [retirement home] in Milan, Onorino remembered that, every day, the teacher Salvatore Principato would come to his shop "to be shaved," bringing propaganda material that he would very secretively leave with his brother (Principato and Patti 1985, 9).

We could list many other names of people who were active in the Socialist Party, by then the PSIUP, and who were arrested with Principato between July 4, when Maria Arata was arrested, and July 9, 1944, when the Pirelli factory worker Eraldo Soncini was arrested.

As with Anna Botto and in many other cases, tips were provided by people who had been considered the most trustworthy and least suspicious collaborators.

Salvatore was arrested on the afternoon of Saturday, July 8, 1944, on Via Cusani, where no weapons were found, only clandestine printed material. He was taken to the prison in Monza on Via Mentana. He was violently interrogated by the Fascist police and the SS. One of his arms was broken.

We do not know much about his final days. On April 19, 1946, his wife, Marcella, declared to the Allied Command:

> I went to visit him twice while he was being detained and the last time I saw him alive was on August 1, 1944. After my visit, I tried to contact some officers in order to obtain my husband's release but I was always told to speak with Lt. [Siegfried] Werning. I was never able to get in contact with this man who, as far as I could understand, had a squad of Italian SS at his command and was in charge of interrogating the prisoners. These interrogations were conducted in a brutal manner because one time, when I went to visit my husband, his arm was in a cast and when I asked him why he told me they had broken it during an interrogation. When I went to Monza, on August 9, I learned that my husband had been transferred to San Vittore prison in Milan the day before. So I went to the Albergo Regina for a visitor's pass but I was sent away without being able to see anyone who had any kind of authority.[16]

Her daughter, Concettina, added:

> We were permitted a visit and went to the prison in Monza. They took us into a basement. There were other people with us, relatives of other prisoners. We didn't know them and everybody kept silent, in part because, nearby, *Repubblichini* [members of the Italian Social Republic of Fascist Italy—translator's note] in civilian clothes were watching us and never took their eyes off us for a moment. [. . .] A small door opened and the prisoners entered. My father had lost weight, his beard was long, his left arm was in a cast and in a sling. We hugged tightly. I don't remember what we said to each other, insignificant things, for sure. Two Fascists stood behind us, holding machine guns. [. . .] Before he disappeared through the door he had entered from, he turned back a moment; he looked at us once more and raised his free hand in a sign of farewell. They sent us out right away and we left in silence. My mother and I held each other tightly by the arm and we walked until we had turned the corner, out of sight of everyone. Then we burst into tears. Because we sensed we would never see him again (Principato 2010, 33–34).

In early August, Principato and Soncini were transferred from Monza to San Vittore, Ward VI, Room 8. In that same cell, according to the files at San Vittore, there was twenty-year-old Renzo Del Riccio, who was also

142   *Chapter 12*

executed by firing squad in Piazzale Loreto; his uncle Mario Del Riccio; and Mario Follini and Alessandro Zappata, who were reportedly deported to Germany the following August 17. Follini, a factor varnisher from Cogliate who avoided execution at the last moment, and Zappata, a prison guard at San Vittore, died at Hersbruck, a subcamp of Flossenbürg, on November 16, 1944, and February 22, 1945, respectively (Geloni 2002, 44).

At 4:30 a.m. on August 10, a number of prisoners, including the teacher Principato, were woken up and mustered in the main corridor of San Vittore prison. They were loaded onto a convoy made of five trucks plus one car and taken to Piazzale Loreto, with a short detour to a large building in Milan, perhaps to load the execution platoon made of roughly twenty-five or thirty Italian Fascist soldiers from the "Ettore Muti" legion. When the trucks arrived, they made the fifteen prisoners get out and revved the trucks' engines to cover the sound of the gunfire.

Since then, the story of Salvatore Principato is tragically linked to that of the fourteen other men in one of the most heinous and emblematic massacres in Milan's history during the twentieth century. They did not stand trial and only realized their destiny at the very last moment. They have gone down in history as the Fifteen Martyrs of Piazzale Loreto: Antonio Bravin, Giulio Casiraghi, Renzo Del Riccio, Andrea Esposito, Domenico Fiorani, Umberto Fogagnolo, Tullio Galimberti, Vittorio Gasparini, Emidio Mastrodomenico, Angelo Poletti, Salvatore Principato, Andrea Ragni, Eraldo Soncini, Libero Temolo, and Vitale Vertemati (Borgomaneri 1997, 139–46; Cenati and Quatela 2007; Castoldi M. 2007b; Chiorri Principato 2014, 147–70; Scirocco 2014).

After the Liberation, Marcella taught school for only one year, even though she had given private after-school lessons throughout the Fascist period; she immediately asked to take over her husband's role in the Resistance, and starting in November 1944, she assumed the position of logistical director in the Socialist Party. In a written note, she remembered not only the secret meetings with Lelio Basso to prepare the uprising, but also the constitutive act of the Matteotti Fund that was stipulated with Lelio Basso at Via Silvio Pellico 12, in the studio of the lawyer Blasco Morvillo in November 1944 to help the families of the fallen and the deported (Chiorri Principato 2014, 11). One year later, Lelio Basso confirmed the episode in a written presentation of *Pro Fondo Matteotti*, an art exhibit held at the Galleria Guglielmi in Milan from November 25 to December 7, 1945. He recalled the summer of 1944, the atmosphere that was "oppressive with terror," when he was called on to assume the direction of the Socialist movement in Milan and felt "the duty to immediately organize assistance for the families of the political victims, whose number grew day by day." With this in mind, he created the National Giacomo Matteotti Fund

during a meeting held in the studio of the lawyer Blasco Morvillo; the widow
of one of the martyrs of Loreto, Signora Principato, was also present and she
offered to fill the place in the struggle that had been left vacant by her husband.
I proposed the name and the goal of the initiative, and they were unanimously
approved (Basso L. 1945, 4).[17]

From that moment, Marcella never ceased running the project: organizing
couriers to San Vittore prison; hiding fugitives, who were often forced to
change houses every night and always had to stay at the homes of trusted
people; helping some find work, albeit temporary. The member of the GAP
[Group of Patriotic Action] Giovanni Pesce remembered her in one of his
books as "tireless" and "heroic" (Pesce 1983, 88).

After the Liberation, on May 26, 1945, the town of Vimercate voted unanimously to change the name of Via del Littorio to Via Salvatore Principato.
The director of studies of the Leonardo da Vinci elementary school, Piero
Bianchi—proof of his anti-Fascist soul, despite the regulation black shirts
he occasionally wore—remembered Principato on March 1, 1945, in *L'Ora
della Scuola, Olocausti: Salvatore Principato*. On August 10, 1946, the
teacher Andrea Tacchinardi unveiled a commemorative plaque on his house
at Via (today, Viale) Gran Sasso 5 in Milan. That same day, in his hometown,
Piazza Armerina, the urban stretch of the provincial road no. 15 that runs
parallel to Via Giacomo Matteotti was named after him. On April 25, 1947,
Ugo Guido Mondolfo unveiled a bust in his memory, the work of the Socialist
sculptor Alfeo Bedeschi, in the atrium of the Leonardo da Vinci elementary
school. After those first two years of effective anti-Fascist unity, for Salvatore
Principato and for the other teachers recounted in this book, it was the beginning of a period of progressive and sometimes strategic forgetfulness.

NOTES

1. The article is reproduced in its entirety.

2. The concluding quote is from Dante: *Inferno* XXVII, v. 120.

3. To Merli, the pseudonyms in the letter are "undeciphered." Today, we can
interpret them, thanks above all to the book Zucàro 1988, 44, 189. "Caio" is Luigi
Veratti, a doctor and former Socialist councilor in the Caldera council, the uncle of
Roberto; "Socrate" is Salvatore Principato; "Italo" is Romeo Ballabio, an industrialist from Parabiago; "Negretto" is probably Dino Luzzato. From other documents,
which Zucàro might not have seen, but which date to the spring of 1938, "Negretto"
appears to be Mario Antonio Bianchi, the son of Pietro and of Chiesa Virginia, born
in Chiasso on March 27, 1909, and domiciled in Geneva, who studied medicine in
Pavia (Archivio Centrale dello Stato, Ministero dell'Interno, Direzione Generale della
Pubblica Sicurezza, Divisione Polizia Politica. Materie, b. 116, fasc. 2).

144   *Chapter 12*

4. Aristide Cagnoli, born in Sarzana on July 22, 1889, a bachelor and office worker, was the nephew of Alfredo Bonazzi, who lived in the same building at Via San Gregorio 6.

5. See Archivio di Stato di Milano, Gabinetto Prefettura I versamento, b. 430, *Diffusione clandestina 1932–1935 "Giustizia e Libertà."*

6. See Archivio di Stato di Milano, Gabinetto Prefettura I versamento, b. 426, *"La libertà 1932."*

7. See Report by Francesco Nudi to "S. e. il capo della Polizia / Roma," dated Milan, February 24, 1933, and the letter by the informer Silvio dated February 16, 1933, conserved in the Archivio Centrale dello Stato, Ministero dell'Interno, Direzione Generale della Pubblica Sicurezza, Divisione Polizia Politica. Materie, b. 116, fasc. 2.

8. Typewritten manuscript conserved in the Chiorri Principato Castoldi Archive.

9. There is also a report on Villa by the prefect to the Ministry of the Interior dated March 31, 1930, at the Archivio Centrale dello Stato, Casellario Politico Centrale, b. 5419. He was the son of Pietro and Giulia Strada, he was born in Gambara (Brescia) on December 6, 1884, but was a resident of Milan starting in 1926.

10. Archivio centrale dello Stato, Sezione Tribunale speciale, b. 456, fasc. *Salvatore Principato*, cc. 11–12.

11. A copy of the sentence is conserved in the Chiorri Principato Castoldi Archive.

12. The motivation reads: "Since a nucleus of enemy soldiers had momentarily re-occupied a section of the trench, at the head of a few soldiers, he courageously threw himself into a counterattack, repulsing the adversaries and capturing about fifteen prisoners. Mount Vodice, May 31, 1917."

13. During the 1970s, Alfredo Barberis was the editor of *Corriere dei Ragazzi*, when a thirteen-year-old boy, Giulio from Sulmona, wrote him a letter asking him about his "anti-Fascist" choices. In his reply, Barberis recalled the education and the example of his own teacher. This is an excerpt from his letter, which was published in issue no. 39 of *Corriere dei Ragazzi* on September 28, 1975, in the column "La posta, ragazzi!"

14. All the testimony quoted here are typewritten or handwritten documents conserved in the Chiorri Principato Castoldi Archive.

15. Alberto Franchino, born in Piazza Armerina on February 11, 1896, director of studies starting in 1936, died in Milan on October 17, 1952; Ines Saracchi, born in Milan on March 19, 1877, director of studies starting in 1920, died in Milan on December 14, 1963: registry notes from documents conserved in the Chiorri Principato Castoldi Archive.

16. Declaration conserved in the file n. 2167, cc. 283–284, della Sezione investigativa del Comando alleato, copy conserved in the Chiorri Principato Castoldi Archive.

17. A few copies of the booklet are conserved in the Archive of the Fondazione Lelio e Lisli Basso Issoco, Fondo Lelio Basso, serie 22, *Organismi di assistenza*, b. 1.1, Fondo Matteotti.

Bibliography

Agosti, Aldo. *Rodolfo Morandi. Il pensiero e l'azione politica*, Bari: Laterza, 1971.

Allason, Barbara. *Memorie di un'antifascista 1919–1940*, Rome-Florence-Milan: Edizioni U, [1946].

Amorth Antonio, Antonicelli Franco, and others. *Dal 25 luglio alla Repubblica, 1943–1946*, edited by Giuseppe Rossini, Rome: Eri, 1966.

Antonioli, Maurizio. *Vieni o maggio. Aspetti del Primo Maggio in Italia tra Otto e Novecento*, Milan: FrancoAngeli, 1988.

Arata Massariello, Maria. *Il ponte dei corvi. Diario di una deportata a Ravensbrück*, Milan: Mursia, 1979.

Ardeni, Pier Giorgio. *Cento ragazzi e un capitano. La brigata Giustizia e Libertà "Montagna" e la Resistenza sui monti dell'alto Reno tra storia e memoria*, with the collaboration of Francesco Berti Arnoaldi Veli, preface by Luciano Casali, Bologna: Pendragon, 2016, new expanded ed.

Arian Levi, Giorgina, and Montagnana, Manfredo. *I Montagnana: una famiglia ebraica piemontese e il movimento operaio (1914–1948)*, preface by Amos Luzzatto, Florence: Giuntina, 2000.

Barberis, Alfredo. 2012. "Il maestro del «no» al fascismo. Salvatore Principato." *Nuova Antologia* 147, n. 2264 (October–December), 195–200.

Bassani, Giorgio. *Cinque storie ferraresi*, Turin: Einaudi, 1956.

Bassani, Giorgio. *Within the Walls*, translated by Jamie Mckendrick, London: Penguin Classics, 2016.

Basso, Antonio, ed. *Dizionario di cultura politica*, Milan: Autas, 1946.

Basso, Antonio. *Responsabilità della pace. Cultura e pragmatismo pacifisti di un militante senza bandiere. Saggi editi e inediti 1919–1976*, selected and introduced by Ugo Basso, Casale Monferrato: Piemme, 1987.

Basso, Lelio. *Solidarietà*. In *Galleria Guglielmi dal 25 nov. al 27 dic. 1945. Mostra d'arte contemporanea. Pro Fondo Matteotti*, Milan: Tipografia Gilardoni-Chiesa-Gallazzi, 1945, 3–5.

Beccaria Rolfi, Lidia, and Bruzzone Anna Maria. *Le donne di Ravensbrück*, Turin: Einaudi, 1978.

Beccaria Rolfi, Lidia, and Maida Bruno. *Il futuro spezzato: i nazisti contro i bambini*, Florence: Giuntina, 1997.

146 *Bibliography*

Belli, Ferruccio. 1998. "Storia di Anna Botto maestra di Vigevano," *Triangolo rosso*, 18, n. 3 (July), 21.

Bellini, Gianpaolo. *Dal Sabotino alla Sormani. Storia di una vita Giovanni Bellini*, Como: Nodolibri, 2013.

Berrini Pajetta, Elvira. *Ogni ora, ogni minuto dai quaderni 1909–1948*, preface by Natalia Ginzburg, Turin: Turingraf, 1981.

[Berrini] Pajetta, Elvira. *Compagni*, Varese: Pietro Macchione Editore, 2015.

Bertolo, Bruna. *Maestre d'Italia*, Turin: Neos Edizioni, 2017.

Bianchi, Arturo. *A Noi! Storia del fascismo pavese*, Pavia: Luculano Anastatica, 2004.

Bissolati, Leonida. *La lega delle Nazioni e la politica italiana*, Rome: "Vie nuove," 1919.

Bocchetti, Matteo Alfredo. *La scuola elementare nel ventennio fascista: direttive politiche, didattica, cronache degli insegnanti*, Bari: Giuseppe Laterza, 2013.

Boero, Pino, and De Luca, Carmine. *La letteratura per l'infanzia*, Rome-Bari: Laterza, 1995.

Borgomaneri, Luigi. *Hitler a Milano. I crimini di Theodor Saevecke capo della Gestapo*, Rome: Datanews, 1997.

Botto, Anna. Typewritten manuscript *Anna Botto*, edited by the Municipality of Vigevano and the didactic association of Gambolò, n.d. [post 1979], conserved at the Archivio della Fondazione Memoria della Deportazione di Milano, Fondo Aned, c. 9.1, b. 206, fasc. 6, *Serie Organi e pubblicazioni*. The text, whose information was referenced in the *Fascicolo personale della maestra elementare Anna Botto* (Archivio 1 Circolo didattico di Vigevano) and that publishes various testimonies.

Callegari, Pasqualina, ed. *Il coraggio della libertà: la scuola milanese durante il fascismo e la resistenza*, edited with the collaboration of Linda Candia Untersteiner, Giudi Faini Cavalli, Concettina Principato, Maria Sofia Silva Strada, introduction by Mario Silvani (Research promoted by the Istituto Didattico Pedagogico della Resistenza di Milano), Novara: D'Imperio Editore, 1991.

Cambosu, Salvatore. 1959. "Ricordo di Angela Marchi Maccioni," *Il Ponte*, 15, n. 10 (October), 1331.

Canali, Mauro. *Le spie del regime*, Bologna: il Mulino, 2004.

Canera Gragnani, Maria Luisa. 1980. "Capelli bianchi a vent'anni," *Triangolo rosso*, 7, n. 3 (March–April), 10.

Castoldi, Aurelio. *Gianni Olal. Romanzo per ragazzi*, illustrated by Riccardo Bandirali, Milan: Edizioni La Vetta, 1945.

Castoldi, Aurelio. 1947. "Lo studio gratuito e gli insegnanti ben pagati," *Il Proletario. Settimanale della Federazione provinciale milanese del Partito socialista italiano di unità proletaria*, n. 3 (July), 2.

Castoldi, Massimo. 2002. "Le ragioni di Gianni Olal. L'onomastica in un romanzo di Aurelio Castoldi (1892–1967)," *Rivista internazionale di onomastica letteraria*, 8, n. 2, 423–36.

Castoldi, Massimo. 2003. "Il balilla e Romoletto: il ribaltamento allusivo in una commedia di Aurelio Castoldi," LG Argomenti, 39, n. 2 (April–June), 65–71.

Bibliography

147

Castoldi, Massimo. 2007 (a). "«Flores apparuerunt in terra nostra». Il maestro socialista Salvatore Principato e il giovane padre Luigi Reginaldo Orlandini da Lizzano," *Nuèter*, 33, n. 65 (June), 45–51.

Castoldi, Massimo. 2007 (b). "10 agosto 1944. I martiri di Piazzale Loreto nella memoria di tre poeti: Alfonso Gatto, Salvatore Quasimodo, Franco Loi," *Poetiche. Rivista di letteratura*, 9, n. 1, 77–102.

Castoldi, Massimo. *Voci del dissenso. Giuseppe Latronico e Aurelio Castoldi*, in *Piccoli eroi. Libri e scrittori per ragazzi durante il ventennio fascista*, edited by Massimo Castoldi, Milan: FrancoAngeli, 2016, 149–67.

Castoldi, Massimo. 2018. "Alcide Malagugini e un'idea di scuola," *Tempo Presente*, 448–50 (April–June), 16–26.

Catarsi, Enzo. *"Critica sociale" e i maestri*, in Tomasi, Tina and others. *Scuola e società nel socialismo riformista (1891–1926). Battaglie per l'istruzione popolare e dibattito sulla "questione femminile,"* Florence: Sansoni, 1982, 39–94.

Cavalli, Libero, and Strada, Carlo. *Il vento del Nord. Materiali per una storia del Psiup a Milano, 1943–45*, preface by Libero Biagi, Milan: Franco Angeli, 1982. (a)

Cavalli, Libero, and Strada, Carlo. *Nel nome di Matteotti. Materiali per una storia delle brigate Matteotti in Lombardia, 1943–45*, preface by Libero Biagi, Milan: FrancoAngeli, 1982 (b).

Cazzola, Marco. *Alda Costa. Scritti e discorsi (1905–1921)*, Ferrara: Spazio Libri, 1992.

Cenati, Roberto, and Quatela Antonio. *Alle fronde dei salici. 15 vite per la libertà. Milano—Piazzale Loreto, 10 agosto 1944*, Anpi. Milan: Provincia di Milano, 2007.

Ceva, Bianca. *Tempo dei vivi 1943–1945*, Milan: Ceschina, 1954.

Chierico, Pier Vittorio, and Resegotti Paola. *L'Istituto pavoniano Artigianelli di Pavia, 1892–1967. Storie di ragazzi e di mestieri*, Pavia: Pime, 2013.

[Chiorri] Principato, Marcella. 1977. "Una gita verso Sondrio . . . ", *Critica Sociale*, 79, n. 1–2 (February–March), 36.

Chiorri Principato, Marcella. *Storia di un comitato. Il Comitato Onoranze Caduti per la Libertà. Milano 1945–1956*, edited by Massimo Castoldi, Milan: FrancoAngeli, 2014.

Colin, Mariella. *I Bambini di Mussolini. Letteratura, Libri, Letture per l'Infanzia Sotto il Fascismo*, Brescia: La Scuola, 2012.

Cozzi, Walter. 1964. "Ricordo di Camillo Baldelli e di G. Battista Ceccherelli," *Rassegna di Storia*, 5, 51–54.

D'Ascenzo, Mirella. *Tra centro e periferia. La scuola elementare a Bologna dalla Daneo-Credaro all'avocazione statale (1911–1933)*, Bologna: Clueb, 2006.

D'Ascenzo, Mirella. *Casucci Casimiro e Fiorelli Gildo*, in *Dizionario Biografico dell'Educazione 1800–2000*, vol. 1 (A–K), Milan: Editrice Bibliografica, 2013, 303–04, 555.

De Amicis, Edmondo. *Primo maggio*, part 1, chap. 9, in *Opere scelte*, edited by Folco Portinari and Giusi Baldissone, Milan: Mondadori, 1996.

De Dominicis, Saverio Fausto. *Linee di pedagogia elementare, per le scuole normali e i Maestri*, part 2, *La vita interna della scuola*, Rome-Milan: Società ed. Dante Alighieri, 1906.

148   *Bibliography*

De Felice, Renzo. *Mussolini, il fascista. La conquista del potere (1921–1925)*, Turin: Einaudi, 1965.

De Unamuno, Miguel. *Commento al Don Chisciotte*, prologue by the author, translation into Italian from Spanish and notes by Gilberto Beccari, Lanciano: Carabba, 1913.

Detti, Tommaso. *Fabrizio Maffi. Vita di un medico socialista*, Milan: FrancoAngeli, 1987.

Di Michele, Andrea. *Squadrismo e primo fascismo a Bolzano*, in *Erinnerungskulturen des 20. Jahrhunderts im Vergleich—Culture della memoria del Novecento a confronto*, edited by Hannes Obermair and Sabrina Michielli, Bolzano: Stadtarchiv Bozen-Archivio Storico della Città di Bolzano, 2014, 47–54.

Fantozzi, Giovanni. *Monchio 18 marzo 1944. L'esempio*, Modena: Edizioni Artestampa, 2006.

Fava, Sabrina. *Percorsi critici di letteratura per l'infanzia tra le due guerre*, Milan: Vita e Pensiero, 2004.

Ferrario, Clemente. *Le origini del Partito Comunista nel Pavese (1921–1926)*, preface by Ernesto Ragionieri, Rome: Editori Riuniti, 1969.

Ferro, Giovanni. *Milano capitale dell'antifascismo*, Milan: Mursia, 1985.

Fiori, Cesira. *Una donna nelle carceri fasciste*, preface by Umberto Terracini, Rome: Editori Riuniti, 1965.

Fontana, Carlo. *Dal forno alla cattedra. Un capitolo delle memorie della mia vita*, Milan: Tip. Sacchi, 1956.

Fontana, Ciro. *All'ombra di Palazzo Marino (1941–1981)*, Milan: Mursia, 1981.

Fontana, Josef. *Unbehagen, Südtirol unter der Zivilverwaltung*, vol. 1, *August 1919–28. Oktober 1922*, Innsbruck: Wagner, 2010.

Fortichiari, Bruno and Malatesta, Mario. *Abigaille Zanetta 1875–1945*, Milan: Saita, 1948.

Galli, Gallo. *I Principii della Scuola Fascista con particolare riguardo alla Scuola Elementare*, Milan: A. Milesi & figli, n.d. [1935].

Galoppini, Annamaria. *Le studentesse dell'Università di Pisa (1875–1940)*, in *Fuori dall'ombra. Studi di storia delle donne nella provincia di Pisa, secoli XIX e XX*, edited by Elena Fasano Guarini, Annamaria Galoppini, Alessandra Peretti, introduction by Elena Fasano Guarini, Pisa: Plus Pisa University Press, 2006.

Garosci, Aldo. *Vita di Carlo Rosselli*, Florence: Vallecchi, 1973, vol. 1–2.

Geloni, Italo. *Ho fatto solo il mio dovere . . .* , memoirs of Italo Geloni, a former political deportee in concentration camps, Pisa: Aned, 2002.

Ghizzoni, Carla. "Il Maestro nella scuola elementare italiana dall'Unità alla Grande Guerra," in *Maestri e istruzione popolare in Italia tra Otto e Novecento. Interpretazioni, prospettive di ricerca, esperienze in Sardegna*, edited by Roberto Sani and Angelino Tedde, Milan: Vita e Pensiero, 2003.

Gibelli, Antonio. *Il Popolo Bambino. Infanzia e Nazione dalla Grande Guerra a Salò*, Turin: Einaudi, 2005.

Giovana, Mario. *Giustizia e Libertà in Italia. Storia di una cospirazione antifascista 1929–1937*, Turin: Bollati Boringhieri, 2005.

Gobetti, Piero. *Felice Casorati pittore*, Turin: Piero Gobetti, 1923.

Bibliography 149

Goria, Giulio, ed. *Mamma Pajetta*, Rome: Editori Riuniti, 1964.

Greco, Valentina. 2005. "Lidia Beccaria Rolfi. La costruzione di una biografia nel passaggio dalla memoria alla testimonianza," *DEP. Deportate, esuli, profughe. Rivista telematica di studi sulla memoria femminile*, 2, 11–35.

Gruber, Alfons. *L'Alto Adige sotto il fascismo*, Bolzano: Athesia, 1979.

Guderzo, Giulio. *L'altra guerra. Neofascisti, tedeschi, partigiani, popolo in una provincia padana. Pavia 1943–1945*, Bologna: il Mulino, 2002.

I deportati pavesi nei lager nazisti, essays and testimony by Donata Brianta, Alessandra Ferraresi, Pierangelo Lombardi, Carlo Sacchi, Elisa Signori, presentation by Giulio Guderzo (Collana di monografie degli "Annali di Storia Pavese," 1), Pavia: Tipografia Litografia Luigi Ponzio, 1981.

Inzerillo, Giuseppe. 1976. "La maestra Alda Costa «vedetta sovversiva»," *I problemi della pedagogia*," 22, n. 6 (November-December), 1131–36.

Inzerillo, Giuseppe. *Una vedetta «sovversiva»: Alda Costa*, in *La cultura ferrarese fra le due guerre mondiali*, edited by Walter Moretti, Bologna: Cappelli, 1980, 49–58.

Latronico, Giuseppe. *Il libro dei treni. Aneddoti, notizie, impressioni, ricordi*, Turin: Utet, 1935.

Latronico, Giuseppe. *Il libro delle ore gioconde. Giuochi e passatempi*, illustrated by Filiberto Mateldi, Turin: Utet, 1936.

Latronico, Giuseppe. *Periscopio*, Milan-Rome-Varese: Istituto Editoriale Cisalpino, 1941.

Latronico Giuseppe and Bruno Paolo Arcangeli. *Lingua d'oggi. Novissima grammatica italiana illustrata per la scuola media*, illustrations by Mario Zampini, Milan-Rome-Varese: Istituto Editoriale Cisalpino, 1943.

Lechner, Stefan. *Der «Bozner Blutsonntag»: Ereignisse, Hintergründe und Folgen*, in *Erinnerungskulturen des 20. Jahrhunderts im Vergleich—Culture della memoria del Novecento a confronto*, edited by Hannes Obermair and Sabrina Michielli, Bolzano: Stadtarchiv Bozen-Archivio Storico della Città di Bolzano, 2014, 37–46.

Le donne nel Parlamento della Repubblica dalla Consulta alla vii Legislatura. Research group: Anna Miserocchi, Beniamino Altezza, Daniela Chiassi, Mario Mammuccari, Rome: Fondazione Cesira Fiori, n.d.

Lega, Carlo. *Le mie strade. Seconda edizione riveduta e aumentata*, Ferrara: Editrice Alba, 1981.

"Lidia Rolfi. Una memoria per il futuro (Atti del Convegno, Cuneo, 20 febbraio)." 2016. *Rivista dell'Istituto storico della Resistenza e della società contemporanea in provincia di Cuneo "D. L. Bianco,"* 90 (December), 13–134.

Lollo, Renata. *Sulla letteratura per l'infanzia*, Brescia: La Scuola, 2003.

L'Università popolare di Pavia, Pavia: Tipografia popolare con legatoria, 1925.

Maccioni, Mariangela. *Memorie politiche*, edited by Raffaello Marchi, Cagliari: Della Torre Istituto Superiore Regionale etnografico, 1988.

Maffi, Fabio. *Vecchio nido. Affetti e ricordi*, Milan: Corticelli, 1939.

Maiorca, Bruno. *La cattedra del duce. Vita della scuola elementare fascista tra cronaca, liturgia e ideologia*, presentation by Antonio Santoni Rugiu, Cagliari: Anppia, 2000.

150   *Bibliography*

Majerotti, Rita. *Il romanzo di una maestra*, edited by Lucia Motti, Rome: EDIESSE, 1995, with two essays by Maria Teresa Sega, *Passione d'amore e passione politica nella formazione di una «donna nuova», 1876–1915*, and by Maria Antonietta Serci, *Una maestra ribelle in Terra di Bari (1916–1946)*.

Maniaci, Davide. 2018. "Anna Botto la nostra maestra. E quel ricordo incancellabile," *L'informatore* (Vigevano) (April 5), 18.

Matteotti, Giacomo. *Scritti sul fascismo*, edited by Stefano Caretti, Pisa: Nistri-Lischi, 1983.

Merli, Stefano. *Fronte antifascista e politica di classe. Socialisti e comunisti in Italia 1923–1939*, Bari: De Donato, 1975.

Merlin, Lina. *La mia vita*, edited by Elena Marinucci, Florence: Giunti, 1989.

Micheli, Mino. *I vivi e i morti*, preface by Mario Bonfantini, Milan: Grafica Micheloni, n.d., later, Milan: Mondadori, 1967.

Mignemi, Adolfo. *Fumetti e giornali per ragazzi*, in *Immagine coordinata per un impero. Etiopia 1935–1936*, Turin: Gruppo editoriale Forma, 1984.

Molinari, Aurelio. 1924. "La Gioiosa: casa di liberi studi e di svago per i figli dei cooperatori e degli operai," *La cultura popolare*, 14, n. 6, 5–24.

Monina, Giancarlo, ed. *Il movimento di Unità proletaria (1943–1945)*, Rome: Carocci, 2004.

Pagani, Severino. *Storia della editoria giovanile in Italia negli ultimi cento anni*, in *Letteratura giovanile e cultura popolare in Italia. Atti del Convegno svoltosi a Torino dal 2 al 4 giugno 1961 sotto il patrocinio del Comitato Italia '61*, Florence: La Nuova Italia, 1962, 89–146.

Peretti, Alessandra. *Da Odessa a Pisa: una donna medico tra interessi pedagogici, diritti della donna e impegno sociale*, in *Fuori dall'ombra. Studi di storia delle donne nella provincia di Pisa, secoli XIX e XX*, edited by Elena Fasano Guarini, Annamaria Galoppini, Alessandra Peretti, introduction by Elena Fasano Guarini, Pisa: Plus Pisa University Press, 2006.

Pesce, Giovanni. *Il giorno della bomba. Racconti*, Milan: Gabriele Mazzotta, 1983.

Principato, Concettina. *"Siamo dignitosamente fiere di avere vissuto così." Memoria della Resistenza e difesa della Costituzione. Scritti e discorsi*, edited by Massimo Castoldi, Ravenna: Giorgio Pozzi Editore, 2010.

Principato, Concettina, and Patti, Giovanni, ed. *Due scelte in tempi difficili: Mino Micheli, Salvatore Principato*, Milan: Circolo culturale Gaetano. Salvemini, 1985.

Puglielli, Edoardo. *Abruzzo rosso e nero*, Chieti: Centro studi libertari Camillo Di Sciullo, 2003.

Quarzi, Anna Maria, ed. *La maestra da Alda alla Clelia di Giorgio Bassani*, Sabbioncello San Pietro (Fe): 2 G Editrice, 2004.

Ranucci, Imelde. *Lagrime e sangue. 8 settembre 1943–30 maggio 1945*, Modena: Teic, 1979.

Ravà, Autunno. *Alda Costa, educatrice-combattente-martire. Trent'anni di stolta persecuzione poliziesca*, edited by the Ferrara chapter of the Italian Socialist Party, Ferrara, n.d.

Ravera, Camilla. *Diario di trent'anni, 1913–1943*, Rome: Editori Riuniti, 1973.

Rebellato, Elisa. *La scala d'oro. Libri per ragazzi durante il fascismo*, Milan: Unicopli, 2016.

Rosada, Maria Grazia. *Le Università popolari in Italia 1900–1918*, Rome: Editori Riuniti, 1975.

Rossi, Ernesto. *Una spia del regime. Carlo Del Re e la provocazione contro Giustizia e Libertà*, nuova edizione a cura di Mimmo Franzinelli, Turin: Bollati Boringhieri, 2000.

Roveri, Alessandro. *Dal sindacalismo rivoluzionario al fascismo. Capitalismo agrario e socialismo nel Ferrarese, 1870–1920*, Florence: La Nuova Italia, 1972.

Roveri, Alessandro. *Costa Alda*, in *Il movimento operaio italiano. Dizionario biografico, 1853–1943*, edited by Franco Andreucci and Tommaso Detti, Rome: Editori Riuniti, 1976.

Santoni Rugiu, Antonio. *Maestre e maestri. La difficile storia degli insegnanti elementari*, Rome: Carocci, 2007.

Sarfatti, Michele. *Gli ebrei nell'Italia fascista. Vicende, identità, persecuzione*, Turin: Einaudi, 2000.

Scarano, Federico. *Tra Mussolini e Hitler: le opzioni dei sudtirolesi nella politica estera fascista*, Milan: FrancoAngeli, 2012.

Scirocco, Giovanni. *Piazzale Loreto, 10 agosto 1944*, in *Culture della memoria e patrimonializzazione della memoria storica*, edited by Cristiana Fiamingo, Milan: Unicopli, 2014, 127–43.

Sema, Paolo. *El Mestro de Piran. Ricordando Antonio Sema, la vita, la famiglia, l'insegnamento tra l'Istria e Trieste a cavallo di due guerre*, Tricesimo (Udine): Aviani, 1995.

Stevani Colantoni, Angela, and Barberini, Carlo Antonio. *Una figura di militante internazionalista Abigaille Zanetta maestra a Milano tra guerra e fascismo*, Milan: Pantarei, 2016.

Svevo, Italo. *Saggi e pagine sparse*, edited and with a preface by Umbro Apollonio, Milan: Mondadori, 1954.

Tacchinardi, Andrea. *Introduzione* a *Fabio Maffi. L'uomo e le opere*, Milan: Labor, 1956.

Telò, Giovanni. *Chiesa e fascismo in una provincia rossa. Mantova, 1919–1928*, presentation by Franco Molinari, Mantua: Istituto provinciale per la storia del movimento di Liberazione nel Mantovano, 1987.

Telò, Giovanni. *Con la lucerna accesa. Vita e assassinio del maestro mantovano Anselmo Cessi (1877–1926)*, Mantua: Gianluigi Arcari editore, 2000.

Tomasi, Tina. *Istruzione popolare e scuola laica nel socialismo riformista*, in Tomasi, Tina and others, *Scuola e società nel socialismo riformista (1891–1926). Battaglie per l'istruzione popolare e dibattito sulla "questione femminile,"* Florence: Sansoni, 1982, 7–38.

Tunesi, Natalia, and Morani, Carlo. *Carlo Fontana: pioniere del socialismo, maestro antifascista, primo Sindaco di Magenta nell'Italia repubblicana*, preface by Massimo Castoldi, Magenta: La Memoria del Mondo Libreria editrice, 2016.

Valeri, Mario. *Letteratura giovanile e cultura popolare in Italia dal 1861 ai giorni nostri*, in *Letteratura giovanile e cultura popolare in Italia. Atti del Convegno svoltosi a Torino dal 2 al 4 giugno 1961 sotto il patrocinio del Comitato Italia '61*, Florence: La Nuova Italia, 1962, 19–88.

Vanni, Renzo. *Fascismo e antifascismo in Provincia di Pisa dal 1920 al 1944*, Pisa: Giardini, 1967.

Vecchi, Angelo. *Abigaille Zanetta*, Milan: Unicopli, 2017.

Villari, Litterio. *Storia della città di Piazza Armerina*, Piacenza: Casa Editrice La tribuna, 1987, third ed. revised and expanded.

Zonca, Paolo. 2004. "La scuola festeggia i 70 anni, ne parliamo con Angelo Taschera che di anni ne ha 99. Vita da maestro elementare: «Vi racconto il mio Leonardo»," *la Repubblica* (April 28), ix.

Zucàro, Domenico. *Socialismo e democrazia nella lotta antifascista, 1927–1939*, Milan: Feltrinelli, 1988.

Index

Agazzi, Achille, 72
Agosti, Aldo, 127, 145
Agostini, Livio, 56
Albasini Scrosati, Vittorio, 128
Albasini, Luigia, 75
Albert I of Belgium (*King*), 110
Albertarelli, Rino, 69
alcoholism, xvi, 9, 37, 95
Alighieri, Dante, 86, 88, 143
Allason, Barbara, 105, 145
Altezza, Beniamino, 149
Amati, Olga, 87
Amorth, Antonio, 117, 145
Anarchism, 7, 70, 79
Andreucci, Franco, 151
Angoletta, Bruno, 99
Annunziata, Giovanna, xxii
Antelmi, Attilio, 129
anti-clerical polemic, xii, 19–20, 76, 90
Antonicelli, Franco, 117, 145
Antonietti, Gaspare, 103
Antonioli, Maurizio, 92, 145
Apollonio, Umbro, 151
Arata Massariello, Maria, 140, 145
Arcangeli, Bruno Paolo, 110, 149
Ardeni, Pier Giorgio, 138, 145
Ardigò, Roberto Felice, 20–21, 26
Arrivabene, Antonio, 20, 22, 23
Associations and Unions:

Catholic Teachers Association
    Tommaseo, xii–xiii, 19
Catholic Teachers Association
    Vittorino da Feltre, 17, 19–22
Giustizia e Libertà, 56, 72, 85,
    102, 127–131, 133, 135, 144–
    45, 148, 151
Humanitarian Society (Milan),
    76, 88
Italian Teachers Union, ix–x,
    xiii, xix, xxiii, 2, 7–8, 10, 20,
    35–36, 53, 60, 62, 79
National Teachers Association,
    xii, 2, 17, 19–21, 35–36,
    59–60, 68, 78–79
Popular University, 56, 81, 95–98,
    103, 106, 149
Teachers Association Roberto
    Ardigò, 20–21
Atomo Cosciente. *See* Zanetta, Abigaille

Badini, Angela, 139
Balabanoff, Angelica, xx
Baldelli, Camillo, xxiii, 147
Baldelli, Maria Luisa, xxiii
Baldisserotto, Anna, 124
Baldissone, Giusi, 147
Ballabio, Romeo, 128–29, 143
Banderali, Attilio, 63

Index

Bandino, Francesco, 41
Bandirali, Riccardo, 90, 146
Baraldi, Francesco, 27
Barberini, Carlo Antonio, 64, 151
Barberis, Alfredo, 136, 144, 145
Bargagna, Italo, 7
Barni, Dario, 140
Bassanesi, Giovanni, 128
Bassani, Giorgio, ix, 25–27, 39,
    145, 150
Basso, Antonio, 72, 107, 145
Basso, Lelio, 142–145
Basso, Ugo, 145
Bauer, Riccardo, 105, 128
Beccari, Gilberto, 148
Beccaria Rolfi, Lidia, xviii, 145, 149
Bedeschi, Alfeo, 143
Belli, Ferruccio, 117, 146
Bellini, Gianpaolo, 72, 146
Bellini, Giovanni, 72, 146
Bellone, Virgilio, 63
Belloni, Ernesto, 63
Benedetti, Fulvio, 107
Benzoni, Alberto, 128–29, 132
Berardelli, Pier Celestino, 118
Berio, Laura Simona, 120–22, 125
Bernadot, Marie-Vincent, 49
Berrini Pajetta, Elvira, xix–xx, 64, 146
Berrini, Mariuccia, xix
Berrini, Mosè, xix
Berta, Giovanni, 108
Bertana, Luigi, 72
Bertini, Cesare, 38
Bertolo, Bruna, xviii–xxi, xxiv, 146
Bertoni, Carlo, 121
Biagi, Libero, 147
Biamino, Carlo, 14
Bianchi, Arturo, 104, 146
Bianchi, Mario Antonio, 143
Bianchi, Piero, 133, 137, 143
Bianchi, Pietro, 143
Bianchini, Laura, 117
Bissolati, Leonida, xvi, 12, 70, 146
Blum, Léon, 49
Bocca, Assunta, 118

Bocchetti, Matteo Alfredo, xiii, 146
Bocchini, Arturo, 72, 130–31
Bodini, Domenico (*priest*), 18
Boerchio, Abele, 97
Boero, Pino, 99, 108, 146
Boito, Arrigo, 56
Bonaguro, Anna, xxii
Bonazzi, Alfredo, 128–29, 132, 144
Bonfanti, Luigi, 18
Bonfantini, Mario, 150
Bordiga, Amadeo, 59–60
Borghi, Sandro, xxii
Borgomaneri, Luigi, 142, 146
Borra, Maria, xxv
Borsi Rossi, Livia, 123
Bottechiari, Nino, 26
Botto, Anna, xvii–xviii, xxiii, xxv, 115–
    25, 141, 146, 150
Botto, Giuseppe, 125
Bottoni, Virginia Apollonia, 89
Bravin, Antonio, 142
Breitemberg (*Count*), 15
Bresciani, Enrico, 23
Bresciani, Italo, 12
Breviglieri, Adalgisa, xix
Brianta, Donata, 149
Broggi, Ambrogio, 129, 132
Bruno, Pietro, 130–31
Bruzzone, Anna Maria, xviii, 145
Bubani, Domenica, 79
Busca, Maria Ida, 97

Cagnoli, Aristide, 129, 132, 144
Caio. *See* Veratti, Luigi
Calamandrei, Piero, 51, 107
Callegari, Pasqualina, ix, xxvi, 106–
    7, 146
Calzecchi Onesti, Temistocle, 54
Cambosu, Salvatore, 41, 51, 146
Cammeo, Carlo Salomone, ix–x, xviii,
    xxiii, 1–11, 60–62, 79
Camosci, Renato, 21
Canali, Mauro, 132, 146
Canera Gragnani, Maria Luisa, 121,
    123–24, 146

Index 155

Canevari, Emilio, xxv, 93
Canova, Antonio, 109
Carbone, Giovanni, 117
Carducci, Giosue, xvii, 86, 95
Caretti, Stefano, 150
Caria, Efisio, 49
Carlantonio, Biagio. *See* Maffi, Fabio
Carli, Rudolf, 12
Carnevali, Virginio, xvi, 58
Casiraghi, Giulio, 142
Casorati, Felice, 106, 148
Cassoni, Dino, 2
Castoldi, Alcide, 97
Castoldi, Aurelio, xvi–xviii, 72, 87,
    89–104, 111, 146–47
Castoldi, Carmela, 89, 103
Castoldi, Gaetano, 89–90
Castoldi, Giovanni, 89, 103
Castoldi, Giulia, 89, 103
Castoldi, Giuseppe, 89, 103
Castoldi, Ines, 89, 103
Castoldi, Maggiorina, 97, 101
Castoldi, Massimo, 94–95, 100–101,
    138, 142, 146–47, 150–51
Castoldi, Raffaello, 89, 96, 103
Castoldi, Serafino, 89, 103
Casucci, Casimiro, xv–xvi, 147
Catarsi, Enzo, xiii, 147
Cavallari, Brenno, 80–84, 88
Cavallari, Mario, 39
Cavalli, Libero, 56, 85, 101, 104,
    140, 147
Cavallotti, Giorgio, 107
Cavani, Ugo, 132
Cazzola, Marco, 27, 29–34, 36, 40, 147
Ceccherelli, Giovanni Battista,
    xxiii, 147
Cellario, Mario, 133
Cena, Ernesta, xxi
Cenati, Roberto, 142, 147
Cereghino (*priest*), 117
Cessi, Alessandro, 21
Cessi, Anselmo, xvii–xviii, xxiii,
    17–23, 151
Cessi, Carlo, 17

Cessi, Gelasio, 17
Cessi, Giulia, 17
Cessi, Iginia, 17
Cessi, Maria, 19
Ceva, Bianca, 116, 122, 147
Chiassi, Daniela, 149
Chierico, Pier Vittorio, 90, 147
Chiesa, Virginia, 143
Chiorri Principato, Marcella, x, 84, 107,
    113, 128–29, 132, 135–36, 142, 147
Chiorri, Amilcare, 111, 135
Chiorri, Filippo, 136
Chirici, Ginetta, xxiv
Ciampi, Enrico, 4
Ciarlantini, Franco, 101
Cino. *See* Moscatelli, Vincenzo
Ciucci, Giuseppe, 7–9
Ciuti, Cafiero, 7
Codignola, Tristano, 107
Colajanni, Napoleone, 133
Colin, Mariella, xiii, 147
Communism, xix–xxii, 4, 7, 21, 49, 60,
    62, 64, 71, 83–84, 96, 103
    Livorno Congress, 3–4
Comte, Auguste, 26
Concentration camps and prisons:
    Auschwitz, xxi
    Bolzano, 122–23
    Dachau, 123
    Flossenbürg, 142
    Hartheim Castle, xxi
    Hersbruck, 142
    Mauthausen, xx–xxi, 140
    Ravensbrück, xviii, xxiii, 115,
        122–24, 140, 145
    Risiera di San Sabba
        (Trieste), xxiv
    San Vittore (Milan), 59–60, 67,
        122, 141–43
Corridoni, Filippo, 79
Corriere dei Piccoli, 98–99
Costa, Alda, ix, xvii–xviii, 25–40, 51,
    56, 60, 147, 149–51
Costa, Alessandro, 27, 39
Costa, Amelia, 27, 39

156 *Index*

Costa, Andrea, xvi
Costa, Linda, 27
Costa, Vincenzo, 27
Cottone, Carmelo, 41, 51
Cozzi, Walter, xxiii, 147
Credaro, Luigi, xii, 78, 147
Crespi, Carlo Alberto, 118–19
Croce, Benedetto, 26
Croce. *See* Gamberoni, Tullio
Crupi, Attilio, 12

D'Agostino, Filippo, xx–xxi
D'Angelo, Vincenzo, xxii
D'Ascenzo, Mirella, xvi, 147
D'Aste, Vittorio, 101
D'Azeglio, Massimo, 109
Dalzini, Santa, 22–23
Daudet, Alphonse, 70, 73
De Amicis, Edmondo, xv, 37, 82, 89, 119, 147
De Dominicis, Fausto Saverio, 43, 147
De Felice, Renzo, 83, 148
De Luca, Carmine, 99, 108, 146
De Stefani, Alberto, 15
Deffenu, Luigino, 46
Deganutti, Cecilia, xxiv
Del Riccio, Mario, 142
Del Riccio, Renzo, 141–42
Dell'Acqua, Carlo, 72
Della Frattina, Gustavo, 72
Detti, Tommaso, 77, 148, 151
Dettori, Giovanni, 48
Di Michele, Andrea, 11, 148
Di Vona, Quintino, 140
Dickens, Charles, 70, 73
Dizionario Enciclopedico Moderno (Labor), xvii, 70–73, 75, 87, 101
Don Alvaro. *See* Fontana, Carlo
Don Quixote by Carlo Fontana, 86
Dossetti, Giuseppe, 117
Dupré, Giovanni, 109–10

education of adults, xi–xii, xix, 56, 81–82, 95–98, 102
Einaudi, Luigi, x

Elmo, Luciano, 124
Enciclopedia del Ragazzo Italiano (Labor), xvii, 87, 101–102
Epplée, Ide, 54
Ercoli, Daniele, 72, 87–88, 101–102
Errante, Vincenzo, 107
Esposito, Andrea, 142

Fabietti, Ettore, 106
Faini Cavalli, Giudi, 146
false charity, 56–57
Fantozzi, Giovanni, xxiii, 148
Faravelli, Giuseppe, 85, 128–30, 132
Farinacci, Roberto, 15
Fasano Guarini, Elena, 148, 150
Fascist culture and propaganda:
    collaborationism and treachery, 49, 72, 120–22, 131–33
    defamation, 33–34, 37
    fascist teaching of history, xiii–xv, 86
    fascist teaching of physical education, xiii–xv, 45, 108
    forced Italianization, 11–12, 16
    publication of foreign literature, 70, 73
    interventionism, 59, 79
    March on Rome, 15, 22, 97
    Opera Nazionale Balilla, xv, 47, 98–99, 108–9
    police confinement (internal exile), xviii–xxi, 25–26, 38–40, 49–50, 56, 62, 67, 139
    racial laws, xx, xxiv, 134
    reclamation of books, ix, xvii, 35, 70, 99, 110
    Roman salute, 37, 47
    squadrismo, 3–4, 6–7, 13, 17, 20–21, 36, 83, 96, 108, 148
    warrior's education, xiii–xv, xvii, xix–xx, 6, 10, 33–35, 37, 43–44, 55, 58–59, 69, 79–80, 108, 111
Fava, Sabrina, 108, 148
Ferraresi, Alessandra, 124, 149

Index

157

Ferrari, Nino, 137
Ferrari, Novemi, 134, 137
Ferrari, Teobaldo, xxiii
Ferrarini, Giuseppe, 140
Ferrario, Clemente, 96, 103, 148
Ferro, Giovanni, 128, 148
Fiamingo, Cristiana, 151
figure of Balilla, xvii, 105, 108–9
Fiorani, Domenico, 142
Fiorelli, Gildo Enrico, xv–xvi, 147
Fiori, Cesira, xxi, 148–49
First World War, x–xi, xiii, xix, 6, 11,
  20, 26–27, 32–34, 43, 49, 58–59, 79,
  93, 95, 108, 136–37, 139
Fogagnolo, Umberto, 142
Follini, Mario, 142
Fontana, Carlo, xvi–xviii, 72, 75–88, 93,
  101, 139, 148, 151
Fontana, Cesare, 82, 84
Fontana, Ciro, 75, 79, 84, 86–88, 148
Fontana, Francesco Napoleone, 75
Fontana, Joseph, 13, 148
Formenti, Camillo, 76, 80, 82, 84, 88
Formentini, Ubaldo, 106
Fortichiari, Bruno, 54, 56, 58–60,
  62, 148
Fortunato, Giustino, 105
Foscolo, Ugo, 86
Fossati, Carlo, 116, 118, 125
Franceschi, Omero, 20
Franchino, Alberto, 139, 144
Frederick I (*Emperor*), 86
Freinet, Célestin, 62
Frigerio, Antonia, 124

Gaiaschi Pettenghi, Rosa, 121–24
Galimberti, Tullio, 142
Galli, Gallo, xiii–xv, 10, 148
Galoppini, Annamaria, 1, 148, 150
Gamberoni, Tullio, 33
Gandolfini, Enrico, 20
Garberini (*teacher*), 119
Garibaldi, Giuseppe, xvii, xx, 18, 53,
  109, 135
Garosci, Aldo, 130, 148

Gasparini, Vittorio, 142
Gasti, Giovanni, 37
Gatti, Pietro, 121
Gaviglio, Danilla, xxv, 119
Geloni, Italo, 142, 148
Ghinaglia, Ferruccio, 93, 96, 103
Ghisellini, Igino, 39
Ghizzoni, Carla, xii, xiii, xxvi, 148
Giacobbe, Dino, 48–49
Giacobbe Sechi, Graziella. *See* Sechi
  Giacobbe, Graziella
Gianni Olal by Aurelio Castoldi, 100–
  1, 146
Gianturco, Luigi Emanuele, 101
Gibelli, Antonio, xiii, 148
Ginzburg, Natalia, 146
Giolitti, Giovanni, xii, 15
Giovana, Mario, 56, 85, 130, 148
Giudice, Maria, xix
Giuffrida, Graziella, xxiv
Giunta, Francesco, 15
Gobbetti, Cristina, 66
Gobetti, Piero, 17, 70, 102, 105–6,
  112, 148
Goria, Giulio, xx, 149
Gragnani, Ernesto, 121
Gragnani Canera, Maria Luisa. *See*
  Canera Gragnani, Maria Luisa
grammar books, 72, 110
Gramsci, Antonio, xix, 62, 103
Gravelli, Asvero, 112
Greco, Valentina, xviii, 149
Gregorio Tognaga, Noemi. *See* Tognaga
  Gregorio, Noemi
Gregotti, Giovanni, 60
Griziotti, Benvenuto, 94
Griziotti, Giacomo, 66
Gruber, Alfons, 15, 149
Guderzo, Giulio, 117–18, 120–21, 149
Guerri, Quinto, 12

Haeckel, Ernst, 26
Heart by Edmondo De Amicis, xv, 37,
  68, 89, 119
Hofer, Andreas, 14

158 *Index*

hygiene in the schools, 9, 32, 37, 78

illiteracy, xi–xii, 32–33, 61
Innerhofer, Franz, xviii, xxiii, 11–16
Internationalism, 5–6, 33, 48, 54, 60,
  62, 67, 91–92
Italo. *See* Ballabio, Romeo

Jewish tradition, 1, 70–71, 108
Joan of Arc, 109–10
Jori, Lamberto, 72

Krupskaya, Nadezhda, 62
Kuliscioff, Anna, 55, 59

Labor day (May first), xv–xvi, 39, 67,
  82, 92–93, 102
La Scala d'Oro (Utet), 107–9, 151
Latronico, Ettore, 105
Latronico, Giuseppe, xvi–xviii, 87, 90,
  101–2, 105–12, 139, 147, 149
Lattes, Bruno, 26
Lavagnini, Spartaco, 4
Lazzari, Costantino, 59
Lechner, Stefan, 11, 149
Lega, Carlo, 39–40, 149
Lenin (Vladimir Il'ič Ul'janov),
  70–71, 103
Leo XIII (*Pope*), 18
Leoni, Eugenio, 18
Leoni, Giovanni, 117
Levi, Giorgina Arian, xx, 145
Liberalism, xi, xix, 15, 17, 19, 108–9
Libicus, 2–3, 6
Lizzeri, Angelo, 22
Locatelli, Adriana, 117
Locatelli, Giuseppe, 72
Lollo, Renata, 108, 149
Lombardi, Pierangelo, 149
Lombardo, Ivan Matteo, 140
Lombroso, Cesare, 68
Lupetti, Giulia, 6–7
Lusignoli, Alfredo, 81–83
Lussu, Emilio, 48–49
Luzzato, Dino, 143

Lycurgus, 110

Maccioni, Bachisio, 42
Maccioni, Mariangela, xvii–xviii,
  41–51, 120, 146, 149
Maccioni, Pietro, 42
Maccioni, Sebastiano, 42
Maffi, Attilio, 66
Maffi, Bruno, 128
Maffi, Fabio, xvi–xviii, 62, 65–70, 72,
  87, 96–97, 101, 149, 151
Maffi, Fabrizio, 62, 66, 96, 103, 148
Maffi, Felicita, 66
Maffi, Francesco, 66
Maffi, Giotto, 66
Maffi, Luigi, 66–67
Maffi, Orazio, 66
Maffi, Quirino, 66
Magrini, Luciano, 132
Maida, Bruno, xviii, 145
Maiorca, Bruno, xiii, 149
Maj De Dionigi, Pamela, 59
Majerotti, Eugenio, xx
Majerotti, Rita, xx, 150
Malagugini, Alcide, 93, 96, 103, 147
Malatesta, Mario, 54, 56, 58, 148
Malavasi, Gioacchino, 132
Malnati, Linda, xviii
malnutrition, xi, 9, 28–29, 61
Malot, Hector, 70, 73
Malvestiti, Carla, 117
Malvestiti, Mila, 117
Malvestiti, Pietro, 129, 132
Mammuccari, Mario, 149
Maniaci, Davide, 119, 150
Marchi, Raffaello, 47, 51, 149
Marescalchi, Arturo, 101
Mariani, Emilia, xviii
Mariani, Gusmano, 7
Mariani, Vittorio Emanuele, 54
Martelli, Achille, 49
Massariello Arata, Maria. *See* Arata
  Massariello, Maria
Mastino, Pietro, 46, 49
Mastrodomenico, Emidio, 142

Index 159

Mataloni, Jenner, 134
Mataloni, Maurizio Alfredo, 133–34
Mateldi, Filiberto, 149
Matteotti, Giacomo, xi–xxii, 7, 37, 70, 96, 119, 132, 140, 142–45, 147, 150
Mattoni, Italo Giovanni, 98
Maurelli, Armida, xxii
Mazza, Emilio, 98
Mazzini, Giuseppe, xvii, 6, 42–43, 86, 109
Mazzola Zanetti, Maria, 20–21
Menelik II (*Emperor of Ethiopia*), 108
Menichetti, Tito, 4
Merli, Stefano, 127–28, 143, 150
Merlin, Lina, 56, 139, 150
Meucci, Elio, 7
Micheli, Mino, 140, 150
Michielli, Sabrina, 148–49
Mignemi, Adolfo, 99, 150
Miserocchi, Anna, 149
Modigliani, Giuseppe Emanuele, 1, 3, 8
Molinari, Aurelio, 72, 150
Molinari, Franco, 151
Mondolfo, Lavinia, 85
Mondolfo, Ugo Guido, 85, 143
Moneta, Ernesto Teodoro, 55
Montagnana, Clelia, xx
Montagnana, Manfredo, 145
Montagnana, Rita, xx
Montemartini, Luigi, 93, 95
Montessori, Maria, 32
Morandi, Rodolfo, 127–29, 145
Morani, Carlo, xxv, 77–78, 80, 85–86, 88, 151
More, Thomas, 109
Morelli, Cristina, 132–33
Moretti, Walter, 149
Mori, Alessandro (*priest*), 18
Morpurgo, Giuseppe, 108
Morvillo, Blasco, 142–43
Moscatelli, Carla, 64
Moscatelli, Vincenzo (Cino), 64
Moschini, Giuseppe, 20, 22–23
Moulin, Léo, 128
Mugnai, Gino, 4

Muratori, Antonio Ludovico, 109
Murri, Romolo, 19, 112
Mussolini, Benito, xxii, xxvi, 14–15, 70, 79, 111, 119, 136, 147–48, 151

Nathansohn, Giangiacomo, 137
Nazi-fascist massacres:
    Ardeatine massacre, xxi
    Costrignano, xxiii
    Marzabotto, xxiv
    Monchio, xxiii, 148
    Piazzale Loreto, x, xxvi, 88, 111, 142–43, 147, 151
    Susano, xxiii–xxiv
Negretto. *See* Bianchi, Mario Antonio *or* Luzzato, Dino
Neri, Filomena, 53
Nicco, Carlo, 109
Niccolini (*Dr.*), xxii
Nissim Rosselli, Mary. *See* Rosselli Nissim, Mary
Nodari, Achille, 20–21, 23
Nudi, Francesco, 132, 144

Obermair, Hannes, 148–49
Oddo, Giuseppe, 49
Olgiati, Ambrogio, 80
Orlandini, Luigi Reginaldo, 127, 137–38, 147
Orlandini, Ulisse, 137–38
Orlando, Vittorio Emanuele, xii
Orsatti, Francesco, 18, 20, 22
Ortica, Giovanna, 116, 125

pacifism, xiv, 5, 21, 33–34, 43, 45, 55, 58–59, 69, 79, 99, 118, 145
    Conferences of Zimmerwald and Kienthal, 33, 59
Pagani, Severino, 72, 107, 108, 150
Paggi, Mario, 107
Pajetta, Gaspare, xx
Pajetta, Giancarlo, xx, 64
Pajetta, Giuliano, xx
Pajetta Berrini, Elvira. *See* Berrini Pajetta, Elvira

Index

Palazzi, Fernando, 107, 110, 112
Panepinto, Lorenzo, 8
Pansini, Adolfo, 133
Panzini, Alfredo, 110
Pappalardo (*teacher*), 134
Parri, Ferruccio, 107, 121, 128
Pascoli, Giovanni, xvi
Passarone, Giovanni, 83
Pastore, Alceo, 19
Patini, Teofilo, 64
patriotism, xi, xvii, xxii, 5–6, 11, 14,
    17–18, 20, 33–34, 42–43, 61, 66, 80,
    109, 135
pellagra, 19, 28, 61
Pellizza da Volpedo, Giuseppe, xvi
Perathoner, Julius, 13–15
Peretti, Alessandra, 7, 148, 150
Peretti, Giuseppe, 117
Pertini, Sandro, xix
Pesce, Giovanni, 143, 150
Petri, Fausta, xxi
Pettenghi, Mario, 121
Pettenghi, Ugo, 121
Pettenghi Gaiaschi, Rosa. *See* Gaiaschi
    Pettenghi, Rosa
Piazza, Alessandro, 85, 88
Pieraccini, Ottaviano, 140
Pini, Paolo, 85
Pinocchio (ballet) by Carlo Fontana, 87
Piol, Elserino, 136
Pius X (*Pope*), 19
Poggetto, Ines, xxi
Poggetto, Moïse, xxi
Poletti, Angelo, 142
Pollini, Gino, 13
Pollini, Leo, 107
Ponti, Gian Luigi, 137
Portinari, Folco, 147
Prampolini, Camillo, 68
Prezioso, Nicola, 137
price of milk and bread, 80–81, 94
Principato, Concettina, 113, 134–35,
    138–39, 141, 146, 150
Principato, Concetto, 133

Principato, Salvatore, x, xvii–xviii,
    xxiii, 56, 84–85, 88, 102, 107, 111,
    113, 127–30, 132–45, 147, 150
Principato Chiorri, Marcella. *See* Chiorri
    Principato, Marcella
Prosdocimi, Cesare, 13
Puggioni, Maura, 48–49
Puglielli, Edoardo, xxi, 150

Quarzi, Anna Maria, 27, 36, 37, 39, 150
Quatela, Antonio, 142, 147

Ragionieri, Ernesto, 148
Ragni, Andrea, 142
Ragni, Guido, 87
Ramicone, Ettore, xxi–xxii
Ranucci, Imelde, xxiii–xxiv, 150
Rausa, Concetta, 133
Ravà, Autunno, 33, 150
Ravenna, Renzo, 39
Ravera, Camilla, xix–xx, 64, 150
Rebellato, Elisa, 107, 112, 151
Rebolino, Enrico, 120
Reclus, Élisée, 70, 73
Regazzoni, Roberto, 131
Repossi, Luigi, 56, 60
Resegotti, Paola, 90, 147
Reut-Nicolussi, Eduard, 14
Riccobene (*teacher*), 134
Risorgimento, xvii, 18, 20, 66, 86–87,
    103, 109, 134–35, 139
Rodolfi, Armando, 129
Rolfi Beccaria, Lidia. *See* Beccaria
    Rolfi, Lidia
Rollini, Gianfranco, 139
Romoletto by Aurelio Castoldi,
    98–99, 146
Rosada, Maria Grazia, 95, 151
Rosani, Rita, xxiv
Rosselli Nissim, Mary, 6
Rosselli, Carlo, 127, 129, 131, 148
Rosselli, Pellegrino, 6
Rossetti, Francesco, 66
Rossi Borsi, Livia. *See* Borsi Rossi,
    Livia

Index

Rossi, Edoardo, 21
Rossi, Ernesto, 56, 72, 128, 151
Rossi, Giorgio, 95, 97
Rossini, Giuseppe, 145
Roveri, Alessandro, 33, 37, 151
Russo, Nunzio, 133

Sacchi, Carlo, 149
Sacerdote, Gustavo, 8
Salgari, Emilio, xvii, 139
Sand, George, 70, 73
Sani, Roberto, 148
Santoni Rugiu, Antonio, xii, 149, 151
Sapienza, Goliarda, xix
Saracchi, Ines, 139, 144
Sarfatti, Michele, 7, 151
Sartorio Tollis, Giuseppina, 123
Satta, Filippo, 58
Sauro, Nazario, 108
Savoy, Carlo Alberto of (*King of
  Sardegna*), 110
Savoy, Emanuele Filiberto of (*Duke of
  Aosta*), 110
Savoy, Margherita of (*Queen of
  Italy*), 110
Savoy, Umberto I of (*King of Italy*), 110
Savoy, Vittorio Emanuele II of (*King of
  Italy*), 110
Savoy, Vittorio Emanuele III of (*King of
  Italy*), 110
Scapolla, Guglielmo, 121
Scapolla, Nino, 121
Scarano, Federico, 16, 151
Schinelli, Erminia, 19
Schinetti, Pio, xvi
scholastic anthologies, xv–xvi, 72,
  101, 110
scholastic dispersal, 43
school laws, xii–xiii, 63, 78, 147
Scirocco, Giovanni, 142, 151
Sechi Giacobbe, Graziella, 48–50
Second World War, xxiii–xxv, 50, 64,
  87–88, 102, 110–11, 117, 123–24,
  136–37
Sega, Maria Teresa, 150

Selis Delogu, Luisa, 51
Sema, Antonio, xix, 151
Sema, Paolo, xix, 151
Serci, Maria Antonietta, 150
Serlupi, Domenico, 4
Signori, Elisa, 149
Sillini, Maria, 123
Silva Strada, Maria Sofia, 146
Silvani, Mario, 146
Silvino. *See* Villa, Carlo
social Catholicism, xi–xii, xviii–xix, 3,
  17–22, 54, 107, 116–18, 129, 132
social justice, 21, 55, 61–62, 65, 67, 69,
  100, 118, 130, 137
Socialism, xi, xv–xvi, xix–xx, xxv, 1,
  3–5, 8, 14, 17–20, 26–27, 35, 37–38,
  54–56, 60, 65–68, 75–76, 79–80, 82,
  84–85, 87, 88, 89–90, 93–97, 100–
  103, 111, 119, 127, 129–30, 132–35,
  139–40, 142–43
  Genoa Congress, 66
Socialist novel, 100–1
Socrate. *See* Principato, Salvatore
Soncini, Eraldo, 140–42
Spalla, Nello, 23
Spencer, Herbert, 26
Stalin (Iosif Vissarionovič Džugašvili),
  62, 70–71
Starace, Achille, xxiii, 11–13, 15
Stevani Colantoni, Angela, 54, 64, 151
Stizzi, Amulio, 2, 7
Storchi, Amilcare, 27
Strada, Carlo, 56, 85, 101, 104, 140, 147
Strada, Giulia, 144
Strada Silva, Maria Sofia. *See* Silva
  Strada, Maria Sofia
Sturzo, Luigi, 133
Sturzo, Mario, 133
Svevo, Italo, 25, 40, 151

Tacchinardi, Andrea, ix–xi, xix, xxiii,
  xxv, 8, 53, 65–66, 68, 72–73, 85, 87,
  101, 139, 143, 151
Tacchinardi, Pietro, xxv
Tagliagambe, Ugo, 2

Index

Tappeiner, Franz, 14
Taschera, Angelo, 139, 152
Taytu. *See* Walatta, Mikā'ēl
Tedde, Angelino, 148
Telò, Giovanni, 17, 21–23, 151
Temolo, Libero, 142
Terracini, Umberto, 148
Terruzzi, Lodovico, 131
Tibaldi Chiesa, Mary, 108
Tobino, Mario, xix
Togliatti, Palmiro, xx
Tognaga Gregorio, Noemi, 123
Tomasi, Tina, xiii, 147, 151
Tombari, Fabio, 110
Tonon, Anna, xxvi
Tonon, Giuseppe, xx
Topolino, 98
Töpffer, Rodolphe, 70, 73
Torrente. *See* Fontana, Carlo
Toscanini, Arturo, 84, 87
Toso, Mario, 117
Treves, Claudio, 8
Treves, Eugenio, 108
Troncon, Gino, 136
Trotsky, Léon 49, 70–71
Trotti, Clelia, ix, 25–27
Tunesi, Natalia, xxv, 77–78, 80, 85–86, 88, 151
Turati, Augusto, 12
Turati, Filippo, xv, 59, 70, 79
Turati, Nino, 76

Unamuno, Miguel de, 86, 148
Untersteiner, Linda Candia, 146

Valeri, Mario, xv, 151
Vanni, Renzo, 3–4, 7, 152
Vassalle, Vera, xix
Vecchi, Angelo, ix, 54–60, 63–64, 152
Veratti, Luigi, 143
Veratti, Roberto, 56, 96, 128, 132, 140
Verdi, Giuseppe, 54, 56, 86

Vergnanini, Antonio, 69
Vertemati, Vitale, 142
Vescovi, Umberto, 23
Viganò, Maria, xxii
Villa, Carlo, 132, 144
Villa, Pietro, 144
Villari, Litterio, 133, 152
Viotto, Domenico, 140

Walatta, Mikā'ēl (Taytù), 108
war (civil) in Spain, 46, 48,
war in Ethiopia, xvii, 46–47, 99, 107, 109
war in Libya, 43, 55, 59
war of Liberation, xviii–xix, xxi, xxiii–xxiv, 18, 64, 88, 107, 117–21, 140–43
women's rights, xii, xix–xx, 18, 30, 38, 54–55, 58, 60, 64, 91–92
workers' rights, xii–xiii, xvi, 3, 5, 14, 29, 42, 54–55, 59, 67, 76, 78, 80–82, 85, 89, 90–94, 96, 98, 100, 103, 128, 130, 133, 137

Zaballi, Caterina, 27
Zampini, Mario, 149
Zanardelli, Giuseppe, 19
Zanetta, Abigaille, xvi–xviii, 10, 36, 53–56, 58–60, 62–64, 148, 151–52
Zanetta, Bartolomeo, 53–54, 57
Zanetta, Erminia, 54, 63–64
Zanetta, Giacinta, 54, 64
Zappata, Alessandro, 142
Zega, Agata, xxii
Zeni, Bruno, 15
Zibordi, Gaetano, xv
Zibordi, Giovanni, 72
Zirardini, Gaetano, 34
Zonca, Paolo, 139, 152
Zucàro, Domenico, 132, 143, 152
Zuffi (*Dr.*), 37

About the Author

Massimo Castoldi, philologist and literary critic, as well as a scholar of Pascoli, Manzoni, and Renaissance poetry, has also concentrated on the memory of anti-fascism and the critique of its contemporary historical sources. He teaches Italian philology at the University of Pavia. His book *Insegnare libertà* won the 2019 *The Bridge Book Award.*

Gail McDowell, an Italian-to-English translator, has studied in the United States, Switzerland, and Germany. She lives and works in Italy.

www.ingramcontent.com/pod-product-compliance
Lightning Source LLC
Chambersburg PA
CBHW030301280325
24158CB00002B/39